Chicken Soup for the Soul®

I Can't Believe My Cat Did That!

Chicken Soup for the Soul: I Can't Believe My Cat Did That!
101 Stories about the Crazy Antics of Our Feline Friends
Jack Canfield, Mark Victor Hansen, and Jennifer Quasha

The publisher gratefully acknowledges the many publishers and individuals who granted Chicken Soup for the Soul permission to reprint the cited material.

Front cover photo courtesy of iStockphoto.com/bigworld. Back cover photo courtesy of Photos.com.

Cover and Interior Design & Layout by Pneuma Books, LLC
For more info on Pneuma Books, visit www.pneumabooks.com

Distributed to the booktrade by Simon & Schuster. SAN: 200-2442

Publisher's Cataloging-in-Publication Data
(Prepared by The Donohue Group)

Chicken soup for the soul : I can't believe my cat did that! : 101 stories about the crazy antics of our feline friends / [compiled by] Jack Canfield, Mark Victor Hansen, [and] Jennifer Quasha.

p. : ill. ; cm.

Summary: A collection of 101 true stories from people about the incredible things their cats have done, from funny to fearsome, from heartwarming to heroic.
ISBN: 978-1-935096-92-4

1. Cats--Behavior--Literary collections. 2. Cats--Behavior--Anecdotes. 3. Cat owners--Literary collections. 4. Cat owners--Anecdotes. 5. Human-animal relationships--Literary collections. 6. Human-animal relationships--Anecdotes. I. Canfield, Jack, 1944- II. Hansen, Mark Victor. III. Quasha, Jennifer. IV. Title: I can't believe my cat did that!

PN6071.C3 C456 2012
810.8/02/03629752   2012939988

PRINTED IN THE UNITED STATES OF AMERICA
on acid∞free paper
21 20 19 18 17 16 15 14   06 07 08 09 10

Chicken Soup for the Soul®

I Can't Believe My Cat Did That!

101 Stories about the Crazy Antics
of Our Feline Friends

Jack Canfield
Mark Victor Hansen
Jennifer Quasha

Chicken Soup for the Soul Publishing, LLC
Cos Cob, CT

Contents

①

~My Favorite Yarn~

②

~Impawsable~

❸
~Miss Congeniality~

❹
~Mr. Right~

❺
~Stalk to You Later~

❻

~I'm Just Staff~

❼

~A Good Mousekeeper~

8
~Love Me, Love My Cat~

9
~Out of the Box~

10
~Eight Lives and Counting~

I Can't Believe My Cat Did That!

Chapter 1

My Favorite Yarn

Bandit Steals a Kitten

One cat just leads to another.
~Ernest Hemingway

With nothing more than a few cardboard boxes, assorted fears and misgivings, and a cat named Bandit, I moved into my grandparents' old house to start an uncertain new life. After a long and painful breakup with my boyfriend of four years, I fled from the city to the comforts of the little house where I always found love when I was growing up. Even with both grandma and grandpa gone the house still held their warmth and traces of their scents.

Bandit paced through the rooms, mewling unhappily while I unpacked my clothes and put them away. He clearly preferred the airy apartment we had left behind. He leaned against my legs and looked up at me, pleading with me to explain why his world had suddenly been turned upside down. I bent over and scratched behind his ears. "It's going to be okay, Bandit. This house has always been filled with love. We are going to be happy here. You'll see."

The sudden rap on the front door startled both of us. I opened it and stared into the face of a young woman with the reddest hair and the most ginger-colored freckles I had ever seen. Her smile lit up her face and her eyes twinkled as if pure joy spilled from them.

She thrust a plate of brownies at me and said, "Hi, I'm Brandi and I live next door." The wonderful aroma of chocolate made me realize how hungry I was. Anxious to make my first friend, I grabbed the plate and opened the door wide.

"I need a break and these are perfect," I chattered. "Come inside and I'll make some coffee and we can get acquainted."

She only hesitated a second before stepping inside, her smile growing even wider. "I can't stay long," she said, reaching down to scratch Bandit under his chin.

"I have a cat too," she said, following me into the kitchen. "She had kittens four weeks ago. You should come over and see them. They are so cute. I'll have to find homes for them soon."

I shook my head. "Bandit is all the cat I need."

Brandi grinned, looking at the black oval around Bandit's eyes that stood out in startling contrast to his otherwise white fur. "Perfect name."

A couple of days later I was staring down at one of Grandma's flowerbeds, wondering what I should do to tend them. Brandi came outside and called to me. "Come and see the kittens. I promise I won't try to persuade you to take one. Besides, they aren't weaned yet."

Brandi led me to the deck in the back of her house. "Pepper had her kittens here and this is where she seems to want to stay," she said. I peered into the soft bed that Brandi had made for Pepper and her kittens. Two were solid black like her, one was gray-and-white striped and one was a calico. I picked up the calico and held it up for Bandit to inspect. "See the little baby," I crooned. "Isn't it sweet?"

Bandit stared at the kitten for a moment, then stepped forward timidly and gently nudged the kitten with his nose. The kitten mewed softly and Bandit quickly stepped back, never taking his eyes off the kitten as I laid it down next to Pepper.

I got my love of cats from Grandma, who had installed a cat door in the kitchen many years ago. It took Bandit a few days to discover the newfound freedom that the door gave him. Once he discovered that he didn't have to wait for me to open the door for him, he would run full speed ahead to the door and burst through it like a rocket.

One afternoon I was doing laundry when I heard Bandit crying softly. Wondering what was causing his distress, I forgot about folding clothes and hurried to the kitchen.

"Bandit!" I hissed sharply. "What have you done?" Bandit looked up at me guiltily as the tiny calico pawed around in vain, trying to find a teat on Bandit's tummy.

Bandit gave an anguished yowl when I picked up the kitten. "He has to go back to his mama," I said, laughing now. "You don't have what he needs."

Holding the kitten close to my chest, I knocked on Brandi's door. She grinned when she saw the kitten. "Changed your mind, huh? Well, he can't leave Pepper for another week at least."

I laughed. "Bandit brought the kitten into the kitchen through the cat door. I suppose he wants a pet of his own."

Brandi took the kitten from me. "Well, tell him to come back for him next week and I'll let him have it."

"Bandit doesn't need a kitten," I said. "And neither do I."

A few days later as I was making a salad for dinner I looked up just in time to see Bandit slinking through the cat door with the calico in his mouth. He looked at me sheepishly and gently put the kitten down. I sighed. "You can't just kidnap a kitten," I scolded. "Besides, don't you know you're a boy cat? Toms can't have kittens."

Bandit just stared at the kitten in utter fascination, licking his tiny face with his rough tongue. Sighing, I scooped up the kitten while Bandit watched me with anxious eyes. "He has to go back," I said sternly. "We don't need a kitten."

The following Saturday I became concerned when Bandit didn't come back home after his morning excursion. He never stayed outside for very long, but it was after ten and he hadn't returned. I went outside and called for him, but no white cat in a black mask came running toward me.

Brandi walked out of her house and waved to me. "Are you looking for Bandit?" She grinned. "Follow me."

Puzzled, I followed her to the deck at the back of her house. "Sweet, isn't it?" she said, nodding toward Bandit.

Bandit sat beside the bed where Pepper patiently nursed her

kittens. When he saw me, I could swear his eyes narrowed in defiance. If I would not let him bring the kitten home with him, he would stay with the kitten. I shook my head in disbelief.

"He's just going to keep stealing the calico until I find a home for him," Brandi said. "And he's going to be sad when the kitten is suddenly gone." She placed her hand gently on my arm. "I think Bandit is lonely. Haven't you ever been lonely?"

I swallowed past the lump in my throat, thinking of the long, lonely nights I spent in Grandma's old four-poster bed. "So... when can Bandit take the kitten from its mother?"

Brandi scooped up the kitten and placed it in my hands. "Now seems like a good time."

Bandit's tail swung back and forth in joy as he trotted along beside me as we took the kitten home. "You got your way this time," I told him. "But don't you dare try stealing another animal... ever."

~Elizabeth Atwater

Mewsic Critic

A cat has absolute emotional honesty: human beings,
for one reason or another, may hide their feelings,
but a cat does not.
~Ernest Hemingway

My tuxedo cat, Squeakette, greeted me with her usual meow and happy dance around her food bowl when I came home from choir practice one night. I gave my snuggle-puss twenty minutes of undivided attention. We played catch with her favorite mouse until she tired of it and curled up into a black-and-white ball on the sofa.

"Good," I said to myself. "Now I can practice unhindered."

My singing voice fell woefully short of Juilliard standards. Studying opera for two years in the music department at a community college gave me enough confidence to join the church choir.

"The only times you don't have to practice," my voice instructor had said, "are days you don't breathe." According to her standard, I hadn't drawn a breath in more than four years.

"Not quite ready for the Met, am I?" I said to Brian the choir director at my first rehearsal.

"You'll be fine." He offered a wistful smile and placed me in the soprano section, close to the altos. Perhaps I wavered between the two octaves.

Six weeks before Christmas, Brian handed out sheet music to the John Rutter piece he selected for our cantata. As the holiday drew closer, he gave us cassette tapes of the orchestra to practice on our own.

Now Squeakette snoozed peacefully on the sofa behind me. I popped the cassette into the tape player and sat cross-legged in the middle of the living room floor, breaking another opera-teacher rule. Sheet music in front of me, I followed the melody with my index finger. When the music reached the soprano part, I took a deep breath and stretched my torso upward, remembering at least one point my voice professor taught me—go high and come down on the note.

I sang the Latin words in my best soprano voice, "Gloria in excelsis, Deo."

Squeakette sprang out of her nap and rushed at me, meowing.

"Not now, Squeakette. I have to practice." I petted her and continued singing.

She climbed across my legs and, pressed one front paw on my chest, covering my mouth with the other. Her ears went flat, and her eyes turned to amber slits. She scowled her harlequin-mask face. I didn't know cats could frown.

"Are you trying to tell me something, Squeakette?"

I rewound the tape. This time when I attempted to hit the high note, Squeakette bit my elbow. Not a bite that broke the skin, but more of a warning nibble. She stood on her hind legs and put both paws over my mouth.

I stopped the tape and stretched out, patting the floor next to me.

She snuggled in and rested her head on my shoulder.

A newspaper headline flashed in my mind: OPERA SINGER'S CAREER RUINED BY CAT'S PAWS. I chuckled at the thought. Stroking her silky black fur, I said, "Do I tell Brian I can't practice at home because my cat bites me when I sing?"

If cats could speak, she would've answered, "Don't give up the day job, Mom." Instead she purred and kneaded under my arm, her eyes no longer slits. I didn't know cats could smile.

Everyone's a critic, but none quite as honest as my Squeakette.

~Janet Ramsdell Rockey

Edward
the Escape Artist

Freedom lies in being bold.
~Robert Frost

It was my niece Jenna's thirteenth birthday. My sister Gale, alias Mother Goose, decided Jenna was old enough to take care of a pet of her own. She found the perfect kitty, presenting it to her on her special day.

Edward arrived in a crate. The black, brown, and cream-colored Siamese feline gazed around the room in search of its new owner. Jenna was elated beyond words. The two became fast friends.

"Now, we need to keep him in his crate at night until I return all the critters we borrowed for the church program," my sister emphatically said.

Sis was known all over town for the visits she made to nursing homes, orphanages and schools with various animals. Glancing around her living room now, I spied baby chicks swimming in a plastic wading pool along with several bunnies wiggling their noses behind bars and happily munching grass. Soft bleating beckoned me to a corner of the room where a baby lamb rested on a mound of hay.

"Yep, Mother Goose has been up to her old tricks borrowing farm animals again," I murmured, as Jenna stroked Edward until he purred like a motorboat.

That evening things quieted as the animals bedded down for the night. After a long day of uninterrupted attention from Jenna, Edward was placed into his crate for the night. Soon human and animal snores mingled.

I awakened to the sound of excited voices.

"It can't be! Where's my kitty?" Jenna cried, her voice panic-stricken.

"What do you mean 'Where's my kitty?'" her mother asked, yawning.

"Edward's missing!" Jenna wailed.

I hurried to the crate. Sure enough, the cage was empty.

The morning passed quickly as every human in the household searched for the newest family member. When evening rolled around, Edward was still nowhere to be found.

We'd just finished eating dinner, deciding to play a game of *Scrabble*, when Jenna suddenly pointed excitedly toward the cabinet in the center of the room. The door of the cabinet slowly opened, revealing a thin paw batting this way and that. Seconds later, Edward jumped out, gazing around the room until he spotted his dish of cat food in the corner of the room.

"Meow!" he cried, greeting Jenna for the first time that day. The two played happily together until bedtime when Edward was placed into his crate for the night.

The next morning I was once again awakened with excited cries coming from the living room.

"Mom… get in here right away!" Jenna hollered.

Reaching for my robe, I raced into the room.

"What's going on?" Gale cried as she spotted baby chicks swimming in the wading pool, delighted to be free. Baby bunnies hopped around the room in search of something to nibble on while the furry lamb munched on a couch pillow.

"Who let these animals out of their cages?" Gale asked, placing a hand on each hip.

"Don't look at me!" Jenna cried. "Edward scratched at my door and woke me up. He got out of his cage again!"

"Something smells fishy around here and it's not the cat food," Sis remarked.

"Tonight we are going to find out who the culprit is!"

After all the animals were fed and bedded down for the evening, Sis asked her husband Dick to set up the video camera in the corner of the room. The remainder of the evening was spent playing board games and enjoying each other's company until it was time to bid each other goodnight.

The next morning I could hardly wait to find out who'd released the animals from their cages. Could Jenna or Gale's husband be playing a prank? What about my niece Michele or her two small sons?

Already my sister was fiddling with the camera in one hand while holding a cup of strong coffee in the other.

Soon the camera screen revealed the truth as Mother Goose and I gasped in unison.

While the theme song from the movie *The Pink Panther* played in my head, Edward, the Siamese cat, slowly reached a long paw through the wire door, releasing the lock on the crate. Ever so softly he made his great escape, glancing from side to side as he slowly slinked across the room. Reaching the rabbit cage, Edward released the hinge holding the door tightly shut. Soon, bunnies were hopping around the living room once again. Next came baby chicks followed by a bleating lamb. It was a midnight menagerie as the animals celebrated their freedom from captivity.

My sister reached out and gripped my arm. "In all my years of caring for God's creatures, I've never seen anything quite like this...."

I failed miserably at an attempt to stifle the laughter welling up inside.

"Look at it this way, Mother Goose. Edward is definitely a free spirit."

Loud meowing interrupted our conversation as Edward made his way across the living room tile. Reaching out, he latched onto the kitchen cabinet door with a paw. Then gazing into my sister's face, he appeared to be waiting for a response.

"That's the spirit, 'Free Spirit,'" she encouraged.

Edward meowed his approval... then continued his Great Escape.

~Mary Z. Smith

Funeral Home Director

Cats don't belong to people. They belong to places.
~Wright Morris

"**N**o," my father said. "We are not keeping that cat!"

Some people might interpret that message as "No. We are not keeping that cat!" But my sister and I interpreted Dad's message as, "I need a bit more time before we can let that cat into our house." And that was okay. We knew that this cat was a perfect match for our father.

After all, the gray tiger cat with a triangle-shaped chunk missing from his left ear was found in one of Dad's funeral cars, taking an afternoon snooze in a nice patch of sunshine in the back seat.

Dad owned the funeral home located next door to our house, and the cat quickly got into the habit of greeting him on our back steps first thing in the morning. He then escorted Dad to the funeral home, where they worked hard, both Dad and the cat. The cat took on the awesome responsibilities of chasing squirrels, dogs, and other cats from the parking lot, and greeting visitors who needed the company of a loving and sympathetic friend.

At the end of each day, the cat walked Dad home from work. Sometimes Dad would say, "Now, let's not feed that cat," which my mother interpreted as "Please wait until I'm asleep before you sneak him some leftover meatballs."

People attending funerals would sometimes ask Dad about the feline in the parking lot. If they appeared to be cat lovers, Dad would say, "Oh, that's Mr. Gray." If they didn't, he'd say, "That's a neighborhood stray."

Mr. Gray was savvy. He recognized that his ability as an escort, master of parking lot security, and official greeter weren't enough to secure him a new home. So he added a new task, that of printing supervisor. Dad printed his funeral home leaflets in our garage on an 1880's printing press—one that had a plate on top of it that was perfect for Mr. Gray to jump on to make sure that Dad didn't make any errors.

When my father was elected president of the local Rotary club, a newspaper reporter came to the funeral home to interview Dad and take his picture. A couple of days later the reporter called to ask Dad the identity of everyone in the photo. "There was no one besides me," Dad said, but then paused. "Oh, no! By any chance is there a grungy-looking gray tiger cat in the photo?"

When that was confirmed, Dad declared, "That's Mr. Gray. He's an employee of the funeral home."

When that photo appeared in the newspaper, we were delighted. And, when Dad came home from work that evening, he simply said, "Well, if you're going to keep that cat, you'd better get him to the vet for a checkup."

So we did. Mr. Gray was estimated to be three or four years old, and he lived more than a dozen additional years, a most loyal and wonderful friend to our family and the bereaved we served.

~Kelly Boyer Sagert

Jethro

*No one ever really dies
as long as they took the time to leave us with fond memories.*
~Chris Sorensen

Jethro came into my life many winters ago as a stray. I would be
in my house, sitting before the fire with my beloved Daisy, who
was quite happy to have me to herself. She had neither the need
nor the desire for anyone to interrupt our cozy twosome. As we sat
cuddled up together Jethro would jump on the outside windowsill
and peer inside, crying for our attention. At first, I would slip outside
to take him some food. I'd pet him awhile and try to coax him into
the garage for warmth. Sometimes he'd take me up on that offer, but
mostly he just wanted to be inside our house, instead of outside looking in.

Daisy would react with predictable fury when she saw Jethro
outside the window. She would hiss and growl, swat at the glass, and
try to impress upon him that he was neither wanted nor needed.

Eventually, I would sneak Jethro inside while Daisy slept in
another room. Seeming to know that he had to be quiet, Jethro
wouldn't meow or make a sound. He would get his fill of food, then lie
contentedly on that big couch that he had first spied from the window,
happy and secure in his new world.

Of course, Daisy soon caught on that he was slipping inside. She
could smell his presence, even after he left. So I began to let him in

right in front of her, reasoning that she would soon grow to love him as I had.

Jethro became a full-fledged member of the household, with all the rights that came along with it. Much to my surprise, he adored Daisy. He followed her from room to room, slept as close to her as she would allow, and was never far from her side, no matter how much she protested. Of course, Daisy did not share his enthusiasm. She would swat him away when he got too close, glare at him when he walked by, and generally treat him with the disdain that only a cat can pull off so successfully.

Although she never loved Jethro, Daisy did grow to tolerate his presence and life went on. Over the years, I moved a couple of times, married and had a son. Through each change in my life, my beloved kitties came along for the ride. Their relationship never changed. Jethro went on adoring Daisy, and she went on tolerating him in her own way.

At nineteen years of age, Daisy developed kidney failure. I took her to our vet and tried everything possible to save her, but she was just worn out. I finally had to make that horrible decision to have her put down. I still remember leaving the house with her the final time, stooping over to let Jethro give her one last little sniff. When I came home without her, Jethro was lost. He searched the house for a couple of days, and then settled into what I can only call a depression. He would lie in a corner of our living room, shielded from sight by a large chair, barely eating or drinking. I would try to coax him out, but he would have none of it.

After a few weeks, he began to come around a bit. He didn't isolate himself as much, and began to act more normally. I thought he was getting over his grief and forgetting about our Daisy. Life went on.

Approximately fourteen months after we lost Daisy, I was cleaning out a drawer and found some old VHS home movies. I popped one in our player and there was Daisy. We had taped her lying on our son's bed as I read him a bedtime story. Every time I would speak, she would roll around and meow at me. On the tape, my son and I were laughing at her as her sweet little meows filled the room.

From upstairs, I heard Jethro come running down the steps at full speed. He had heard his Daisy and was looking for her. I couldn't believe my eyes. This cat, which had never paid attention to anything on a television screen before, saw his beloved Daisy and stood on his hind legs, touching the screen with his front paws and meowing back at her. He stood mesmerized until I turned the television off. I sat there stunned as I realized the depth of Jethro's grief for his friend, and his still constant love of her.

I tried replaying the tape later to show my husband Jethro's reaction, but this time there was nothing. He seemed to have figured out she wasn't really there, but the memory of that moment has never left me. We lost our beloved Jethro almost two years to the day that Daisy passed. Their ashes are now together in a small urn, and while I feel that Daisy tolerates this last indulgence, I'm sure Jethro's heart soars.

~Lynn Rogers

Sassy Was a Lady

Always the cat remains a little beyond the limits we try to set for him in our blind folly.

~Andre Norton

My next-door neighbors were in their mid-seventies and very much into a healthy lifestyle. Part of their regime was a five-mile walk every day. One spring day, while out watering, I saw them striding toward me, heading for home in their blue-and-white jogging suits. They walked to my front gate and handed me a very small gray bundle of fur and told me that the kitten had been following them for at least six blocks, so they decided to bring it to me.

We have a huge area about a half a mile from the house that is designated for community gardens. They told me that the kitten saw them walking past the gardens and jumped out of the bushes and ran to them meowing. They tried to put it back inside the garden fence, but it kept coming out.

They walked away briskly, figuring that the little fur ball would give up and go back inside to its surely wild mother, the gardens being full of feral cats. It didn't. The tiny paws beat the pavement as fast as they could to keep up with the pair, mewing all the way. Finally they relented and decided to bring the little vagabond to me.

I didn't want another cat since I was on the road a lot with my business, but my daughter said she would help with the kitten. The neighbors also traveled a lot, but they said they would share in her upkeep if I would let them take her to their house when their grand-daughters came over to visit. I agreed.

Although very tiny, she was completely weaned and eating regular food. She immediately showed my old tomcats who was boss, and she walked right up to my Husky/Samoyed mix Lady, like a flyspeck on the nose of an elephant, smacked her away from her food, and started chowing down on Lady's meal. We laughed and named her Sassy.

The first thing we did was to take her to the vet. After a full checkup and her shots, the vet gave us bad news. Sassy was FIV positive. She would need special care, and even immunizations would not help her. Her first germ could be her last. He recommended we put her down, rather than go through the stress and expense of trying to keep her healthy. After a short confab, my daughter and I decided she was worth the risk. Sassy fought to find a family and we were not going to deny her.

Sassy was no ordinary cat. She got a kick out of alarms, particularly the stove timer. As soon as she was large enough to jump, she figured out how to move the timer dial on the back of the stove to make the timer alarm go off. She'd delight in setting it and jumping down to wait for it to go off so she could watch someone rush into the kitchen to turn off the noise. She was so persistent that I had to put duct tape over the dial.

Sassy visited the neighbors whenever their granddaughters came to visit. The girls would come over and ask if Sassy could play, and I'd hand her over. Sassy was always gentle with the girls. At the end of the day, they'd bring her back. I often wondered if being with the girls and watching them taught her the best trick in her bag.

Sassy started avoiding the cat box. I cleaned it and so did my daughter, and we both noticed there was less to clean. We started searching and sniffing around the house, and within days we tracked her down. She was using the toilet in our front bathroom. My daughter was first to figure it out, and I didn't believe her.

I'd heard of people potty training cats, but had never heard of a cat potty training itself. But sure enough, my daughter pulled me to the bathroom door, and as I peeked in, there was Sassy, poised over the commode, doing her thing. Afterward, she walked daintily around the toilet seat, scratching at it as if she were covering up her deposit with cat litter.

I went into the bathroom and flushed the toilet, figuring it would scare her away from the toilet and back to her litter box. It didn't. She sat on the rim of the seat and watched as I flushed.

After that day, we tried to keep the front bathroom door closed, figuring it would force her back to using the litter box. We only got a messed up paint job on the front of the bathroom door. Sassy would stand, scratch at the doorknob and meow until someone opened the door for her. Then she would rush in, jump on the toilet and relieve herself. She would paw at the handle to try to flush it until someone came in and did it for her. From the time she was two until she passed away in her sleep at seven years old, Sassy refused to use a cat litter box and only used the toilet.

I hope the toilets in kitty heaven are easier to flush than down here.

~Joyce A. Laird

Friends After All

*Some people say man is the most dangerous animal on the planet.
Obviously those people have never met an angry cat.*
~Lillian Johnson

Miss Goldie wasn't happy when Lucky Dog joined the family. Though she'd also been a stray when we welcomed her, the elderly cat wasn't as generous when the gentle Rottweiler-Lab-Chow-mix arrived. Her hair was always up.

It took some time for the black dog to settle in with us. He was leery of trusting anyone since he'd been pushed from a moving truck and abandoned. We bonded after he enjoyed a steady diet of food and fresh water, games of fetch, and walks through the neighborhood.

Miss Goldie wasn't amused. She hissed at the too-thin dog at every opportunity. He took it in stride by simply looking at her with soulful eyes. He plopped on the floor at my feet and propped his head on my leg. Miss Goldie glared at Lucky and flattened her ears.

I could almost hear her say, "Don't get too comfortable, Lucky. You're not staying."

But as the months passed, Miss Goldie and Lucky Dog developed a routine. They ate their food side by side. On a good day, Miss Goldie ignored Lucky. Most days, the hair stood up on her back when he got too close for her comfort.

Miss Goldie was all about comfort. First she focused on grooming. After licking her paw, she picked at a tuft of fur. When finished, she jumped on the porch swing, flexed her claws, and kneaded the cushion. Then she stretched out for her afternoon nap. But always keeping one eye open, guarding her turf.

"How are things between the cat and the dog?" my friend Natalie asked while stroking Goldie's soft fur. Goldie purred, but kept her eyes on the black dog in the distance.

"I doubt we'll be a family any time soon. I think the best we can hope is that Miss Goldie will learn to tolerate Lucky," I said. "He's still skittish," I added, wondering how anyone could hurt a dog, especially one as smart and sweet as Lucky. "He is good around Goldie. Very gentle."

I watched Lucky Dog prance across the grass with his head held high, tail straight, and his tongue lolling. A neighbor's large thirteen-year-old chocolate Lab, Mollie, waddled behind him, ears flapping. They played together often.

Miss Goldie glared at them when they approached, but she held her spot on the swing.

In no time, Lucky and Mollie tussled by the porch. Lucky barked. Mollie growled. Lucky snapped at Mollie's ear. She yipped. Mollie bit at Lucky. He snarled and bared his teeth. They rolled on the ground, bodies tangled, and sand clung to their thick coats. The musky scent of dog slobber and sweat permeated the air. The playful scuffle escalated and had become a full-on dogfight.

"Lucky!" I yelled. "Mollie! Stop!"

Before I could utter another word, Miss Goldie flew through the air. Her deep, low yowl turned into a shriek. A flurry of orange-and-white fur and outstretched claws pounced between Lucky and Mollie. Lucky stopped in his tracks. Mollie hesitated and cocked her head. Goldie bowed her back, hissed, and then smacked the stunned Lab on the nose with repeated one-two punches. Mollie yelped and headed for the safety of home.

For a moment I couldn't speak as I watched Miss Goldie turn to Lucky Dog as though to say, "Don't worry. Everything's okay now. I'm here to protect you." I shook my head.

"I can't believe Goldie did that," I muttered.

Natalie raised a brow and echoed my thoughts. "That was unbelievable."

But no more so than in the evening when I spotted Miss Goldie curled up against Lucky Dog's back. Who could have imagined it? We had turned into a family after all.

~Debra Ayers Brown

A Swan Tale

Every cat is special in its own way.
~Sara Jane Clark

Years ago I decided to take a two-week cruise on Lake Ontario in my twenty-three-foot sailboat. There was no one at home to pet sit, so I took with me my cats: Twinkle Toes, a black-and-white; her mother, Dusty; and a barn cat, Miss Piggy. Since it was a bit crowded with the four of us aboard, I thought Twink, my bravest and most stubborn cat, might enjoy a stroll ashore on one of the Toronto park islands.

Leaving the others on the sailboat, I put Twink in the dinghy and started rowing. As we neared the shore I noticed a large male mute swan had left his mate and batch of baby cygnets, and was gliding across the water toward us with a considerable bow wave, half-raised wings, and a nasty glint in his eye.

Thinking of Twink, I turned the boat and stepped up my stroke, and the swan responded by picking up his own pace. He had us on the run now. I rowed faster but he gained steadily. I shoved Twink behind me to the front of the dinghy, and as we neared the safety of the yacht, the situation suddenly deteriorated.

Seeing that we were about to escape, the swan spread his wings, flapped them furiously, and ran across the water at us hissing. I grabbed an oar and stood up in the tippy little boat to do battle to the death. Tales of swans breaking a man's wrist with a blow of their wing, capsizing canoes, and drowning children flashed through my mind.

I hoped I could beat him off with the oar. He slowed down when he saw me on my feet. I decided to try to make an escape again, and sat down to sprint under oars. We were still six feet away from the sailboat when Twink jumped for her life. She missed.

She plunked into the water just as I got alongside the hissing swan, still a few yards astern. I grabbed for her but I was too late. She swam away around the boat's stern, where the swan was heading, too.

I thought she was finished, as I scrambled out of the dinghy onto the sailboat, taking an oar with me in case the bird followed. I feared he would grab Twink and push her under the water.

I'd barely gotten into the cockpit when Twink reappeared on my side of the boat, having swum completely around it in about four seconds. Somehow she had escaped the swan.

I reached down, grabbed the slippery wet cat, and threw her through the open companionway into the cabin, then turned to repel all boarders.

The swan declined. He sat just astern hissing like a boiler, threatening and posturing furiously, determined that the cat would never get off that boat alive to threaten his young again.

It's been many years since I sailed with those three cats. Twinkle Toes and her mother Dusty now rest at the edge of my garden, but when I walk by the two stones marking their graves I remember Twink's stubborn courage and toughness.

~Susan Peterson Gateley

My Forever Cat

Death leaves a heartache no one can heal,
love leaves a memory no one can steal.
~From a headstone in Ireland

Snowball came to me as a Christmas gift when I was seven years old. She was part of my life until I was twenty-seven. Having a pet through all your growing-up years and into adulthood creates a remarkable bond. Snowball was a beautiful white cat with lemon-yellow eyes and a perfectly shaped pink nose. She was unique not only in her exceptionally good looks, but in her remarkable intelligence and devoted attachment to me.

When I was in elementary school, most days Snowball would follow me as I walked a mile to school. As I walked along the sidewalk, she would sneak through the shrubbery in all the front yards along the way. I could watch her from my classroom window, playing in the school courtyard all day. She would follow me home at the end of the day in the same manner.

Our bond was so strong that whenever I was upset or sick, she would always seek me out and sit by my side, never budging, until I felt better. When I would visit a friend, she would follow me and sit on their windowsill and wait for me. Later, in high school when I started driving to school, she would wait on the porch for me. She recognized my car and would run to greet me at the curb.

Snowball was a neighborhood sensation because of the way she loved to ride in the front basket of my bike and go trick-or-treating with my group of friends on Halloween. Sometimes, she would sit all day, obliviously basking in the sun in the middle of our street, forcing the neighbors to give up waiting and tapping their horns only to patiently laugh and drive around her.

She was remarkably courageous and fierce, too. Snowball loved to chase straying large German Shepherds and Sheepdogs out of our yard like a rodeo rider. We laughed as she rode on their backs, claws dug in, as they galloped, yelping for mercy all the way down the street.

Snowball eventually became a devoted mother of two litters. I was the only human she trusted to handle her babies right after their birth.

When I grew up and moved across the country I took her with me. Even at the advanced age of nineteen years, she was so youthful and full of energy that she chased after lizards on my apartment patio by running horizontally up the walls.

I cannot relate the details of her untimely illness and death because, even to this day, so many years later, it breaks my heart to think about that chapter of our lives. She lived to the age of twenty, but doubtlessly, she would have lived many more years if not for certain circumstances.

I was so devastated by the loss of my feline soul mate that it took me eleven years before I could accept another cat into my life. And during those years, I had this strong feeling that somehow, somewhere, she was still close by. It was a pervasive feeling that she was still with me, that her spirit was omnipresent and watching me.

I still have her ashes in a tea tin that I keep in a box in my closet. I couldn't bury her, for I did not know where I would be living years later and did not want to leave her behind and far away from me.

Two years after Snowball's death, my first child, Nicholas, was born. By the time he was two years old he was already gifted spiritually. I did believe he had amazing clairvoyant talent. For example, I would be sitting, writing out a grocery list, and thinking that I needed strawberries. And at that moment, my eighteen-month-old son would come toddling over and say, "Mommy, don't forget strawberries!"

One day, he was playing on the floor inside my closet. When he came out, I asked, "Nicky, what are you doing in there, sweetie?"

My son said, "Mommy, I'm playing with a pretty white cat!"

It took me completely by surprise. I had never mentioned Snowball's existence to Nick. I asked him, "What is a cat doing in my closet, Nicky?"

He replied, "She said that she's watching over you, Mommy."

~Lisa Wojcik

Out on a Limb

It is surmounting difficulties that makes heroes.
~Louis Pasteur

Early on a crisp October morning, I stood on our back deck and shivered. The temperature had dipped below freezing for the past two nights, unusual for an Oregon autumn, but it matched my mood.

A day earlier my sixteen-year-old, Nate, had been caught smoking near the high school. He and a friend had climbed into a tree to hide their activity. Now he was suspended from school for a week. My hands stuffed in my jacket pockets, I clenched my jaw. I couldn't believe it. He had embarrassed the whole family. I felt ashamed.

His ten-year-old sister, Alyssa, tugged my sleeve. "Mom," she said frantically, "I can't find Oliver. He's gone!" Oliver was her orange-and-white shorthaired tabby kitten, rescued a few weeks before from a collection of cats our neighbors kept.

Alyssa had used her ten-year-old cuteness until I agreed to let her adopt one of the healthier kittens. Because he was an orphan, she'd named him Oliver and given him a bright red collar.

"We have to find him, Mom!" Her eyebrows bunched with worry. "I can't go to school until Oliver's home safe!" She burst into tears.

The patio door opened. Nate, his hair spiked into a Mohawk, walked out onto the deck where we stood. He was dressed in black, with a spiky dog collar around his neck. A dog collar! He generally did well in school, but lately seemed rebellious. Why couldn't kids stay in that cute stage?

He tousled his sister's hair and asked, "What's wrong?"

She shot him a look and wiped her tears away. "Ollie's gone!" she wailed. "Get Ollie back, okay Nate?"

"Are you kidding? I can't find him," he replied, shrugging. I drilled him with The Look. He sighed loudly. "Okay. I'll try."

Try! If he tried a little harder at school instead of getting into trouble, I'd be a lot happier. I sent Alyssa off to school, promising to scour the neighborhood. Nate, suspended from classes, was to clean the garage as partial penance. He slunk away to do his chore. I swept leaves from the deck, scanning the horizon, listening intently.

Then I saw it: a glint of red near the top of our neighbor's towering fir. Ollie's bright red collar. But the tree was almost one hundred feet tall. How could a kitten climb so high?

"Oliver," I yelled over and over. Cold air stung my eyes each time I searched the dark boughs. Finally, a faint mew floated down. Somehow Ollie was stuck in the tallest tree in our neighborhood on the coldest morning of the year. The poor kitten clung to a branch at least seventy-five feet up. I ran inside and called the fire department.

I was shocked when the dispatcher said, "Sorry, we don't rescue kittens from trees. That's on TV. Try the utility company."

I ran back outside to comfort Ollie. He mewed every time I shouted his name, but now other voices joined in. Several large crows circled around, their caws loud and coarse. They dived at Oliver, again and again. I hurried back inside to phone the utility.

"You're outside the city limits, ma'am," the woman said. "We don't service your area. And anyway our ladders only extend fifty feet."

I tried not to cry. "Doesn't anybody care about a poor kitten?" I imagined Ollie cowering in terror on the branch while the mob of crows tried to peck him.

By noon the sun was out, but things in the tall fir were no better. All morning I'd been running outside every few minutes, alternately praying and trying to coax down the frightened kitten. Yet no matter what I did, Ollie wouldn't budge.

To make matters worse, the tree was in our neighbor's fenced back yard and he was away at work. He also owned two huge dogs that were fierce enough to warrant a "Beware of Dog" sign. I doubted any kitten could survive another freezing night without food or water.

Three hours later my voice was reduced to a hoarse whisper. I'd screamed at the crows and kept up a pep talk for Ollie, whose own cries were getting fainter by the minute. I told him to hang in there, and visualized that poster of a kitten hanging from a bar by its paws.

The crows must have had a nest near where he clung, for they didn't let up. Their black shiny wings shone as they struck and Ollie yowled in pain each time. How much more could the poor thing take?

When our neighbor finally got home, school was over. Alyssa would be home any minute. I called to Nate, still toiling away in the garage, and we raced next door. The man secured his dogs and brought out his tallest ladder, but the top step was still about six feet below the bottom branch of the tree.

I knew from the incident at school that my son was an expert climber. But I couldn't dwell on his mistakes now. "Don't worry Mom," Nate said. He clambered up the ladder, grabbed the bottom branch and hoisted his body up. I smiled at him.

Nate scaled the huge tree toting a Strawberry Shortcake pillowcase, to keep Ollie from scratching or jumping, just as Alyssa burst into the yard. We prayed for Nate to be sure-footed, and Alyssa screamed at the crows to leave her kitty alone. Finally her big brother descended, a squirming lump inside the pillowcase.

Alyssa hugged Nate. "You're my hero!"

By some miracle, Oliver only suffered a couple of cuts on his face where the crows had attacked. The tiny orange-and-white fur ball was cold and hungry, but he gobbled some food and water, crawled into Alyssa's lap and fell asleep.

I slipped into the garage. The entire space had been tidied and swept, and Nate stood to one side, his chin resting on the handle of the push broom. In the commotion of rescuing the cat, I hadn't noticed that my son's hair was still spiked but the dog collar was gone. Still, he wouldn't look at me.

"Son," I said, "I hope you won't keep smoking—cigarettes can kill you."

He held up a hand. "I know, I know, it was stupid." He shook his head. "I'm sorry I disappointed you."

I placed my hand gently on his shoulder. "I was going to say that what you did was heroic—rescuing Ollie that is. I love you and I'm proud of what you did to save the kitten."

"Really?" The rebellious glare softened to a contrite smile.

"Just don't go climbing trees for the wrong reason, okay?" I said and we laughed.

Later Oliver padded into the kitchen and rubbed against his rescuer's leg, as if to say, "Thanks." Nate stroked Ollie's ears. Heroes, I thought, aren't hard to find. You just have to be willing to go out on a limb.

~Linda S. Clare

I Can't Believe My Cat Did That!

Chapter 2

Impawsable

The Gymnast

Play is the beginning of knowledge.
~Author Unknown

When I adopted Leo J. as a six-week-old kitten, I could never have imagined that I was adopting a world-class gymnast. Named Leo for his leopard-spotted coat, my little friend would amaze me in ways I didn't know possible.

One hot summer afternoon, the UPS driver pulled up to our home and dropped off a large cardboard box. My mother had ordered my father a pair of tennis shoes, and she told me to leave the box close to my father's favorite spot on the couch for him to open later that evening.

My father opened the large shipping box to find the shoebox inside, and shoved the larger box to the side in his eagerness to try out his new shoes. After strutting around the living room for a little while, Dad came back to discard the boxes.

He crumpled up the tissue paper from the shoebox, and the packing paper from the shipping box, and placed both inside the large brown shipping box.

After closing the top of the box and shimmying the paper inside, Dad noticed something unusual. My little Leo, who had been aloof during the fashion show of my dad's new shoes, now began to wiggle his hind haunches as if preparing to pounce. Noticing this slight movement, Dad shimmied the box—which was right in front of him—again.

What happened next was something that my father, mother, and I could never have predicted. Leo J. took off in a gallop, heading straight for my father and the box. Instead of doing a normal cat thing and trying to jump inside the box, Leo jumped just before reaching the box, did a somersault over the top of the box, and landed on his back in my father's arms!

This cat had not only managed to catch all of us off guard, he had calculated his trajectory path, velocity, height, and mass perfectly to pull off this most amazing stunt!

Seeing this most bizarre sight, my dad insisted on trying his set-up one more time. Again, Leo wiggled those hind haunches, took off in a gallop for my father, and somersaulted perfectly over the box and into my father's arms. It is from this athletic stunt that Leo J. has earned his reputation as a world-class gymnast.

~Lisa Kirkpatrick Mueller

Ride of a Lifetime

Down deep, we're all motivated by the same urges.
Cats have the courage to live by them.
~Jim Davis

Our family cat Scuber liked riding in, and on, cars. We were fine with his riding in the car, but the times he secretly rode on the car terrified us.

Once he rode to work with my dad. After a coworker announced there was a cat walking around the office, my dad went to take a look. "That's my cat!" he exclaimed. Another time he rode on my mom's car to my grandparents' house. My mom had no idea until she was leaving and heard a "meow" coming from across the street. She looked up to see Scuber, gazing at her from the neighbors' front yard.

But our favorite Scuber story happened right after my grandfather had come for a visit. As he drove home on the four-lane highway, he noticed two college-age girls in the car to his left waving and smiling at him. He waved and smiled back, assuming they were just being friendly or possibly admiring his new midnight blue Signature Lincoln Town Car. After all, it was the luxury car to have in the mid-eighties, with power seats and windows, leather interior and keypad entry. His even had the optional canvas roof that mimicked the look of a convertible.

He turned his eyes back to the road, but couldn't help noticing that the girls were still waving. Becoming a little embarrassed, but flattered nonetheless, he acknowledged them again. Still, they stayed next to him and soon began mouthing words and pointing at him.

An exit was coming up, so he decided to take it and see if the girls would follow him. They did not so he decided to examine the car. Nothing could have surprised him more than what he saw. There was Scuber, his fur sticking straight out and his claws still latched onto the cloth roof of the Town Car.

The cat was a little shaken up, but aside from that he was unharmed. My grandfather scooped him up and put him gently in the back seat, where he rode with him back to our house.

We all had a good laugh picturing Scuber hanging on for dear life to the roof of the car, while my grandfather, oblivious to this, relished the attention he and his car were receiving from the two young ladies.

~Jane Barron

Lipstick and Kisses

Cats are designated friends.
~Norman Corwin

C.C. stood for "Crazy Cat" and I won her friendship by offering her bites of a Krystal Cheeseburger. Little did I know that this cat would become my officemate, my second shadow, and my best friend. C.C. was, however, very particular about her company. Coming from a home where she received little attention, C.C. most certainly preferred to have only one close companion at a time. I happened to be the companion that she chose. If anyone else came near her, C.C. would growl, hiss, and behave like someone had just committed a major crime.

I have never met a cat that liked to have things as neat and orderly as C.C. did. After repeatedly finding permanent markers by my bedroom door for a few days in a row, I finally discovered that this crazy feline was trying to tell me that a box of permanent markers had spilled in my office/spare bedroom. C.C. was trying to clean up the mess one marker at a time!

One morning, I started my day with my usual routine. I got dressed and then headed into the bathroom to put on my make-up. As usual, C.C. was by my side to make sure that I was following all of the regular protocols.

For some reason, though, she disappeared after I got my foundation on and evened out. After putting on my eye shadow and mascara, I started to hear an unusual ruckus coming from my office.

I was in a hurry this particular morning, so I didn't pay much attention to the noises. However, it soon became apparent that C.C. was on a mission. Almost as if she knew that I was nearing the end of my make-up routine, she came strutting down the hallway meowing in the most garbled way that I have ever heard. She sounded like a human trying to talk with their mouth full.

I was alarmed. What if she was choking on something?

C.C. reached the doorway at the exact time I turned around. I looked down at her and said, "C.C., honey, what's wrong?"

What I saw next absolutely amazed me. As if to answer my question, C.C. sat down, spit something gold out of her mouth, and looked up to me as if to say, "See what I did? I'm helping you!"

This Crazy Cat had gone into my office and found a tube of lipstick that I needed to apply next — which I had left on my desk!

Through tears, I thanked this special girly girl. And you better believe that I did wear that shade of lipstick!

C.C. passed away a few years ago, but she did leave me with another memory that I still hold dear to my heart. After many years of lifting up my chin to blow kisses at this crazy girl, in her final year of life on this earth, she did actually pick up on this gesture and started lifting up her own chin as if trying to blow kisses back at me. Was C.C. really crazy or was she an extremely attentive and smart feline? As for me, I vote for the latter, and there is certainly nothing crazy about that!

~Lisa Kirkpatrick Mueller

A Hug for Harry

There are few things in life more heartwarming than to be welcomed by a cat.
~Tay Hohoff

"**M**rs. Hamilton, I'm Harry. The rental office sent me over to put up your ceiling fan," announced the man through the screen door of my apartment.

Oreo and Cookie, my feline roommates, scattered to find hiding places from the suspicious looking person in khaki work clothes. Riding across the country caged in a car was unnerving. Having every room filled with boxes, and strange looking birds and trees in the yard was frightening. And now there was a stranger invading their new home in Florida.

"That's great. If you need to get into the attic crawl space, there is a pull-down staircase in the closet," I explained, as I led him to the back bedroom where the fan was to be installed. The curious cats followed at a safe distance, peeking in from the living room to see who this man was and what he was doing.

Harry took off his hat and scratched his bald head as he surveyed the job and my cluttered bedroom. "I'll get the fan and a ladder from the truck while you finish up in here."

"Nice looking cats," Harry remarked, returning to the living room. Oreo dove behind the sofa and Cookie scrambled to the top of a mountain of boxes.

Oreo and Cookie were littermates whose mother belonged to a

coworker in Tennessee, from where I had just moved. Rumor was that their daddy was a roadie with a famous country music star.

They were a day old when we saw them for the first time, curled up in the back of a closet where they were born. My daughter picked Oreo's name because of his sleek black-and-white fur. After we got them home, Cookie seemed an obvious name for his sister. Cookie was matte-gray with a stub tail, while Oreo had what seemed like an extra long tail. They were easygoing, but each had a unique personality.

"Harry, if you have a key, I'm going to head out to work. But I need to warn you about the cats," I said, searching through a box for my shoes. "The gray cat, Cookie, is a climber. If you go into the attic, please be sure to pull the stairs up behind you so she can't follow you up there. She loves to explore, and who knows how long it would take us to get her back down."

"No problem." Harry chuckled.

"The black-and-white cat is Oreo," I continued, anticipating the usual reaction. "This may sound strange, but he may try to jump from the floor to your chest to give you a hug. He doesn't have front claws, so he won't hurt you."

Without saying a word, Harry stopped in his tracks and looked at me doubtfully. Shaking his head, he continued walking out the front door.

A few minutes later Harry came back in.

"Huh!" I heard him say from the living room.

I looked in and saw an amazed Harry. Oreo had jumped on him and was clinging to him now, with his paws wrapped around Harry's neck and his head tucked under Harry's chin. It was a giant hospitable hug, letting our returning visitor know that he was welcome.

"He really does do that!" Harry grinned, petting the purring Oreo.

~Maryanne Hamilton

The Great Escape

Turn your wounds into wisdom.
~Oprah Winfrey

My sister phoned me from the Humane Society to tell me about a tiny orange-and-white kitten with bright blue eyes and a sad little meow. His mother had died after being hit by a car but her young kittens had been found and saved.

"All his brothers and sisters were adopted except him," Jennie said, adding, "he's all alone." She paused, careful not to make any connection between the kitten's situation and my own. My family was worried that I was lonely, or at least on the verge of lonely, those days.

I had recently moved to Portland, Oregon to take a job as a residential counselor in a lock-down treatment facility for teenage girls who were battling mental illness and substance abuse. The job proved to be exhausting, putting me into situations for which even the best college degree couldn't have prepared me. My family knew that even more challenging for me than my new job, was trying to recover after a painful breakup that preceded my move.

"May I please give this kitten to you for your birthday?" Jennie asked excitedly. She knew that I had longed to have a cat of my own, but my previous boyfriend was severely allergic and getting a cat had been out of the question. Since our breakup, there was no reason for me to wait anymore, but I still reserved hope that we'd reunite.

Despite my hesitation, my curiosity drove me to visit the Humane Society and I was drawn to the kitten immediately. Jimmy was soon on his way to his new home in my small studio apartment.

The following year of cat ownership was demanding, and I had a lot to learn. Jimmy had lost his mother too early. He had trouble figuring out how to eat and toilet independently. I managed to feed him using an eyedropper, and frequent sponge baths helped with his other difficulties. Despite my nursing, Jimmy often bit and scratched me unexpectedly. I found myself diagnosing my cat with psychological disorders similar to those that impacted the teenage clients with whom I worked during the day. I wondered if Jimmy would ever feel at home with me.

Not surprisingly, some of my clients began asking me about the scratches on my arms. Many of the girls had a history of self-harming or cutting their skin to deal with their traumatic pasts, many had been in abusive relationships, and many had participated in gangs or destructive behavior in the community. They looked upon my scratches with concern and suspicion. To calm the girls, I began telling them stories about Jimmy and my efforts to raise him. Over the course of the following year, I brought in pictures of Jimmy as he grew into a very large tabby, bigger than some small dogs.

Some clients hung onto my stories about Jimmy more than others. The girls were ordered into treatment with the belief they should be rehabilitated rather than incarcerated in juvenile detention, yet many of them still fought fiercely against the treatment process and the staff. Those girls who most longed to return to their previous lives on the streets would inevitably join together, creating secret schemes to escape the locked facility. Their plans usually involved attacking a staff member, stealing the keys we all carried around with us, and fleeing out the doors into the night.

Fortunately, I was never physically assaulted while working at the facility, but when clients did escape, I spent weeks worrying about them. Usually those same girls were found and returned to the facility, some with a very different perspective after experiencing indescribable hardships while on the run.

One evening in April, I returned to my studio apartment after a particularly difficult day at work. I called hello to Jimmy, as I always did when I got home. Jimmy never came when he was called, so my ritual was more about saying his name than waiting to hear his feet padding toward me in response. My sister had been right—having Jimmy comforted me during the times I could have felt lonely as my heart mended. I walked across the room and sat down on the narrow window ledge that ran the length of my studio. That spot was my favorite place to relax after work because I could watch people walking on the street below. Jimmy often squeezed his huge furry self up on that ledge when I wasn't there.

Jimmy? I scanned my eyes around my studio, this time taking a closer look for him. It was difficult not to see him in such a small space. I began looking in the few places he could actually hide, but my apartment was empty.

I had left the windows open while I was at work. The windows had no screens and I had a sinking realization of what must have happened. Jimmy had either fallen out, having grown too chubby for the window ledge, or he had tried to make a great escape to the streets far below, like my clients at work. I craned my neck outside and peered down.

While cats tend to fall on their feet, how could Jimmy survive a drop from a third floor apartment onto cement? Even if he had survived the fall, Jimmy was a house cat, with no experience on the streets. How could he manage the traffic, the other animals, and all those people? Jimmy barely put up with me some days!

Instead of discovering the worst, I saw Jimmy huddled in the shrubs below, his fur shining bright and orange like an emergency cone. He was clearly alive, but cowering in fear as cars rushed nearby. Shoeless, I ran out and swooped him up in my arms. Instead of scratching me, Jimmy relaxed and pressed against me while I bounded up the stairs to our apartment. Jimmy remained calm, in shock perhaps, as I took him to the veterinarian for a checkup, where I was assured that he was okay.

I realized that even more than surviving the fall, it was astonishing that Jimmy hadn't bolted the moment his feet hit the ground. He could have been hit by a car or ended up at the Humane Society again. Something special had held him to that spot, telling him to wait for me to come home. Had Jimmy finally learned to trust me?

The next day, I had my most valuable Jimmy story to share with the clients at work. Like Jimmy, these young women knew what it was like to want to run away or to stage a great escape, believing it to be the easiest option. Sometimes, we find ourselves falling and we're not even sure how it happened. In any case, life is not only about having the ability to land on our feet. We have to know when to stay put and to accept help from people who we trust. I hope that perhaps some of the clients who listened to Jimmy's story were encouraged to stick with their treatment, accept help from the staff, and forego escape attempts.

~Sally Desouza

Trainhopping

It is in the nature of cats to do a certain amount of unescorted roaming.
~Adlai Stevenson

Fisk means "fish" in Danish, or so a friend told us after we had already named the black-and-white, half-grown cat we found on our doorstep one morning. The first day, we gave our friendly visitor milk. He was still there the next day, and the next. By that time we were giving Fisk bowls of minced meat.

"It seems to want to live here with us," I said.

"We should put notices around the neighbourhood in case anyone has lost it," Barney, my husband, suggested.

We did that, but no one called, and Fisk stayed. Outside we played tag with him in the yard around the vegetables, and inside we played chase the feather. He was now part of our family, but we put our name and phone number on a little blue collar around his neck as he still wandered off sometimes.

I would get phone calls from old ladies and other neighbours wanting to come get him after he had invited himself into their houses and sat purring on their knees. Once the local train station staff called, saying he was wandering around the station.

A few months later, our first baby was born. I was very busy with my new son, and probably giving Fisk less attention than usual.

One evening in December it was snowing lightly. The phone rang.

"Hi, do you have a cat called Fisk?" a man's voice asked.

"Yes," I answered.

"Well, a black-and-white cat with your phone number on a tag around his neck has just jumped into my car. I'm in the station car park at Hatfield."

Hatfield was the next town down the railroad.

"That's incredible," I said. "We live in Welwyn Garden City. I know he tends to wander, as he used to be a stray, but how on earth has he got to Hatfield?"

"Well, as I looked down the platform, I saw a cat jump out of the train I just got out of," the man said. "He must have followed me to my car. When I opened the door, this little cat leaped in as if he owned it."

We both were laughing so much we could hardly speak.

"I shut him in the car to make this phone call to keep him safe," the man said when he had controlled his laughter enough to talk. "Look, I'll bring him back to your place. Where do you live?"

"But, surely," I said, "you must have just got off the train at Hatfield because you are on your way home. You're in the next town down the line. You won't want to drive all the way back here. Why don't we wait until my husband comes home, and he can drive over and get Fisk." This was getting surreal.

"Well, don't worry, it's no problem. I'll just bring him over now. What's your address?"

I told him, and some time later the doorbell rang, and there was Fisk in the arms of this kind man, struggling to get free.

By this time, Barney was home. We both thanked the driver standing out there in the snow.

"Would you like to come in, have something to drink, or some supper?" I asked, amazed at the trouble he went to for Fisk and us.

"No, it's okay, I've got to get home now before this snow gets bad," he replied.

He waved goodbye as he disappeared into the snowy darkness.

~Caroline M. Brown

The Odd Couple

In ancient times cats were worshipped as gods; they have not forgotten this.
~Terry Pratchett

Hadaash was a regal cat. With long brown fur and a tail that rivaled a raccoon's, he demanded attention whenever he crossed a room. He was poised, fastidious and, dare I say, sophisticated. Perhaps that is why he had little tolerance for our brown Poodle, Smokey, undoubtedly one of the dumbest dogs that ever lived.

While Hadaash seemed to have a command over the outdoors, the outdoors seemed to have a command over Smokey. We would open the door, and before Hadaash could put one sure step outside, Smokey would nearly bowl him over in an attempt to escape the confines of the house. The Maine Coon would just glare at him with obvious disdain.

One evening, after filling their bowl with fresh water, my husband watched Hadaash's refined movements as he drank. A moment later, Smokey came barreling into the room, thirsty for a drink of his own.

Pushing Hadaash aside, Smokey proceeded to lap up the water from the bright red bowl they shared. With just a moment of hesitation, Hadaash looked down at the dog, lifted his left paw and shoved Smokey's head into the bowl.

Sputtering, the Poodle shook the water from his brown curls and looked at the cat sitting regally beside him. Hadaash seemed to understand that the dog was blaming him for this action, so he simply looked at Smokey, and then raised his eyes toward my husband, as if to blame the human for the dunking.

If ever there was a time we wished for a video camera, it was then. However, even if we'd had one, we could never predict the actions of such a magnificent cat, especially when in the presence of unbridled idiocy. Hadaash and Smokey, our furry version of the Odd Couple.

--Hana Haatainen Caye

Reprinted by permission of
Bruce Robinson ©2010

The Kibble Shower

After scolding one's cat one looks into its face and is seized by the ugly suspicion that it understood every word. And has filed it for reference.
~Charlotte Gray

Dinner with the family was uneventful that night. Or it was until I heard a noise overhead and looked up, just in time to see cat kibble raining down on us. It landed in our hair, dotted our food plates, and splashed in our milk glasses. Then the kibble was quickly followed by an empty cat food dish, which hit the middle of the table upside down, and wobbled noisily to a stop. We all looked in the direction the kibble bomb came from, but we saw nothing, yet. Almost in unison, we said, "Suki!"

At the sound of her name, our mischievous Siamese cat raised her black silky head just high enough for us to see it over the edge of the catwalk. Being the generous souls that we are, we gave Suki the benefit of the doubt, and assumed this stunt was an accident. But whether it was intentional or not, Suki evidently liked the hoopla she caused, and that night would be the first of many kibble showers.

The problem had started a few months earlier when we moved into our cabin in the woods. Our young Boxer dog, Jake, ate his dinner in the kitchen. He'd attack his food with gusto, pushing his dish all over the room as he emptied it. He'd lick the bowl shiny, then flip it over for inspection in case he had missed something. With that done, he'd go in search of dessert. Cat food! Suki was a delicate eater and chose to pick through her bowl slowly, savoring each bite at leisure.

That is, until the marauding Jake discovered her food. He'd push her away and devour whatever was left in the bowl, as Suki watched helplessly.

We had to find a place where she could eat in peace. The choices were few, and nothing seemed to work out well. Knowing that Jake feared the staircase, we started putting Suki's dish on the landing at the top of the stairs. That worked for a while. Unfortunately, Jake's fear of the stairs was not as strong as his love of cat food. It took some time, and he looked a lot like a swimming turtle as he climbed, but he eventually conquered the staircase. Once again, Suki's food was in jeopardy.

Finally I had a new idea. Jutting out from the landing was a catwalk, about six inches wide, and overlooking the dinner table. It was perfect for Suki, who tended to sit up there anyway, enjoying the warm air that rose from the wood stove. And there was no way Jake could navigate the catwalk. Suki was finally able to eat in peace. In fact, it seemed like she enjoyed her food more than ever, knowing that Jake sat squirming in frustration nearby.

Then, one evening, as we ate big bowls of creamy potato soup, it happened again. A quick movement, a "thunk!" and immediately it rained kibble. We were stunned. When she decided she was finished eating, she gave the bowl a good swat and sent it flying down on us. Clearly, she was amused by the family's reaction because she filed this away in her bag of cat tricks, and repeated it whenever she felt like it.

Without telling us, Dad decided to tackle the Suki problem himself. One evening we sat down to dinner with Suki munching away overhead as usual. Then something hit the table. It was a much bigger, much more disruptive thunk than usual. This time it wasn't kibble, but Suki herself. In a mad scramble to regain her footing and her dignity, she took a quick look around, and then ran off to hide.

"What happened?" we asked. Then Dad explained.

"Look up. Her dish is still there."

He'd replaced her old dish with one of my stepmom's wooden salad bowls, which he had nailed in place on the catwalk. Then he filled it with kibble. He knew Suki couldn't bat the bowl off the landing, but it hadn't occurred to him that when she swatted the bowl, she'd knock herself off. It only happened once. Suki was unharmed, but she learned that lesson quickly, and never again tried to bat her bowl at us.

Years after Suki passed away, I could still see the hole in the landing where the nail held down her bowl. Yes, she could be a pain, but it was impossible not to admire her spunk.

--Teresa Ambord

19

The Storm Shelter

If a cat does something, we call it instinct; if we do the same thing,
for the same reason, we call it intelligence.
~Will Cuppy

I n mid-May in Arkansas anything can happen weather-wise, and one night it did. It started out a typical day, with a beautiful blue sky, clouds on the horizon, and temperatures still in the bearable range. I was going about my normal routine when I noticed our cat Flower marching across the room with one of her kittens in her mouth. I gently took the kitten away from her and put it back in the basket in my brother's room where the kittens "lived." Five minutes later she did the same thing again. Again I took the kitten away from her, but this time swatted and scolded her. A few minutes later, she returned again.

I was curious so I let her go and watched. She took the kitten into another room, and then over to a wooden nightstand that was missing the top drawer.

Flower is a mostly white calico with short legs and a long plume of a tail; she looked pretty cute as she sat on her hind legs and tried to raise herself high enough to drop the kitten into the bottom drawer of the nightstand. Her big golden eyes glowed with determination as she tried to figure out the best way to accomplish her goal.

Understanding what she wanted now, although not understanding why, I emptied the bottom drawer and put a soft blanket inside it. Then I moved the drawer into my brother's room, placing it where

Flower's kitten basket had been. I carefully transferred the kittens from basket to drawer, Flower watching me intently.

When I was done, she hopped into the drawer with the kittens and lay down to let them nurse, purring loudly. I had to admit, the nightstand did make a better place for the kittens—with the hard wooden top and sides it was protected from drafts and anything that might be accidentally dropped. I praised her for her intelligence and beauty and went back to what I had been doing before we started the Great Kitten Relocation.

That evening, storms rolled in. As we watched the OKC Thunder basketball game on TV real thunder rumbled outside. Lightning flashed across the sky. The wind blew and the rain came down—a nice thunderstorm! We left the front door open to enjoy the fresh air and watch the storm.

Then the weather changed. The wind went from twenty miles an hour to at least sixty—then it blew harder still. Rain blew horizontally, coming six feet into the house. We struggled to close the door, and as we pushed, I gasped… everything outside had turned into a complete blur. The door finally closed, we stared at each other in shock. We listened to the storm rage outside, and then heard a loud crack and pop nearby. All the lights went out.

Less than fifteen minutes later, the storm had passed. The wind calmed and the rain was just a soft patter. We breathed a sigh of relief. The electricity was still off when we went to bed, but we were confident it would be back on by morning.

Morning brought a few shocks, but still no electricity. There were huge trees uprooted all around us. The ground around the big walnut tree in the front yard was cracked and raised—we nearly had a tree in our living room!

The neighbor behind us couldn't get out of her house until the landlord sent someone with a chainsaw to help. She also lost part of her roof—we found it in the churchyard across the street. Power poles looked like toothpicks, cracked and broken on the ground. Oddly enough, the two trashcans we had set out by the curb were still there, untouched. Most of the town was without power and stayed that way for three and a half days.

Word started getting around about what we already suspected—a tornado had come through our little town. And as happens so often with night storms, the sirens never went off. But Flower knew it was coming. Hours before it happened, that little cat knew we were in for more than just a regular old thunderstorm and she wanted her babies safe.

After that night, the nightstand with the missing drawer, which has since been home to three more litters of kittens, became known as The Storm Shelter. And Flower became known as the smartest cat we know.

~Linda Sabourin

20

The Real Max

Cats come and go without ever leaving.
~Martha Curtis

Max was a beautiful longhaired cat. His shiny black-and-gray striped coat was distinctive. I could always tell our Max from the other neighborhood cats. It was like recognizing your child, bundled up on a cold winter's day with just a patch of skin showing. I just knew!

Max was an outdoor cat, but he loved his warm indoor house and our family. Needing his private outside time, Max enjoyed being let out in the evening, free to roam the neighborhood and seek out his favorite cat haunts. He would come home when called, usually on the third holler.

One evening when Max didn't respond to my third call we all worried. This wasn't like our Max. Perhaps he had been catnapped. We told our children Max probably wandered too far and got lost, and we would do our best to find him.

The next morning we put up flyers with Max's picture and our telephone number, offering a reward. Everyone helped tape flyers to trees and telephone poles. It seemed that the entire state of New Jersey knew that Max was lost. Neighbors called at night to see if Max had been found.

A week passed and I was heartbroken when we received a call from a local pizza parlor, some six blocks away, telling us Max had been found dead. He was run over by a car in front of their restaurant window. I hesitated telling my kids, knowing there was no easy way to convey this sad message.

My husband and I drove to the pizza parlor to pick up the remains of our dear Max. "He's in the pizza box, by the curb," the proprietor said. "We picked him up with a shovel and put him inside the pizza box. We're sorry for your loss."

Peeking inside the cardboard box we saw a dead, flattened cat. Yes, it looked like Max.

Max would love this—he always liked to lick the sauce off our slices of pizza.

We placed Max's remains inside the garage for safekeeping. We intended to break the news of Max's demise to our children that evening, and bury him in our flower garden the next day.

"Mommy, mommy," came a cry from my eldest son. "Did you forget to bring in the pizza?" And there stood Steven, in the middle of the kitchen, holding the pizza box with our dead cat Max inside.

Not knowing whether to laugh or cry, I grabbed the box and told the children to sit down as I had some sad news to tell them. They all cried, but were relieved to know that Max didn't suffer and experienced a quick death. Since I was too upset to prepare dinner that night we actually did order a pizza.

The next morning, my husband dug a big hole in the garden and the boys made a cross from Popsicle sticks. We all said a few kind words about our beloved Max as he was lowered into the ground. Vicki, my daughter, covered the grave with handpicked flowers from the garden. This lovely funeral and tribute to Max would have made him happy.

A month later, a Max lookalike showed up at our front door, thin, hungry and meowing. We had buried the wrong cat. We all agreed that our family provided the unknown, homeless, run over cat with a four-star funeral.

My children kissed and brushed Max and were elated to have him home again, no matter how he got there. I wondered which one of his nine lives he used up making the journey home. To celebrate his return, we called for another pizza, with extra sauce for Max.

~Irene Maran

I Can't Believe My Cat Did That!

Chapter
3

Miss Congeniality

Trade You

I am as vigilant as a cat to steal cream.
~William Shakespeare

"Hang on a second, sweetie," I said, pushing the door closed with my foot. "Let me put these bags down first and then I'll pet you."

Luna wove figure eights through my legs, meowing for attention. I dropped my keys on the desk as I walked by. The jingling caught her attention. She jumped up on the desk, swatting at the keys. Maybe I could get the groceries to the kitchen without tripping over her. Crash! I looked back over my shoulder. She'd knocked the keys to the floor and had them in her mouth.

I couldn't help but laugh. She looked so cute. The key chain was in her mouth and the keys themselves hung between her front legs like a metal tutu. She waddled off, the keys dragging the floor under her belly.

After I put the groceries away, I went to find Luna and my keys. She was in the living room playing with a toy mouse. But my keys were gone. I searched all over but couldn't find them.

"What in the world did you do with my keys?" I asked her. She just looked at me with her big green eyes, rubbed against me, and purred. When my son came home, he helped me look. We tore the house apart trying to find them.

We looked under the couch and behind the loveseat. We found some loose change but no keys. We looked under the beds and behind the refrigerator. We found a lost bottle opener but no keys. We looked under the stove and in the cabinets—still no keys.

Luna must have thought my keys were really something special because she hid them in a really safe place. Unfortunately, she wasn't about to show me where. I finally gave up and had new keys made.

A month later, I was working on a craft project with a long leather string. Luna was fascinated with it. She kept grabbing the string and trying to run off.

"No way," I told her, taking it from her for about the tenth time. "If I let you out of my sight with this, it'll be like my keys. I'll never see it again."

She looked at me for a moment and stalked out of the room with her nose in the air. A few minutes later she returned with my keys in her mouth and dropped them at my feet. I stared wide-eyed as she jumped up on my desk, grabbed the leather string, and darted off.

It was almost as if she were saying, "Trade you."

~Kimber Krochmal

Nature Calls

The cat is the only animal which accepts the comforts
but rejects the bondage of domesticity.
~Georges Louis Leclerc de Buffon

When we moved to our new home in Alabama, our three indoor-only cats quickly discovered the pleasures of a screened-in porch—all the smells, sights and sounds of the great outdoors without any of the dangers.

Our boys, Cujo and Laser, were content to laze on the porch watching the squirrels, birds and chipmunks that were always in the yard. Fluffy, however, the oldest and most adventurous of our trio, wanted more. She was always looking for a way to sneak out into the big wide world so we could never open any door to the outside before checking to see whether she was lurking in the vicinity.

I guess it was bound to happen. One evening, just a few months after we moved in, my husband was on his way out to the grill with his hands full. Fluffy came dashing out of nowhere, darted around his legs and in a flash was out the door and into the woods.

We had adopted Fluffy from the shelter when she was just nine weeks old. At five years old, she had never been outside in her life. My husband and I spent hours calling her and looking for her, but to no avail.

Anyone who has ever had a feline family member knows that if a cat does not want to be found, you are not going to find her. When it got dark, there wasn't much we could do except go inside and hope she found her way back. I was terribly worried about her having encounters with other animals, getting hit by a car or just getting lost.

I didn't get much sleep that night, so at about 4:00 a.m., I decided that I might as well just get up. Since it is so quiet around our neighborhood at that hour, I thought I would go outside, and maybe I would be able to hear Fluffy if she was crying in distress.

I flipped on the outside light and looked out the window. To my great relief and joy, there was Fluffy, apparently no worse for the wear, sitting on the back sidewalk. I ran to the screen door and flung it open. As I did, Fluffy came bounding along the sidewalk and up the steps.

This is like something out of a corny movie, I thought as she ran full-speed toward me.

She ran toward me and past me, up the stairs, and straight to her litter box.

Apparently no one had ever told Fluffy that it was okay to relieve herself outside.

Fluffy did little except sleep for the next twenty-four hours. Whatever adventures she had that night, they certainly wore her out. In the thirteen years since that great escape, she has never again made an attempt to get out and commune with nature.

~Nancy Kucik

Our Striped Spot

She clawed her way into my heart and wouldn't let go.
~Missy Altijd

My striped cat Spot was small in stature but large in spirit. I tried to keep her an indoor cat, but she was insistent. I eventually made peace with the fact that Spot was an indoor/outdoor cat. I worried about her constantly when she was outside, but there was no arguing with Spot.

Spot and I first lived in a beautiful part of Los Angeles called Topanga Canyon. Topanga has miles of wide-open spaces and rolling hills where dogs, coyotes, rattlesnakes and all sorts of wild animals roam—so Spot fit right in.

I loved Topanga but I was scared of the pack of dogs that ran through the canyon. These dogs were domesticated, but on occasion they acted unpredictably. I froze when they'd surround me at the mailbox. Usually they were friendly, but sometimes one of the dogs would snarl and then the others would too.

One afternoon, Spot and I were sitting on our porch and the dogs ran into the driveway. I heard Spot hiss and saw the fur on her back stand up. I tried to grab her, but Spot charged down the stairs directly toward the dogs.

A few months earlier, these dogs had killed our neighbor's cat, Sweet Pea, so I was terrified. I yelled for Spot to stop, but she increased her speed. I should have run after her, but I was so afraid that instead I covered my eyes and held my breath. I heard a yelp, and when I peaked through my fingers, I saw the dogs running away—and Spot strutting down our driveway.

Spot wasn't always heroic, though. Sometimes she was downright ornery. Veterinarians in particular had a hard time with Spot, but that's partly because they underestimated her. Spot had always been good with her first vet because he too had "temperamental children" as he described Spot. He knew how to soothe Spot and she never gave him trouble.

One day when I brought Spot in for routine shots her regular doctor wasn't there. I told the receptionist that maybe we should come back because Spot was a handful, but she insisted that the new vet was also good with difficult animals.

When the new vet walked in, I told her Spot's history, but she assured me not to worry. I tried again. The woman looked at me like I was insane.

"Look, I handle Rottweilers, Dobermans and Pit Bulls on a daily basis so this isn't going to be a problem. I'm just going to start by taking Spot's temperature," she replied.

"You're going to take her temperature?" I exclaimed. "You definitely do not want to take Spot's temperature. Let's just do the shots."

After the vet insisted that she would go ahead, I turned my back and said, "I'm sorry, I can't watch."

The next thing I heard was a low, deep growl and an angry hiss. When I turned around, Spot's eyes were dilated and she was staring down the vet, who now had blood dripping from the tip of her nose to her upper lip.

We had to find a new vet.

The only time the strength of my will matched Spot's was when she and I were living in a South Bay condo. The condo had wall-to-wall white carpet that was expensive to shampoo so my roommate and I only deep cleaned the carpet once a year. I remember coming home one day after the carpet had been cleaned and admiring how great it looked.

Not wanting to track any dirt into the condo, I left my shoes at the door, said hello to Spot and got in the shower. When I got out of the shower I saw a gray cat sitting outside the bathroom door. I was momentarily confused. Spot was the only cat living in our condo, but Spot wasn't gray, she had stripes.

Then I saw little gray footprints all over the freshly cleaned white carpet and realized that Spot had gotten in the fireplace, rolled around in the ashes, and then walked all over the wet carpet, leaving gray, sooty paw prints from one end of the condo to the next.

I grabbed Spot by the scruff and said, "You're getting a bath, young lady, and I don't want to hear a peep out of you."

Spot knew I was serious because she allowed me to put her in the bathtub and scrub her from head to tail without struggling. Once I dried her off, she went under the bed and watched me clean the soot off the carpet one paw print at a time. It took me three hours.

Years later Spot and I met Tom. Tom was handsome and sweet—he brought me flowers and Spot toys so we both adored him! Eventually, Tom and I got married and the three of us became a family.

Tom loves cats and to my amazement, he did the impossible and tamed Spot. As she'd curl up against his chest to go to sleep, we'd joke that she'd gone from being "The Topanga Terror" to becoming "The South Bay Softie." She let Tom brush her and would sit with him for hours in his music studio as he wrote songs. Beyond a shadow of a doubt, Tom won Spot's respect—and Spot stole Tom's heart. Spot remained "my baby" but she became Tom's best friend.

At the age of fourteen, Spot's kidneys failed. On the dreadful day that we had to put Spot to sleep, I held her gently and whispered, "Mommy loves you" as the vet administered the lethal injection. Tom bit his lip as Spot faded away and sighed, "She was my best friend." Holding Spot's body, I sobbed while I watched Tom crumble; he shook and cried uncontrollably. It was hard to believe that my ornery little terror had ended up being such a softie that she had become Tom's devoted companion.

~Rebecca Hill

The Island Cat

You will always be lucky if you know how to make friends with strange cats.
~Proverb

We had only been on the island of Saint Thomas for a day. Newly married and excited to explore, Tom and I sat on the balcony of our rental condo overlooking Coki Beach and sipped wine for breakfast. This was the good life. Tom, getting ready to begin medical school, and I, his bright-eyed new wife, will always remember this moment. Not only because it was picture-perfect, but also because it was when our cat, Essie, entered our lives and made us a family.

She sashayed up to our second-floor balcony bellowing a high-pitched meow for attention. We backed away at first with fearful thoughts of feral island cats, but she wasn't deterred. Stretching her long, slender legs, she casually opened her mouth to yawn and bared her large teeth. I yelped and gathered my knees to my chest, wondering what she would do next.

Moving smoothly, like a dancing ballerina, she shimmied up against Tom, as if to claim him as her property. Then she jumped onto the table and stuck her head in his wine glass. He pulled her away and, much to my chagrin, put her on my lap. She began to purr and knead my legs. Then she lowered herself onto my lap and rested—where a pool of drool that could only be traced back to her mouth began to form.

We laughed while wondering if she had rabies or some strange disease. Later we would discover that Saint Thomas is a rabies-free island.

What kind of a cat just runs up to a random stranger, sticks her head in their wine glass and drools?

Suddenly this strange, spotted cat with a wild-eyed look intrigued me. She certainly wasn't afraid of us and I began to feel like we shouldn't be afraid of her either.

We ran into the condo and took some fish out of the freezer, cut it into bite-sized pieces, and brought it onto the balcony. We watched her devour it as we stroked her soft fur. With a final slurp and lick of her lips, she rid the porch of any evidence of food and looked around expectantly.

We left the condo that morning and spent the next eight hours snorkeling and enjoying the ocean. When we returned, Essie was lying on the balcony and eagerly leapt to her feet to greet us.

For the next couple of weeks we had a routine. Essie would join us for meals and then lie on our laps. We lavished her with meals of fish and lunchmeat and whatever else we had that would satisfy her.

Five days before we were supposed to leave the island Tom finally said what both of us had been wondering. "Should we take Essie home with us?"

"You said it," I said accusingly, though secretly excited by the thought of bringing our new family member home.

"You were thinking it," he replied, smiling. We went to bed nervous at the prospect of bringing Essie home, and wondered how to even start the process. The next morning we awoke expecting to find Essie on our balcony waiting for her usual morning meal, but she wasn't there. When we couldn't find her we began to worry.

"What if she got hit by a car? What if she was taken in by animal control?" I ranted. We resolved that it must not have been meant to be—but not before searching the local beaches and roadsides. After seeing no sign of Essie, we drove back to our condo with a glimmer of hope that she would be waiting. She wasn't.

It wasn't until 10 p.m., when we were sitting on our balcony mourning our loss, that we heard the familiar high-pitched meow. We jumped up and down, excited that we had our cat back. We brought her into the condo, something we had been resisting because it was not ours, and slept with her through the night.

In the morning we called the airlines to find out how to fly a cat from Saint Thomas to Michigan. The process was surprisingly simple, and after clearing her health with the local vet and ensuring that she wasn't someone else's cat, we boxed her in a small airline-compliant crate.

After twelve grueling hours we arrived home. When my parents picked us up from the airport their jaws dropped as we walked toward the car carrying a cat. We had left a couple, but returned a family of three. All because of an island cat with the will to adopt us as her family.

~Ayesha Schroeder

Guru Kitty

Commit to be fit.
~Author Unknown

"Hey cat, careful, you'll scrunch my papers." Naomi, my sleek, black kitty, ignored my warning and plopped into my lap. She kneaded the papers several times with her paws and settled in.

"Sorry. They're important." I set her on the floor and smoothed the papers as best I could. They were important indeed—a report on my bone density scan that showed osteopenia. The doctor warned if I didn't take action I was a likely candidate for osteoporosis. I pictured a cabinet full of medications and a future where I had to be on constant vigil not to fall and fracture something. I had to take action, and fast.

Naomi leapt back onto my lap.

"Seriously, cat. Quit messing with the papers." I ruffled the fur between her ears and set her on the couch beside me.

"Meow." She turned her head to stare at me with her round, green eyes.

I started to read the lab report for the tenth time.

"Meow." She extended one slender paw and whapped my arm.

This was atypical Naomi behavior. Could she be trying to tell me something?

"You have an idea, Miss Naomi?" I ruffled the fur between her ears.

"Meow." She tiptoed to the other end of the couch where she sat, turned her head away from me, and began licking her back.

"Is that advice?" I couldn't lick my back in a million years. And if I could, what would that have to do with my bones?

Naomi stopped grooming herself and looked at me. Her expression was a mix of disgust and disdain.

I thought a minute. "I get it. Flexibility."

She revved her gravelly engine until she had a loud purr going.

I was so impressed with her advice that I set the lab report on the lamp table, got up from the couch and did something I'd been putting off for years. I called the yoga studio a friend attended and registered for a weekly class. I resolved to take exercise classes at our local recreation center too.

With one more glance at the papers, I went to the kitchen to prepare dinner. A wedge of three-layer chocolate cake left over from a granddaughter's birthday beckoned me from the counter. I got a fork and prepared to dig in for some quick energy before I started cooking.

Before I could take a single luscious bite I felt Naomi rub against my leg. Naomi isn't a cat who rubs against legs. I leaned down, swooped her into my arms, and scratched the white spot in the center of her black chest.

"Hey, Miss Kitty, what are you doing?" I asked. "I hope you don't have your eye on that cake. Chocolate is bad for kitties."

"Meow," she answered.

"Okay, so it's bad for humans too."

"Meow." She blinked her eyes.

"Are we talking a diet for me?"

Again she rumbled into a purr.

I thought of the articles I'd read about the benefits of whole grains and green leafy vegetables. "I don't have to give up cranberry orange muffins and mochas, do I?"

She rumbled on. Who was she to talk? Or rather purr. Holding steady at eight pounds, she refused all kitty snacks and had maintained the same weight and waistline for fifteen years. I couldn't say the same for me. More importantly, geriatric for a cat, she could spring on any counter in the house. Nutrition had to have something to do with that.

I set Naomi on the floor and put an inverted bowl over the chocolate cake so I wouldn't be tempted.

Naomi stretched and walked across the kitchen. "Meow, meow," she said, looking back at me from the doorway into the hall.

"I need to make dinner. Do you have more advice for me?" I supposed with all the controversy I'd read in articles about the treatment of bone density, a cat's advice might be as good as any.

"Meow." She twitched her tail.

"I'm coming."

In the master bedroom Naomi went immediately to a shoebox lid of cat toys near our bed. She lay down on her side, stretched one paw into the lid, and batted a cloth mouse, sending it flying. Then she pounced on it and batted it directly toward me.

"I'll play 'cat and mouse' with you." I surprised us both when I lay down near Naomi and knocked the mouse her way.

"Meow," she said with a tone that implied, "look at you relaxing and having some fun." She whopped the mouse back to me.

I sent it scurrying in front of her nose.

She flicked the toy just out of my reach.

I scooted for it and flipped it back so quickly it whizzed by her head.

Naomi's ears flattened and she pounced on it before batting it back. We'd have to try out for the cat and mouse Olympics. I was Type A to the max, which couldn't be good for my bones, not to mention my cardiovascular system. I should do this every night.

I crept closer to Naomi, snaked out an arm and pulled her close.

She lifted her head, rubbed her cheek against mine, and burst out with her loudest purr yet.

"You're better motivation than any article I've read," I said, my lips against her tiny damp nose. Naomi was a nice name, but maybe I should start calling her Guru Kitty.

~Samantha Ducloux Waltz

Sophie's Touch

A friend is one of the nicest things you can have,
and one of the best things you can be.
~Douglas Pagels

Everett slammed the door and flounced on the couch, sending Sophie, his cat, vaulting for quieter territory. "I hate it when they do that! Hate it! Hate it! Hate it!" he fumed through splotchy red cheeks damp with sweat.

"Do what?" I asked, sitting beside my ten-year-old.

"Nothing."

"Oh," I said, stroking his hair.

Annoyed, he shrugged my hand away. Then, as if to make his point, he turned his back to me, pulled his legs tight against his body, and wrapped his arms around himself.

"You seem awfully upset about 'nothing.'"

"I'm not upset," he said, digging his chin resolutely into his knees.

"Mad, maybe?"

"No! Can you leave me alone, Mom?" he said, looking back at me a little apologetically. "Please?"

"Yeah," I sighed. "I'll give you some space, but it's important to talk to somebody about the stuff we feel strongly about, even if it's not to a parent." I hoped he was listening. "Okay?"

He grunted. My son is not one for many words when something

is bothering him, so I took his response as a yes and headed to the kitchen.

For an instant, I had visions of being a cookie-baking mom and imagined whipping up a batch of double-chocolate-chip Toll House. Not wanting to add to his list of "nothing," I simply sprinkled chocolate chips on a dollop of peanut butter and returned to the living room a few minutes later.

Everett wasn't on the couch anymore. At first I thought he'd gone back outside to settle the "nothing" with the other kids. Then, I heard him whisper. I scanned the room and saw him kneeling beside the rocking chair that Sophie claimed after she had fled the couch.

He'd put his head down on the seat cushion and was running his hands through her fur like I'd tried to do with his hair. From the snippets I could hear across the room, I could tell he was sharing his burdens about the neighborhood altercation.

I was thankful he was talking to someone, anyone, even a cat, and I was thankful his little snowshoe tabby was a quiet, patient listener who would likely sit and purr as long as he'd pet her and whisper softly.

But there was something missing.

Everett needed someone to respond to him. He needed someone to stroke his hair, or rub his back, to reciprocate his gentle touch. I set the cookie substitute down and took a few soft steps forward, careful not to disturb them. As I knelt down behind Everett, poised to rub his back while he stroked the cat, I saw it. Sophie was licking Everett's forehead and hair, reciprocating his kindness, his gentleness, and his touch.

I stood up, as quietly as I had bent down. Then I backed away, letting boy and cat share the moment alone. As I left the living room, I heard Everett whisper, "Sophie, you're a really good listener." A few minutes later, he was playing a game of ball with the kids on our street, the "nothing" apparently kissed away by a sweet little snowshoe who knew how to listen.

~Mary C. Chace

The Reign of Cleopatra

Cats do not have to be shown how to have a good time,
for they are unfailingly ingenious in that respect.
~James Mason

At age ten I was already a huge animal lover, but had never had a cat of my own. When I visited friends who had cats, I loved to pet their soft fur and feel their happy purr, so I jumped at the chance to cat-sit for two cats when a friend of my mother's offered to hire me.

The indoor cats lived in a single story, second-floor apartment. The male was a gray tabby named Caesar The female was a Siamese named Cleo, short for Cleopatra. All I had to do on each visit was put out food and clean water, scoop the litter box, and keep the cats company for a while.

Everything went well from the very first visit. I had practiced my "Here, kitty, kitty!" but as soon as Caesar heard me put the key in the lock he was on his way to meet me with a "meow" and a dance between my legs. Cleo was more standoffish, but her loud "mer-row" let me know she heard me arrive. She finally made her appearance when she heard the can opener's whirr.

By the time my first cat-sitting assignment ended seven days later, I still didn't have a cat of my own, but I felt like I had two cat friends. Every visit was a blur of leg rubs and happy purrs. I felt like a cat whisperer. I was a natural.

Then one day I got a sad telephone call. Caesar had died unexpectedly. Would I ask my mom if Cleo could stay at our house while her owner was out of town for a three-day weekend? The owner worried that Cleo would be upset if left alone so soon without Caesar's company.

When my mom said okay, I was over the moon. Even though she wasn't mine, I was going to have a cat living at my house! I couldn't wait for my buddy Cleo to arrive.

Although I was glad to see Cleo, she didn't reciprocate the feeling. When she came in the door, I wanted a cat cuddle, but she ran off to explore the house. "Mer-row, mer-row" echoed off the walls.

I had scarcely said goodbye to Cleo's owner before Cleo finished a circle of the first floor. Then, although she had never seen a staircase before, she ran up the bottom set of stairs, barely paused at the landing and bounded up the second flight of stairs to the top. She was on a tear, back and forth, up and down. I tried a "Here, kitty. C'mon, Cleo," patting a spot next to me on the sofa, but Cleo didn't break stride to even look at me. I thought she just needed time to acclimate to her new surroundings.

Over the next few hours, Cleo kept up her wild pace. Up and down stairs, up and over the back of the sofa, always on the move, and always just out of reach. In the past, Caesar had been friendlier than Cleo, but eventually Cleo would come for a scratch behind the ears. There were no scratches for her that day.

Later in the day, I realized the house seemed quiet and I hadn't seen Cleo for a while. "Cleo! Here, kitty!" I called.

She didn't come, but she did answer with her regal "mer-row!"

I was standing by the bottom of the stairs and her voice sounded loud. I looked around but I didn't see her anywhere.

"Mer-row!" Cleo said again.

I looked up and saw her head stuck through the railing at the top of the stairs, directly above my head. The tip of her tail twitched back and forth.

"Careful, Cleo!" I yelled. Could a slender Siamese fit all the way through the railings or was she stuck? I was panicked. If she could fit through, what if she lost her balance and fell? I didn't want to have to explain how I killed my cat-sitting charge.

"It's okay, Cleo. I'm coming." I used my sweetest, most soothing voice and edged up one stair.

Before I got to the second step, Cleo flattened her ears against her head and hurtled through the air. I didn't have to worry about her falling, because she jumped!

I didn't have time to react. Cleo landed on my back and bounced off into the living room in one motion. When I turned the corner to check on her, she was sitting calmly, cleaning her fur as if nothing unusual had happened. I, on the other hand, was a nervous wreck.

I told my mom what happened.

"She's so fast, you probably just didn't see her come down the top flight of stairs," Mom said.

I almost believed her, until it happened again. And again.

The next time I couldn't find Cleo, I tiptoed to the steps and peeked overhead. Sure enough, there was Cleo. Waiting. It had become a game for her. Which would have been fine, except the next time I headed upstairs I was in a hurry and I had forgotten about Cleo's game. As she launched herself into space, I took two stairs instead of one. This time, instead of a smooth bounce off my back, Cleo had to use her claws to steady herself as she sideswiped my head.

"Ow!"

The blood convinced Mom I was telling the truth, and before the day was over, she had the cat land on her head once or twice too. But I didn't celebrate this little victory. We were under attack.

Shy Cleo had gone Rambo. Maybe she was over-stimulated by the excitement of experiencing stairs for the first time. Maybe it was the whole change of surroundings. Whatever it was, Cleo was a fast learner, graduating from novice user to stair ninja in a matter of minutes.

I don't know if we were "prey" or just part of a crazy cat practical joke, but for the rest of the time that Cleo stayed at our house, we had to hold a book over our heads if we wanted to use the stairs. You couldn't always see her, but Cleo lurked in the shadows, waiting to pounce—and she never missed. She never seemed to get tired of waiting either, even if no one came by for a long time. She was a true cat "survivor" willing to outwit, outlast and outplay us.

I wasn't the cat whisperer anymore.

Cleo was in charge.

~Wendy Greenley

My Glory

A bit of fragrance always clings to the hand that gives roses.
~Chinese Proverb

Months after we lost our longtime companion of sixteen years, we were delighted to receive a call from someone who knew of a cat that desperately needed a home. Glory fit into our empty nest immediately. She seemed to get to know us personally. A "designer breed," she is a mix of Ragdoll and Siamese, making her a Ragamese.

She arranges her schedule to meet ours. She watches her favorite television program every night curled alongside us. She goes to get her bedtime snack at the same time as my husband. She loves people and hates unoccupied rooms.

One day, sitting in traffic during the long ride home, I wondered how I had made it through the drawn-out day at work. I was bone-weary by the time I arrived at my dimly lit house. I was in no hurry to go inside since my husband was in the hospital for the third time that year. Hesitantly, I entered to face the quiet.

I threw my jacket and keys down on the table, and with an audible sigh, fell back into the comfortable chair that was the only thing to welcome me.

Much to my surprise, Glory pranced proudly through the hallway with a single rose clenched in her mouth! Dropping it at my feet, she couldn't have possibly known what that meant to me. Could she? Somehow she had removed the flower from the vase and brought it to me—a special delivery that quickly changed my mood. The overturned vase, the water glistening on the mahogany wood, only made me smile.

I have always loved to receive flowers, but never more than that lonely day when I came home from work so dejected and Glory presented me with a rose.

~Verna Bowman

My Talking Cat

Lots of people talk to animals.... Not very many listen, though....
That's the problem.
~Benjamin Hoff, The Tao of Pooh

Home alone, I curled up in a chair to read Mary Higgins Clark's *Pretend You Don't See Her*. Actually alone is not accurate. Two days earlier we'd adopted a three-year-old female cat alternately striped in shades of brown, black, and orange. Sweet Martha, as we christened her, now hid under the bed in the guest room.

Understanding a new cat's need for privacy, we provided her necessities near the bed. A note from a foster parent had accompanied our kitty: "I would have kept her because she's a sweetheart, but I already have four cats and this one is too vocal." So far, this cat with the mouthy reputation hadn't uttered a syllable.

Then I heard, in a perfect rendition of Joan Rivers' voice, "Hal-lo!" I looked down and saw Sweet Martha sitting by my chair. During my lifetime, I'd enjoyed countless cat companions, but I couldn't believe I had one that talked! I tried to coax her into my lap for a long conversation, but she slipped back into hiding.

I couldn't wait to tell my husband Sam about our talking cat, though I know he'd wonder if I'd been into the catnip while he'd been out. As soon as he arrived, Sweet Martha met him with another "Hal-lo."

Sam rewarded her with a dollop of whipped cream, which she

lapped up with obvious pleasure. I phoned our daughter Susan, who lived in a nearby town.

"Guess what, Susan! We have a new cat and she talks! Both Dad and I have heard her!"

"That's nice," she said. Our daughter spoke in a condescending tone that indicated she thought her mother was becoming dotty. She humored me by saying, "I'm pretty busy right now, but I'll come over as soon as I can to meet your..." she cleared her throat, "talking cat."

Sweet Martha couldn't pronounce the letter "S" so Sam was "Am." My name, Alice, came out "Ai-eee." I guess she couldn't manage the "C," though we knew she could produce an "L."

When my daughter finally stopped by, she displayed doubt with tone of voice and choice of words.

"So, you're the so-called 'talking cat'?" she muttered, bending down to pet Martha. The cat ducked this intruder's hand, but responded with a great big "Hal-lo!"

Susan, totally amazed, responded, "She sounds just like Joan Rivers!"

We tried to get her to say "Susan" or call us by the names she'd given us, but Martha stalked off. She let us know that she refused to perform on demand.

Her speaking vocabulary peaked at three English words, yet she showed disdain at our lack of linguistic ability. She seemed to think we were the stupidest creatures on earth because we couldn't understand her when she spoke "Cat."

She'd beg each morning—in Cat—for her cream, then demanded to go outside. She made friends with all the neighbors in our cul-de-sac. Though our city prohibited cats from roaming free, we could not convince Martha, who had been a stray, to comply with this regulation.

We feared neighbors might call Animal Control to capture her while she squatted in their flowerbeds instead of her litter box. Instead she befriended everyone by sharing long discourses in Cat, as she looked each listener in the eye. More than one neighbor commented that he or she had never heard a cat "talk" so much. Some she greeted with "Hal-lo," but mostly she saved that for newcomers to our home.

She became a favorite among the neighborhood children and received invitations to every First Communion and birthday party on the block. Most she refused, preferring to pop into a child's house on her own with a continuous stream of her feline chatter.

When not visiting, Martha hunted birds of all varieties and squirrels that outweighed her. Though we tried to discourage her hunting, she left morning offerings on our porch. One spring the whole neighborhood experienced an invasion of voles. People stuffed mothballs, peanut butter and chewing gum in the unsightly mounds that dotted our pristine suburban lawns. Nothing dissuaded the critters. Martha took matters into her own paws. She began leaving dead varmints on neighbors' porches as well as ours. Even those who didn't really like the garrulous little cat became her fans.

Many volunteered to give Martha a home when we retired from Minnesota to South Texas, but we couldn't leave her behind. For once she didn't utter a sound as she experienced traveling by plane.

Due to the hungry coyote population in our new location, we concluded Martha must convert to Indoor Catism. This new confining life made our cat and us, by extension, miserable. We had deprived her of her favorite activities—hunting and visiting neighbors. She voiced her displeasure loudly. We stood firm until the day I felt so sorry for her, I brought her out to the upper balcony for some fresh sea air. In a flash, she walked down the side of the house—three stories to the yard! Before I could make my way down two flights of stairs, she had removed tail feathers from a seagull and was chasing a lizard in the yard next door.

We gave up. Knowing by now that she did understand every word we spoke, we explained the perils of coyotes. We promised her that we would allow her outside under this condition: she needed to abide by the 8:00 p.m. curfew or become a coyote's supper.

For all the days of her life in Texas, Martha showed up on the front porch at exactly 8:00 p.m. Post-Martha we now share our home with two other adopted cats. Unlike their amazing predecessor, neither has spoken a word of English to us.

~Alice Marks

The Unlikely Gift

The manner of giving is worth more than the gift.
~Pierre Corneille, Le Menteur

All my life I had wanted a pet. So when I got married and set up my own first household, a kitten was at the top of my agenda. Luckily, I learned that another teacher at school had a litter of Siamese kittens born a few weeks earlier. Perfect! When my husband carried me over the threshold, the kitten trotted ahead of us.

After a serious, long discussion — our budget was settled more quickly and easily — the kitten was given the name Tico. Tico the tyke. She was also given everything else a kitten might possibly want. Not just food, but special treats. Not just a comfy bed, but our bed. If we were working on something she had to have the best vantage point. If my husband was painting the door, she was on his shoulder. If I was marking essays, she supervised the allocation of marks. If she wanted to play with the blue pen, I wrote with the red one.

She matured into a cat — but stayed as small as many kittens and just as playful. She knew she was the heart of the household. One tiny, plaintive meow could bring all kinds of good things. We doted on her, probably to excess. Whatever she wanted, it was our pleasure to give her.

Then came our first Christmas. We bought a turkey and I crossed my fingers that I could cook it. We prepared it the night before, all ready to pop into the oven. Tico surveyed every move, nose twitching, ready to assist. It looked as if our first Christmas dinner might be perfect. But overnight I came down with a violent flu. Tossing and feverish, I moved onto the chesterfield under blankets that were alternately too hot and not warm enough.

"You'll have to cook the turkey," I croaked. My husband tentatively got to work in the kitchen. Slowly the aroma of cooking turkey began to permeate the apartment. For me, it only made matters worse.

I had expected that Tico would be in the kitchen investigating and supervising, close to the source of the wonderful aroma and ready to be first to help with taste testing. But she was with me, cuddled into my neck. I would toss and turn over every few minutes. She would quietly move, wait till I settled for the next few minutes and then curl back into my neck. I would turn again, and again she would wait and settle back. It went on all morning.

My husband, meanwhile, checked the cooking. He added water to the turkey innards and boiled them for flavoring for the gravy. The additional aroma added to my woes. I ran to the bathroom yet again. Tico ignored the smells and settled back with me after each bathroom break.

Somehow in the middle of all this I managed to fall asleep. Not much of a sleep—I have vague memories of Tico climbing back and forth across my pillow to keep track of my thrashing. Then I awoke with a strong smell of cooked turkey liver in my nostrils. Tico was sitting up straight, about a foot from my nose. Right beside my mouth was a large piece of cooked turkey liver—her treat from the turkey that my husband had put in her dish.

"Eat it!" her posture said. "It will do you good. You'll like it."

Okay, I was in a weakened state, but the tears flowed. How generous. How giving. The most delicious morsel saved for me when I was ill.

I had sensed that a kitten would bring an emotional richness into my life. I just didn't know she would return our giving with practical giving of her own. I managed to choke back the turkey liver—just. Accepting gifts, even unlikely gifts, is important too.

~Valerie Fletcher Adolph

I Can't Believe My Cat Did That!

Chapter 4

Mr. Right

The Chosen

People that don't like cats haven't met the right one yet.
~Deborah A. Edwards

A cat rescuer in San Diego, whose name I never knew, was often referred to as The Cat Lady since she happily shared her home with twenty-six cats. When she was diagnosed with a severe allergy to cats it was strongly recommended that she find good homes for her furry charges. I was drawn to the unfortunate plight of an altruistic lady who had spent several decades caring for society's discarded felines.

I reasoned with my husband Doug, who did not like cats, that we needed an environmentally friendly exterminator because of our growing problem with roof rats. Although Doug wondered how adopting a new pet would impact our prey-driven white German Shepherd, Kodi, he eventually acquiesced.

I arrived at The Cat Lady's house and braced myself for the smell of twenty-six cats living in one home. I was pleasantly surprised. The Cat Lady ushered me into her spotless and fresh smelling living room where a plethora of cats roamed freely from the ledge on the fireplace, to the top of the bookshelves and all spaces in-between.

Setting myself down on the floor in the middle of the room to get acquainted with the former outcasts, The Cat Lady and I talked while I assessed the parade of critters displaying differing levels of curiosity about me. Some were distantly curious, some playfully accepting, but most tried to nonchalantly sniff the stranger in the midst when I wasn't looking.

During our conversation, The Cat Lady revealed she was broken-hearted about her diagnosis. She felt the weight of needing to place her beloved companions into the right families, and she was experiencing separation anxiety because of it.

She offered to show me her custom-built cat sanctuary, and I agreed since my curiosity was not only limited to the furry critters. The converted garage was like no other I had ever imagined. What was once the family's double-car garage was now an unbelievable kitty-cat playground. She revealed she had spent $10,000 to outfit the entire area to accommodate every cat necessity she could think of and then added a few extravagant luxuries. She wanted the outcasts of society to feel loved and pampered.

Built-in carpeted stairs led to upper walkways, and carpeted plank inclines connected shelves set at differing heights around the area. Carpeted climbing trees stood in all shapes and sizes like a forest. Numerous carpeted boxes of differing sizes had cat-sized openings and provided privacy during nap time. The room had rolling toys and hanging toys and comfy little kitty bed cushions. There were twenty-six covered litter boxes lined up in a row.

Prowling contentedly throughout this Cat Palace were black cats of all sizes. "You have an unusual number of black cats," I observed.

"I won't adopt out the black ones," she stated firmly. "People do bad things to them. I'll keep my black ones and take pills for allergies if necessary."

I felt warmed by this lady's passion to help the former unfortunates.

We returned to the living room and I took up my cross-legged observation point on the floor again in hopes of bonding with our future rat-catcher. I became fond of a playful blue-eyed kitten.

"I'll adopt the cute little gray tabby," I said.

"You can't have that one."

"Excuse me?"

"I won't let them go until they are fixed and declawed," she said.

"We'll have him neutered."

"I won't adopt out any of my cats until they are fixed," she repeated firmly. "You need the white cat over there." My eyes followed her finger pointing to a fur ball lying on the shelf.

"I don't really want a white cat," dismissing her recommendation. "We have a white dog and don't need another white pet. Besides, I hadn't even noticed him until now."

"You need to consider him. That white cat will make you a good rat-catcher and friend."

"No thanks. I really don't want a white cat."

"But that cat wants you."

"How would you know? He hasn't even come down off the shelf to smell me."

"But he hasn't taken his eyes off you since you've been here. I've gotten to know you, your personality and your needs. I can guarantee he will be the best cat for you."

"I don't know." I hesitated, not entirely convinced.

"You may not have chosen him, but he has chosen you."

Finally and reluctantly, I agreed to take the cat.

As my newly acquired white rat-catcher and I departed, The Cat Lady whispered with tears in her eyes, "Bring him back if he doesn't live up to your expectations."

Cautious of how Kodi would react, I apprehensively carried our newly adopted cat into the house. Kodi was lying on his side with his legs stretched out. He didn't bother getting up to check out the unsolicited intruder. Instead, when I set the white cat on the floor, the fearless feline headed straight to Kodi.

It was a recipe for flying fur. Kodi took one look at the critter and with a lick of welcome on top of the cat's head, he laid back down to resume his nap. Then, the confident cat curled up in-between Kodi's legs and made himself at home. I stood there amazed.

I said to Kodi, "Looks like you've got yourself a new buddy."

Doug came into the living room to meet our newest family member. As he sat down on the couch to observe Kodi and the cat sleeping together, I told him about The Cat Lady, her twenty-six cats, The Cat Palace, and the adoption recommendation.

"Sounds like you were chosen to be his new owner," Doug observed. "Looks like Kodi was chosen to be his new buddy."

As if on cue at the end of my story, the slumbering cat woke up, stretched, hurried over to meet Doug. Jumping up beside him, the cat curled up in a ball and started purring. Doug's heart was melting. "Okay, maybe we've all got ourselves a new buddy," he said.

The name Buddy stuck.

That was twelve years ago. The Cat Lady knew her cats. Buddy proved to be the coolest cat ever. He was a skilled rat-catcher and remedied our roof rat problem soon after his arrival. He was extremely friendly. Buddy ran to greet and welcome all of our guests, probably thinking they had come just to admire how handsome and well behaved he was. And Buddy was the sociable center of attention at every gathering at our home as he plopped himself conspicuously in the midst of the festivities.

Buddy has since gone to reside in The Cat Palace in the sky. If a Kitty Hall of Fame is ever formed, we would definitely nominate our beautiful, longhaired, twenty-pound, furry white Buddy.

~BJ Jensen

The Cat Who Taught Me Chutzpah

You learn something every day if you pay attention.

~Ray LeBlond

I can still picture the morning we adopted Eddie. I was sitting with a dozen mewing kittens at the local Animal Rescue League. There was a slight movement between two pillows on the far side of the cage. That's where I found Eddie. He was on his back trying to get some sleep "in this lousy joint" as I imagined an independent cat like he would say.

He was a plain gray tabby, as common as a housefly.

"He's the one," I said to my husband, Bob.

Eddie swaggered to the food bowl, pushing four kittens out of the way.

"But he's so ratty looking," Bob said, picking him up. "And he only has one whisker."

Eddie tenderly pressed his face against mine. Then he put his sharp baby teeth around my gold earring and yanked with the strength of a sumo wrestler. Why did I fall for him so quickly? This cat had chutzpah and he knew how to use it. I would soon find out that there were other vital reasons he was perfect for me.

On Eddie's first day at our home, he got up before Bob and I did. I knew that from the sound of breaking glass. We found him on the mantel where my favorite crystal plate used to be. The floor was covered with glass shards. He quickly put his paw behind a blue china vase and chucked that off the mantel too. At first I felt bad. But that didn't last. Things are just things. Pets are family. Our solution? Velcro. And no more glass on the mantel. Instead we stuck on fake fruit.

Early in his life, I had a spinal cord injury. There were thousands of things I was certain would be impossible for me to ever do again. Eddie's attitude was what I needed. But that would require me believing that I could learn from a cat. Well, I did learn… a lot. I learned that the word "impossible" was nothing other than a word. A word that only carried meaning if I allowed it to. Eddie believed nothing was impossible. And by watching him, nothing was.

At the beginning of my life after my surgery, I saw obstacles as just that—obstacles. And therefore put them on my "can't do" list. But Eddie never accepted obstacles as anything other than challenges. He opened cabinets by putting his paws around the knobs and pulling. Vitamin bottles made great rattling noises on crash landings. We bought childproof magnets at the hardware store. Eddie simply tugged a little harder. Back to the hardware store for hook and eye locks. Eddie flipped the hooks open with one paw. Back to the hardware store for deadbolt locks. He easily slid the bolts to the side. The guy at the hardware store already had combination locks on the counter.

I'll always be in awe of Eddie's tenacity. When barriers thwarted him, he never quit trying. To him, anything could be a toy. He'd unravel entire rolls of toilet paper. So we had to keep ours in a coffee can.

One day, years ago, he found something that should surely go down in the "History of Best Cat Toys" book. I was on the phone with a rabbi. He was asking me about my mother's interests for his sermon at her funeral. I said, "My mother loved painting and…"

That's when Eddie came running in with something in his mouth. He had opened the new box of tampons I bought that morning. He was flinging the tampon in the air like it was a toy mouse. The rabbi asked if I was all right because not only had I stopped talking in the middle of a sentence, I was having an earsplitting laughing fit that I just could not control.

The rabbi assumed I was having a traumatic stress reaction and said, "When we lose a loved one, we're often not in control of our emotions, and that's okay. It's fine to laugh."

That cracked me up even more. I managed to blurt out, "She made jewelry!" before seeing the tampon go flying across the room again. I hung up on the rabbi. Oy vey.

For the past two years, Eddie has been sick. I have spent lots of time massaging him on either side of his face. He always loved that.

On one afternoon, I used my fingers to comb through his lovely full set of whiskers he had eventually grown. That's when I saw the one side effect from the medicine he was taking. As I gently rubbed along his face, all of his whiskers came off in my hands, except for one. I placed them in a tiny needlepoint purse my mother made for me. He came into our lives with one whisker. And that is how he would leave.

A few months ago, on a quiet Sunday afternoon, I kissed his forehead and whispered, "I love you." He looked up at me. His face showed the love he was never successful at hiding.

As Bob softly sang to him, Eddie took his last breath.

While his body was still warm, I cradled him in my arms and rocked him. I held his head so he was nestled against my neck. I whispered, "You came into my life when I needed you the most." Bob was crying as he stood next to us, watching me rock my little soul mate. "Eddie," I could barely speak. "You will always be a part of me."

I didn't want to let him go from my arms. But Bob, so lovingly and slowly, gently took him away. And so, I honor the life and the lessons of my wonderful cat who, from the beginning, stood apart from all the others. My beautiful cat, my Eddie, just a plain gray tabby, as common as a housefly.

~Saralee Perel

Lucifer's Lady

Is not a kiss the very autograph of love?
~Henry Finck

Lucifer was in love with Grandma. Lucky Grandma—she had to be the only human being on the planet who he did love.

Lucifer had come to us as a swaggering buccaneer of a kitten. Dressed in a pristine black-and-white tux with white spats, he was a fine figure of a tom, and he knew it. Normally, I am an excellent judge of character when it comes to cats, but boy, did I make a whopper of a mistake in choosing him. The first night we had him, he jumped on the counter, relieved himself on the carpet, scratched the furniture, and bit someone. Thus his name. We thought that surely, we could cure him of such bad habits. For the second time, I was wrong.

Lucifer grew up to be an attack cat. He hated people, regardless of the fact that they fed him, were responsible for his sleek appearance, and gave him a place to live. He snubbed my every advance. If ever a barbarian refused to become civilized, it was Lucifer. It was like living with a miniature Blackbeard who would whip out all his twenty swords whenever he saw you coming. He didn't believe in sneak attacks, either. His strategy was full frontal assault, no matter how much bigger you were.

The one exception to his hatred was Grandma. From the first moment he laid eyes on her, he was smitten. He would lay down all weapons when she was around, twining happily around her ankles and purring.

Some women have a fatal attraction to the wrong kind of guy. Although she made an excellent choice in Grandpa, when it comes to black-and-white cats, Grandma is a lost cause. And so, the rest of the family looked on in amazement while Grandma was able to snuggle and love the outlaw.

Then came the night he was snubbed.

Grandma and I were standing outside admiring the stars. It was a remarkably clear evening, and it seemed as though you could see the whole of the Milky Way. Lucifer found us in the driveway, and discovering that he was in the presence of his beloved, he put on his best behavior. So, I picked him up. He purred and glared at me.

I was standing right beside Grandma, and seeing his opportunity, Lucifer nimbly stepped out of my arms and right onto Grandma's shoulder. She didn't seem to really notice. He stepped from one shoulder to the other, and still she didn't react.

Finding the lady to be apparently responding so well, and unable to hold himself back any longer, Lucifer reached his nose around planted a whiskery kiss right on Grandma's lips.

I guess I don't blame him. I understand that stars can be romantic. But really, he should have known better. At this sudden show of affection, Grandma shrieked, the cat went flying off into the shadows, and I picked myself up from a spasm of hysterics a few moments later.

Grandma explained afterward that she had thought Lucifer tripping across her shoulders was me putting my arm around her. So the spontaneous smooch was a surprise in more way than one.

As for Lucifer, his pride — if not his ardor — was greatly wounded. But the incident taught him to treat his love with more respect and he made no more such advances.

~L. Stewart

Daddy Cat Steps Up

There is, indeed, no single quality of the cat
that man could not emulate to his advantage.
~Carl Van Vechten

Males are just not nurturers. Well, that's what I thought as a young single mother whose ex-husband was seldom present in the lives of her children. It took a special tomcat to convince me otherwise.

Momma Cat had had five kittens, but one died shortly after birth. She was an outside cat and the skinniest, puniest one I'd ever seen. I could not imagine how she could keep herself alive much less four helpless kittens, but she and they were doing well. No thanks to Daddy Cat who pretty much ignored both kittens and Momma, but was Johnny on the Spot when I poured the cat food. Weeks went by and the kittens' eyes opened. They began to move around the back porch and explore. Just about the time they were being weaned, Momma Cat was killed on the road in front of the house.

I could not imagine how the kittens would survive without her around to protect them, care for them, and supplement the kitten food they were beginning to eat. During the day I had a job and my kids had school. Who would care for them all those hours we had to be away? They were in the rambunctious stage that kittens go through — fast on their feet and into everything.

The first morning we left them, I worried all day about what we'd find when we returned home. Imagine my surprise that afternoon when we drove up and found Daddy Cat curled up with his four kittens on the back porch.

Over the next weeks I was amazed at how well he looked after his offspring. He groomed them, let them climb all over him, and corrected them when they went too far in their play. He treated them a little rougher than Momma Cat had, but they did not suffer for it. They thrived, learned to hunt, and grew into excellent mousers.

As for me, I no longer felt that men couldn't nurture their children just as well as women. Seeing Daddy Cat lick those kittens' ears, cuddle with them for naps, and cuff them when they bit his tail one too many times, showed me that all that's necessary is a willingness to love and put someone else's needs before your own. And if that can be found in the males of the animal world, then human males can do it too.

~Karen Teigen

To Be Chosen

*Are we really sure the purring is coming from the kitty
and not from our very own hearts?*
~Emme Woodhull-Bäche

I t was during a weekend when I was feeling very lonely and rejected that I met a kitten who, for the next eight years, would make me feel loved and chosen. I was born with cerebral palsy, a disease that left me unable to walk, use my hands, or speak clearly. I required the constant care of my parents, who found this task to be quite overwhelming. They made no effort to hide the fact that they felt that God had given them a heavy cross to bear. As I grew older, their words did a number on my self-esteem. I was certain that the only people who could ever love me were people who had to love me.

After my younger brother Brian got married, my parents were thrilled when he and his wife Linda offered to take care of me. These trips would happen twice a year, once in the spring and once in the fall. While I was happy that my parents were getting a much-needed break, knowing what those weekends held in store for me would tie my stomach up in knots.

Although my brother and sister-in-law would urge my parents to go away, once they were gone, Brian and Linda made me feel very unwelcome. They told me that if I loved my parents, I would volunteer to move into a nursing home. As a woman in her early forties, I was not ready to do this.

One fall I did not dread my parents' vacation quite as much as I usually did. Just a few weeks earlier, Linda's cat had given birth to six kittens. My mom had already picked out the kitten that would come live with us. I was looking forward to bonding with Whiskers.

I was thrilled with the way that Whiskers reacted to me. The minute that Brian sat me on their couch, Whiskers jumped in my lap and stayed there, even while the other kittens were playing together. Yes, Whiskers and I were going to be great friends.

"Whiskers really likes me," I said to Linda when she finally came out of her home office to fix my lunch.

"That's not Whiskers," Linda said casually. "That's Baxter and he's been promised to someone else." I was heartbroken. To make matters worse, Linda told me that she had never seen Baxter sit still before. "If the kittens are in trouble, Baxter's usually in the thick of things. He's the clown of the litter."

Over the next few weeks, I often thought of Baxter. That little kitten had wanted to be with me. I prayed that Baxter's new owners would make him feel as special as he had made me feel.

Then a miracle happened. When the lady came to pick up Baxter, the young girl who was babysitting my niece and nephews picked Whiskers instead. That same night, Baxter came to live with us, and he immediately found his favorite seat, my lap. After I went to bed, Baxter got very restless. When my mom showed Baxter where my bedroom was, he curled up next to me and fell asleep.

As Baxter became more comfortable in his new home, I could see why Linda had called him the clown of the litter. He was always getting into trouble. During supper, he would sit on our kitchen trashcan and beg for food. My mom had to watch Baxter when it was time to give our four cats their nightly treat of canned food because he would gobble up his food and then try to steal from the other cats.

Baxter also liked to "help" with chores. Whenever my mom was sewing, he would try to catch the fabric as it came out of her machine. Baxter also thought that he was my personal computer expert. And to be fair, he did teach me a valuable lesson about the computer. When Baxter was around, I made sure that I saved my work often. Within a few months, we were affectionately referring to my darling little kitten as Bad Boy Baxter.

As busy as he was getting into trouble, Baxter never strayed from his main mission in life—to be my loving companion. In the summer, while our other cats were chasing mice, Baxter would climb into our lawn glider and swing with me. When I was taking a bath, he would sit on the edge of the tub; he even let me put bubbles on his face.

One thing that Baxter did especially touched my heart. I have a very big nose, which my family loved to make fun of. Often when Baxter was sitting on my lap, he would gently touch my nose with his paw. I took this to mean that he loved me, big nose and all.

A few weeks after Baxter's eighth birthday, everything changed. The cat who used to steal and beg for food had no appetite. Instead of looking for trouble, Baxter spent most of the day sleeping. A visit to the veterinarian confirmed my worst fears. Baxter's kidneys were failing. The vet put him on antibiotics, and said that if his condition didn't improve within a week, we would have a decision to make. I told myself that the medicine would restore Baxter to the fun-loving cat that he had always been.

Unfortunately, the medicine didn't work. Within a few days, Baxter had to be spoon-fed baby food, and even then we could only get a few bites into him. The Baxter I knew and loved was slipping away before my eyes.

As sick as he was, Baxter still made me feel loved. He would wake up from a dead sleep and run to me when I called his name. On the last night of his life, Baxter found the strength to stumble from my mom's lap into mine. I patted Baxter's almost lifeless body and knew that my touch comforted him. Knowing that being with me was so important to Baxter, that he was willing to use his last ounce of strength to make it happen, comforted me.

Baxter has been gone for thirteen years, but what he gave me will last forever. Thanks to him, I will always know what it feels like to not only be loved and accepted, but to actually be chosen.

~Cynthia M. Dutil

36

The Cat Who Stared Down Mice

The clever cat eats cheese and breathes down rat holes with baited breath.
~W. C. Fields

W e needed a good mouser, so when we learned of barn kittens born not too far from us, off we went. The kind farmer led us into the barn, and like many others in the same situation, when our kitten looked up from the furry litter pile we connected immediately. Big green eyes, orange-and-white stripes and personality galore — he was ours. We scooped him up, thanked the farmer, and took Sam home.

Home was a big, very old, cobbled-together house in the country, and we had just purchased it. At the time there were more crannies and nooks for mice to get into than there were asphalt shingles on the roof.

Someone had installed cabinets under the sink and left four perfectly round holes in the baseboard. We never found out what their purpose was, but when Sam was tiny, he'd scoot into the holes, turn around and poke his head back out. It was super cute, and we called him jack-in-the-box kitty for a while.

There was also an ancient stove along one kitchen wall, and we knew there were plenty of holes and gaps underneath it. I usually fed the cat his food in a small dish on the floor near the stove.

One morning as I sipped my coffee I noticed Sam staring intently at the space under the stove. He wasn't moving a muscle. About twenty seconds elapsed before I saw the cause of Sam's stare. A small mouse scurried from beneath the stove, heading for the food dish. Sam watched until the mouse reached the edge of the dish and with one pounce it was all over for the rodent.

Sam grew quickly and got along well with our dog Boots. They took turns grooming each other, and it was quite a sight to see the dog licking the cat's ears or to see the cat play with the dog's tail. Boots wasn't very interested in Sam's mouse-catching antics, though; I imagine because the dog was far less patient than the cat.

One evening my husband and I came home late and found Sam sitting on top of the portable dishwasher next to the old stove. He was focused on a pan that I'd left after making some marshmallow treats, intending to clean it later. I gave my husband the shhhh sign as we crept up next to the cat.

Following the direction of his piercing stare we saw a mouse, stuck fast in the marshmallow goo at the bottom of the pan. Ewwww. I picked the pan up, and the cat hopped down. I ran hot water over the bottom of the pan and went outdoors where I turned it upside down onto the patio. Sam followed me out, his eyes on the pan all the while. I let the hot water do its work, lifted the pan, and voilà—Sam enjoyed his first marshmallow-covered mouse.

That wasn't the last time Sam had a specially prepared meal. Once my husband came home late to find Sam once again on top of the dishwasher. Since portable dishwashers in those days came with a nice counter top, we kept our toaster there. Sam's focus that night was on the toaster slots. Again, no muscle in that cat's body was moving.

Knowing what the stance and the stare usually meant, my husband walked quietly over to the toaster and pushed the switch down. Sure enough, when things got too warm inside that toaster, the mouse made a scramble for the top. Pop! Right into the waiting paws of a very thankful cat—the reward for his late-night vigil.

We've done lots of work on the old place since then, and nothing can rival our mouse problems of those long ago years. Although our faithful mouser, Sam, is gone now, I hope there are mice in Cat Heaven to keep him as happy as he was in our old house.

~Susan Sundwall

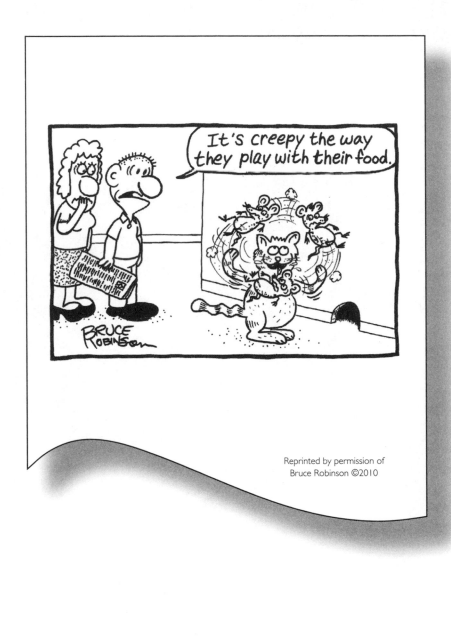

Reprinted by permission of
Bruce Robinson ©2010

37

Parting Gifts

Unable are the loved to die. For love is immortality.
~Emily Dickinson

I married Jake when I married my husband, Doug. Jake, the big orange tabby, had been Doug's cohort through many stages of their lives. During Doug's divorce and single parent years, Jake was his companion and confidant. Jake had broad shoulders and a big heart. His dedication to Doug was obvious, his reluctance to share Doug with me apparent.

It didn't help that I brought to the family a dog of my own—Jimmy, a barkless Boston Terrier whose nubby little tail was slightly off-center, making him appear to move with an alignment problem.

We also inherited a lovely red mixed-breed dog, Holly, when our son-in-law passed away. Then our youngest son brought home Rudy, a domestic, longhaired, tortoiseshell kitten with eyes the color of kiwi fruit. The son left; Rudy stayed.

We had become a four-pet family. Jake, however, was boss and we all knew it.

At twenty-three years of age, Jake began to show signs of decline. He lost weight, seldom strayed far from the house, brought home fewer birds and mice, and had to be carried on our evening walks. We spelled the word "o-l-d" as if keeping Jake from hearing the word would keep it from happening.

Most of his teeth had to be pulled, or were so worn down he could no longer chew. Doug began taking pieces of chicken and fish and giving them to Jake pre-chewed. Their bond of love required selfless sacrifice. Jake would keep going for Doug. Doug would keep cherishing and caring for Jake like a loving son would care for his aging parents.

The day finally came when we knew Jake had no more days left. Doug carried him to the living room where they sat together on the sofa saying their goodbyes. Jake, it seemed, had one final gift to leave for Doug. With all the strength Jake could muster, he called his three siblings to his bedside. From different parts of the house, in response to Jake's feeble meow, came Rudy, Holly and Jimmy. They each positioned themselves on the floor, looking up at Jake.

Jake, turning his head from one furred face to the next, meowed instructions that only his brother and sisters understood. As Jake finished with each, that pet moved on to the place in the house where they had come from when Jake beckoned.

Then Jake said goodbye to Doug.

It was not long before we could see Jake's final instructions being carried out. Holly became Doug's closest buddy, never moving far from his feet and always standing guard outside whatever room he was in. She was a loyal listener when Doug needed a sounding board. Holly's devotion to Doug mirrored Jake's in many ways.

While Holly became the alpha animal, Rudy became top cat. He began sleeping on Doug's head as Jake had done so often. He playfully slid his paws under the bathroom door, enticing Doug to play from the inside, as he had witnessed brother Jake doing. He slept on top of the printer while Doug used the computer. Occasionally, Rudy would walk the cul-de-sac with me when I delivered mail on our own street, as Jake and I had walked together on those few special days.

Jimmy, well he never did walk a straight line, but he began forming a special bond with Doug, even allowing Doug to get close enough emotionally to teach him to bark.

Jake had moved on, but not before ensuring the important parts of his character were endowed to his siblings. In his absolute dedication to Doug, Jake left reminders of their life and love to soothe Doug's grieving soul.

~Karen R. Hessen

Between Friends

Who hath a better friend than a cat?
~William Hardwin

I lay on my bed, curled in the fetal position. Why, of all weeks, did I have to come down with a stomach virus now? Only a few days earlier, I had promised to cover for the other payroll clerk in my department so she could go on a much-needed but impromptu vacation. Authorization for that vacation was based solely on my willingness to process her payroll that week. And now I was laid up. How were those 400 employees going to get paid?

With that in mind, I drifted in and out of a fitful sleep only to awake in the wee morning hours to discover my faithful red tabby, Moo, beside me. Normally I welcomed Moo, encouraged him, in fact, to share my bed. Yet now, even his small body at my feet was irritating. I tossed and turned, seeking a position that would give me some relief. With each movement, Moo drew nearer. Gently, I nudged him away but he kept coming back. Finally, too tired to fight, I gave up. Then my little tabby did something very odd — he lay flat over my aching belly.

Now, Moo had been known to sleep in the most unusual of positions and places: on his back in the middle of the living room floor with all four paws up in the air; under the pillow of his cat bed instead of on top of it; and once, cushioned in my husband's sock drawer. But never had he lain directly on top of me in this fashion. He wasn't exactly what might be termed a lap cat, preferring his own personal space. Moo was independent, his own man, probably the result of his early years as a stray. Yet for some reason, he sought out this spot close to me now.

I must admit that I found the warmth from my kitty soothing. It must have been as soothing, I imagined, as the warmth of my arms had been for him when I found him huddled next to my back door early one winter morning, a stray seeking shelter from the cold and wind. A massive snow had fallen the previous night and his tail was covered in ice. I had held him against my body until he thawed, terrified that his tail, and perhaps other parts of him, had been damaged by exposure. After he warmed, I gently dried his body with a soft towel and fed him an entire can of my best tuna. I'll never forget how he purred afterward, or my relief to see his tail swishing madly as he rubbed his body against my leg. The look in his eyes at that moment spoke directly to my heart. "Thank you friend," it said.

Moo stayed with me throughout that harsh winter and when spring arrived, I imagined he would go back to his rambling ways. Yet, he never did and Moo became a permanent fixture in my home.

As we lay together this night, I felt my stomach begin to calm within only a few minutes and it seemed as though the soft touch of Moo's body was drawing the ache out of me one breath at a time. Within half an hour, I was sound asleep and remained so until I was awoken by my alarm clock. Overnight, after I had fallen into sleep, Moo had resumed his usual position at my feet and when I stirred, he rolled over. Quietly, I slipped out of bed and readied for work feeling a bit weak, but still capable enough to face the day. Before leaving the house, I returned to the bedroom and ran my fingertips through the fur between Moo's ears. He lifted his head and looked back at me with one sleepy eye. Then I bent close, kissed him on his fuzzy cheek, and murmured, "Thank you friend."

~Monica A. Andermann

Adopted

*The husband who doesn't tell his wife everything
probably reasons that what she doesn't know won't hurt him.*
~Leo J. Burke

I stormed out of the house waving my arms and screaming, "Get out of my birdbath, you stupid cat!" The black-and-white feline, hair bristling, arched his back and glared at me. "Didn't you hear me? I said scat, you dumb animal." I stooped to pick up a rock.

The cat had nothing to worry about; there was a reason I didn't make my elementary school's baseball team. I stomped towards the birdbath never considering what I would do if the cat didn't scat. It did—across the yard, through the flowerbed, and up onto the fence. He glowered at me, daring me to take further action, but my hands were empty and I was tired of chasing the animal.

For weeks, the creature had been skulking around our yard, stealing dog food from the bowl on the deck and sneaking onto the birdbath to wash it down. I knew it belonged to the tenant living in the basement of my neighbor's house, but I had not seen her for a while and wondered if she had moved on. I decided to call Rita.

"Rita, your tenant's cat is terrorizing the birds around here. What's up?"

"Oh, the poor dear isn't well at all. I think she and her little girl are moving back to Alberta. She doesn't seem to want the cat and it doesn't get along with my cats."

"Well, I'm tired of it doing its business in my yard. I'm a dog person. I don't like cats."

"I'll see what I can do," Rita promised.

I guess she couldn't do anything because when my husband and I turned into the driveway late the next night, two glowing green eyes stared out at us. The cat scurried out of the way of the car and jumped onto the lowest branch of our mountain ash. I grabbed a stick and started poking at it, hoping it would get the message. Instead, it hissed at me and batted the stick away.

"Brazen, nocturnal animal," I said turning to Don. He laughed. He always laughs at me when I am frustrated. I put the stick down, sighed, and turned to go inside.

"You know, maybe that cat needs a home," Don said. "Perhaps we could adopt it. When we got married you said you were open to getting another pet."

I stared at him. "Are you nuts? I'm a dog person. I don't like cats, and I don't like cat people."

I was beginning to think I had won the war. My birdbath and flower gardens had remained untouched, and I hadn't caught even a glimpse of the cat's shadow since the stick incident three days earlier. Coming to a halt at the end of my driveway, I set the park brake and popped the trunk. Reaching in, I loaded up my arms with groceries to begin the ascent up the stairs to the living level of our home. My arthritic knees didn't like stairs, and by the time I got to the top, my face was scrunched up in pain.

Just as I set one armload of bags down, a black-and-white streak flew past me, across the kitchen floor, and out the gap in the patio door that I had left open. In shock, I dropped the rest of my groceries and ran to look out the kitchen window. There was the cat, nonchalantly lapping water from the birdbath. As if he could sense my glare, he lifted his head and stared straight at me. If I hadn't known better, I would have sworn that there was a smirk on his face. With a swish of his tail, he leaped onto the fence and cat-walked away into the shadows.

I turned back to the mess of bags and the task of putting the groceries away. Rearranging boxes and cans in the cupboard to make room for my purchases, I came across an unfamiliar bag tucked behind my flour. Pulling it out, I stared in disbelief. A bag of cat food. A bag of high-grade, expensive cat food! Stunned, I robotically put the rest of the groceries away, and then plopped down in the living room to wait for my husband to come home.

I heard his car pull up. The front door creaked open. "Honey, I'm home," he called. Silence. I heard his footsteps on the stairs. "Honey, where are you? I'm home." Silence. He was used to me running to greet him. He gave a bit of a start when he saw me in the chair. Then he looked down at the bag sitting at my feet, and a sheepish grin spread across his face. "Oh, you found it."

My mouth dropped open. "How long did you think you could hide it? By the way, when I got home that cat had made itself comfortable inside our house!"

He started to respond, but I cut him off. "You know I don't like cats. And I don't like cat people."

"But, the poor guy was hungry, and he was covered with fleas."

"Oh, great! Now I suppose we have fleas in our house." I shook my head, at a loss for words.

"Don't worry, I bought him a flea collar the other day. Rita was able to catch him and put it on for me."

The atmosphere at 1375 Kerfoot Road was strained that evening. There was a part of me furious that Don had befriended this nuisance, yet something inside me ached for this flea-bitten feline. On one hand, I saw my husband as having no regard for my feelings, but on the other hand I saw a man who had a heart of compassion for the lonely and neglected—it's just that this particular lonely and neglected creature was a cat. I simply didn't know how to feel about this or how to deal with my raw emotions.

Finally, I put my arms around Don's waist and looked up into his face. "Were you serious when you said we should adopt this cat?"

He took a deep breath as if not sure what to say, "I think it's too late. It looks like he's already adopted us."

Curio—we discovered his name from Rita—was skittery and

wouldn't come near. Perhaps he remembered the stick. He would scat whenever I approached him, but I always remembered to leave the patio door open a few inches, and whenever I'd come home, there would be a flash of black and white from the living room, through the kitchen and out the patio door. Don filled the food dish outside every night, and in the morning, the bowl would be empty.

A week later, Don's brother and his family arrived for a visit. On the second day of their visit, six-year-old Becky came inside, Curio dangling like a limp rag doll from her arms. "Look what I found," she said. That's all it took; the cat knew this was his home now. We figure Curio took to Becky because she reminded him of the little girl who had named him and loved him as a kitten.

"May I hold him?" I asked hesitantly. Becky held him out to me, and as I cradled him in my arms and listened to him purr, I wondered what it was about cats and cat people that I didn't like.

That was thirteen years ago. These days, he curls up beside me at night, and like a lullaby, his purring sends me off to dreamland. As I'm typing this, he is lying in front of me, stretched out between the monitor and my keyboard. His shoulder blades stick out and there isn't an ounce of fat on him. He gets a tuna-flavoured pill every morning, but his hyperthyroid condition is taking its toll. He's a senior now, and a lump rises in my throat as I realize it likely won't be long before his purring ceases to soothe me as I type. I smile as I recall just how this old guy adopted us and found a spot in the heart of someone who once didn't like cats—or cat people.

~Linda Mehus-Barber

"I'm a quiet, non-smoker who sheds very discreetly."

Reprinted by permission of Andrew Toos/
CartoonResource.com ©2007

Butter's Ball

Some people think football is a matter of life and death.
I assure you, it's much more serious than that.
~Bill Shankly

I heard the thumping on the roof, followed by a short period of silence, and then there it was again... and again... and again. I knew exactly what was going on. Supper was in the oven so I snuck outside to watch the show.

Our seven-year-old son was tossing a small football onto the roof and then trying to catch it as it tumbled back down. Nearby, haunches vibrating as he squatted in his ready-to-pounce position, sat our striped yellow cat, Butter. Our son's goal was to catch the football before it hit the ground. Our cat's goal was the same.

Nothing infuriated our son more than Butter catching that football—Butter was not only a poor sport, he was a bully. If he got the football, he ran around the yard, teasing the young boy who was pursuing him. Once he was bored with that game, he would dash under the house where he, and the ball, could not be reached. This was almost a done deal. Sooner or later our son would miss, and the game would be over. This created a lot of tension during what should have been a time of leisure.

As I watched, the ball took a wild bounce. Butter sprang into action, leaping high to snatch the ball out of mid-air. The pursuit began. Of course Butter could not be caught or outmaneuvered, but that didn't stop our son from trying. "You stupid cat, give me back my ball!" he screamed at Butter while Butter zigzagged around the yard, crouching and leaping to evade his pursuer. Our son was very quick, but not as quick as our cat. When Butter was finished with the torment he zipped under the house.

My son was as angry with me for giggling as he was at Butter for stealing his ball. He kicked at a dandelion. "It's not funny. He won't give it back."

A few days later, we sat in the den, watching TV. Butter pranced into the den with the football in his mouth. No one could imagine how he had slipped the ball past the whole family or where he had hidden it.

Both our son and daughter would hit the floor where Butter was waiting for the fun of watching them scramble after him, over and behind furniture just to come up empty-handed. Butter could clear each piece of furniture in a single leap or slide under a low area when necessary. He would actually sit and wait for them to catch up with him, so sure was he of his prowess.

Butter did not understand the concept of gravity, and as far as we could see, those laws did not apply to him. He would run straight at a wall, making an impossible last minute U-turn, sometimes banking off the wall. Our children would skid into the wall like they were sliding into home base. Butter would stand in plain sight, waiting for them to recover.

We enjoyed watching this chase so much that my husband and I would momentarily forget our responsibility to stop this chaos and settle the children down. Once we regained our parental senses and control over the household, straightening up the mess, Butter would disappear. When he smugly returned to the den, the football would be missing. My children would search the house over, but never once did they find that football.

Then, one day, the football would just mysteriously reappear. Maybe it would be inside on the floor or on a piece of furniture. Maybe it would be on the lawn or the porch. Butter allowed our son to reclaim his football when Butter felt like it. Sometimes our son would be allowed to play with the football for several days, uninterrupted.

Those days Butter would innocently prance around the yard, seemingly without interest in the boy or the ball.

The day Butter died, the football was missing. And even when we eventually packed up and moved from that house, we never found that football.

~Debbie Acklin

I Can't Believe My Cat Did That!

Chapter 5

Stalk to You Later

Three Does in Tow

*Prowling his own quiet backyard or asleep by the fire, he is still only a
whisker away from the wilds.*
~Jean Burden

It is a snowy late December afternoon. The fire in our living room fireplace is blazing, roast chicken is in the oven and the Patriots football game is on the TV. A perfect scenario.

I get up to check on the roast, breathing in a blast of contentment as I open the oven door; the aroma of fresh rosemary and thyme fills my senses. "Cooked to perfection," I boast to myself.

Moving over to the large picture window in the living room, I look out. The snow is coming down hard with thick flakes steadily falling in front of me.

"Look how gorgeous," I say to my husband, Jack, who looks as though he is just about ready for his second nap. He stands up, stretches and then joins me at the window.

"It is gorgeous. The sunlight is hitting the snow-covered branches, perfectly highlighting the trees. It's almost like a movie set," he says. With that he puts his hands to his mouth and shouts, "Cue the deer." Within minutes, three does peek out from behind the trees in my neighbor's yard across the street. We laugh, not so surprised, as deer are a daily occurrence in our rural neighborhood.

We watch as they approach our house and stop right outside our window. Calmly munching on some pachysandra, they seem so sedate, so comfortable, as if they know they are expected and safe.

Suddenly, one of them looks up and signals to the others. They stiffen, each taking several steps backward, all looking in the same direction. Jack and I look around, concerned. A coyote has been spotted in the neighborhood and we are afraid it is near. If it were, it would probably be sick and hungry.

The three deer take a few more steps back, then look at one another as if to ask, "What should we do?"

All of a sudden, Jack says, "Look."

I look, but don't see what he is seeing.

"Look, there by the oak." He takes my head and points it toward the tree, but lower.

"There," he says, "walking towards the pachysandra."

I look and see our neighbor's cat, a longhaired Maine Coon named Gizmo. He is marching right at the deer. Walking straight toward them purposefully, almost as if he is on a mission. The deer move back a bit more and then stop. Gizmo stops not two yards in front of them. Then, almost in unison, the three does take two steps forward. Then, Gizmo takes two steps toward the does. The four just stand there, staring each other down. It's a standstill.

Finally, Gizmo marches right by them. The three deer look at one another for advice and then the largest one turns toward Gizmo, following him past the side window of our living room.

Jack and I are surprised by this turn of events. We run to the back window to see what is happening. There goes Gizmo, tail up, marching along with a leader-like attitude. I don't know what he is thinking, or what mission he has, but he seems to have a devoted following as we see all three deer come up the rear.

They march single file, through the thickening snow, around the side of the house and down a newly set trail to the nature preserve behind our house.

Jack and I run upstairs to see if we can follow this adventure from a higher vantage point. "There they are," I say, pointing toward the entourage. It is getting darker and increasingly hard to spy. The four disappear into the woods.

"How adorable was that?" I say.

We go back to our roast and our game and sigh at the marvels of animals in the wild, figuring that is the end of that.

The next day the snow has stopped and the landscape boasts a new, clean appearance. I look out the back dining room window at the vast white clearing and see three sets of large tracks coming from the woods. I follow the tracks from the woods toward the house. As they get closer I notice a fourth set of smaller tracks running parallel. Impossible, I think. Gizmo couldn't possibly have spent the night with those deer.

That evening, as the sun is beginning to set, I look out and see our little family of deer across the street. I smile and turn back towards the kitchen when something catches my eye. There, across the street, I see a big ball of gray fur, jumping up and down, swatting something with his paw. Gizmo is throwing what appears to be a field mouse up into the air, over and over again. To his right stand three deer watching intently as if thoroughly entertained. When the show ends, he marches the three does toward our house.

They cross the street and enter our yard. The deer seem to acknowledge me looking through the window, but Gizmo can't be bothered. He is the leader and as such has to maintain an air of dignity, importance, and command... with his three does in tow.

~Jeanne Blandford

The Lion
of Woodhaven

Some people say that cats are sneaky, evil, and cruel. True,
and they have many other fine qualities as well.
~Missy Dizick

Buster was gorgeous—emerald green eyes and a long Persian coat the color of caramel. The day we adopted him from the animal shelter he was no more than a tiny ball of fluff. Who knew he would grow up to be the curse of the cul-de-sac, the bane of the block, the scourge of the sidewalks? He was, after all, a cream puff at home.

Some cats choose to ignore their names, pretending not to hear when you call them home. Buster wasn't like that. He would prick up his ears, stop whatever he was doing, and run for the house the minute he heard me call his name. Once, he stopped dead in his tracks while chasing a mouse and scampered into the house with his tail ramrod straight, purring like a Porsche and rubbing against my leg.

But as much as we loved him, we had to admit that Buster was the meanest cat in Woodhaven. Neighbors called him "Devil Cat," and didn't think twice about turning the water hose on him when he had the bad manners to pick a fight with their cats. Buster was definitely the neighborhood bully.

Then one fateful day, Buster's world turned upside down. It was a Saturday, and I had just come home from the grocery store.

"Can you help me with these bags?" I asked my husband, Terry. He was in the garage brushing the final coat of linseed oil on an old chest he'd refinished, but he put his brush down to help me unload the car. Just as Terry set the last bag on the counter, we heard a loud crash and a horrible yowling coming from the garage.

"What in the world was that?" I asked.

We dashed to the garage, imagining all kinds of terrible things. What we found was the gallon can of linseed oil on its side, a thick, gooey mess spreading across the concrete floor. Buster howled again and we found him hunkered down in a corner, crying like a baby. His body was covered in linseed oil, and he looked like a refugee from a house of horrors.

"You've done it now, buddy," Terry said, shaking his head.

"How in the world will we ever get him clean?"

"Call the vet. I'll try to get Buster into his carrier," Terry said as he grabbed an old beach towel.

Three hours later, we stared in stunned silence as the pet groomer handed us a very different version of our old Buster.

"The vet says he's perfectly fine," the young woman assured us. "I shampooed him four or five times, but finally gave up and just shaved him. It was the only way I could get all the gunk out of his hair." She smiled. "I think he looks like a little lion now, don't you?"

I nodded as she put the shivering cat in my arms. Buster looked exactly like a miniature lion. His head was a shaggy mane, but his legs, body, and tail were sleek and smooth with only a little fluff of hair at the tip of his tail. And even though he looked like a wild beast, there was nothing ferocious about the new Buster. He seemed embarrassed, actually mortified, the epitome of the Cowardly Lion from The Wizard of Oz.

Terry and I couldn't help laughing out loud as soon as we reached our car. Buster crawled to the back of his pet carrier and licked at his paws, feigning nonchalance. The minute we were home, he dived under the bed and hid until after dark.

The next morning Buster refused to go outside. I found his old litter box and made sure he knew where it was. Then I fed him some kitty treats, and held him for a while as I read the newspaper. He purred contently in my lap, but skittered to the bedroom when the doorbell rang. Marilyn, my next-door neighbor, stood on the porch holding a basket of homegrown tomatoes.

"I saw you dash off with the pet carrier yesterday," she said. "Is Buster all right?"

I described Buster's misadventure and then asked, "Want to see him?"

"Absolutely!"

I gathered Buster from under the bed and held him like a baby as Marilyn stared in disbelief.

"That's Buster?" she asked. "Our Buster? The unholy terror of Woodhaven?"

"The very same," I answered.

Buster struggled from my arms and darted under the sofa.

"He doesn't seem quite so ferocious now, does he?"

"I don't think he likes his new look. He won't go outside, and his favorite time of day is when we turn out all the lights and go to bed."

Thirty minutes after Marilyn left, the doorbell rang again. Four little girls stood at my door, begging to see Buster. Marilyn had been on the phone, no doubt, announcing Buster's makeover to everyone in Woodhaven.

"We heard he looks like a baby lion," one girl said with a giggle.

"See for yourself," I answered, coaxing Buster out from under the sofa with cat treats. He scarfed down the treat, glanced up at the wide-eyed visitors, and scampered down the hall to find another hiding place.

The phone rang as soon as the girls left and continued to ring all day as poor Buster's news traveled through the neighborhood. Everyone who'd ever had a run-in with our cat seemed to be having a field day.

"I'm going to start charging admission," I told Terry three days later. "Every kid in the neighborhood has been by to see Buster. Some of them twice."

Buster's hair gradually grew longer, and within a couple of

months he looked more like his old self. When he finally decided to venture back outside though, we noticed a change in his "cattitude." He seemed reluctant to leave our yard and was almost polite when he encountered neighboring animals. Several friends commented that Buster's experience with the linseed oil seemed to have humbled him—a "new and improved" Buster, they said.

Terry and I didn't mind the change, mainly because folks no longer complained about Buster's poor behavior. For years, at our neighborhoods' annual summer block party, discussion would eventually get around to Buster's accident, drawing howls of laughter at the memory. Terry and I laughed, too, not just about the way Buster had looked, but the way he'd acted. Who knew a cat could be embarrassed?

Buster died of natural causes several years later at the ripe old age of thirteen. Word traveled quickly through the neighborhood that our beloved pet was gone. Every neighbor who had ever fussed about our devil cat came to pay last respects to the little lion of Woodhaven, and laugh with us at the fond memory of a very changed cat.

~Ruth Jones

The Dinner Party

The trouble with cats is that they've got no tact.
~Sir Philip Sidney

Twinky and I were soul mates — right from the first time she stared deep into my eyes. We spent all our time together once the busy house emptied each morning. Kids off to school, husband off to work, and the day was ours. She followed me from room to room as I did housework and laundry. She sat and listened if I chatted on the phone. When I went outside to work in my garden, she shadowed me and would take particular pleasure in hiding among my plants. Then she would leap out when I least expected, always eliciting a little scream in return.

In the afternoon, when I made my tea and sat down with a good book or my knitting, she would lie beside me on the couch and purr. That was our cuddle time. If ever I was home alone in the evening, she was my faithful companion. If I went out, she never failed to meet me at the door.

But, as in every close relationship, sometimes you let each other down.

One night, my husband and I had invited three couples for dinner. I was used to entertaining, but it was generally casual and relaxed when we hosted family or old friends. This time we had invited my husband's boss and his wife, along with another business associate and his sophisticated spouse. Everything would be decidedly more formal. I had met all of them at company functions over the years, but had never entertained them in my humble home.

To round out the table I had invited a third couple—my good friend and her husband, a comfortable pair I could depend on to help put me at ease.

I had agonized over the menu, done the baking ahead of time, and had already cleaned the house, but that day I was still running around frantically. Everything had to be perfect. My laidback husband could not understand why I was a nervous wreck.

"It's only a dinner," he said, advising the kids to stay out of my way.

But he forgot to warn Twinky. My poor cat could not understand why I was so upset. We hadn't even had our daily cuddle.

In an attempt to calm me, she repeatedly wrapped herself around my feet as I charged about my kitchen. After tripping over her for the umpteenth time I did the unthinkable. I yelled at the poor little creature to get out of my way, and pushed her out of my path with my foot.

Twinky flew out my kitchen, bewildered and heartbroken, and headed down the basement stairs. I immediately felt terrible, but had no time to dwell on it. I had too much to do.

That evening when the doorbell rang, everything was ready. The kids were all out for the night, and no cat was to be seen. Our guests, leaving their coats and boots at the door, entered noisily and made themselves at home. The wife of the business associate presented us with an expensive bottle of wine, taking care to inform us it should be opened at once and left to breathe.

We chatted in the living room while the wine aired in the kitchen. When we finally sat down to eat, I felt that everything was going well. The meal turned out great, my husband was at his charming best, and our guests seemed to hit it off tremendously. The wine was excellent. I started to relax as my good friend gave me a wink.

That was when the cat reappeared from nowhere and headed straight toward my feet.

"Oh, isn't that cute," remarked my husband's boss. "The cat is playing with his little toy mouse."

I looked at my husband in horror. Twinky did not own a toy mouse.

Twinky put down the very-much-alive mouse at my feet. The mouse ran wildly under the table and then bolted for the living room, with Twinky in hot pursuit.

Pandemonium broke out. Two out of four ladies screamed and leapt to their feet, their husbands looking on bemused. I had never been so embarrassed.

Without missing a beat my good friend turned to me and queried, "Oh dear, did you forget to close the cage again?"

The evening ended soon. Our distinguished guests headed for the door and grabbed their footwear. Where was the mouse now? Hopefully not in anybody's boot.

Our old friends stayed behind to rehash the evening and help us search for the mouse while Twinky watched disdainfully. After that, much to the relief of my family and my cat, I did not attempt many formal dinner parties. And Twinky and I forgave each other—soul mates till the end.

~Virginia Maher

One of the Family

The family is one of nature's masterpieces.
~George Santayana

Our family fell in love with the tiny ginger kitten the minute we saw him. His pointy ears and short legs earned him the name Yoda, after the Star Wars character. Sheba, our young German Shepherd, and Candy, our elderly Maltese Poodle, soon adopted the young cat as part of the family pack. Wherever the dogs were, there was Yoda. Call the dogs, and Yoda came too.

He had grown into a beautiful ginger tom when my husband Rob and I were moving from our home in Krugersdorp, South Africa to Grabouw, a small town 900 miles away. Because we were towing a travel trailer, we planned for it to take three days. For several weeks before we left, we held regular training sessions in the back yard. The two dogs had to learn to go to the bathroom on command, since we couldn't stop at every tree along the way, and Yoda had to learn to walk on a leash, so we could take him out of the trailer in the evenings. His small head slid out of every collar we tried, so we put him in a body harness, which he initially detested, but grew to accept.

Our plans were simple. The dogs were to travel with us in the car, and Yoda would be in the trailer, inside a comfortable carpeted wooden crate with wire-netting sides. Lastly, our other pet, a canary named Pedro, would be in his cage. The vet gave us sedatives for the dogs and cat just in case.

The night before our departure, we locked the animals in the otherwise empty house while we slept in the trailer. We planned to leave at seven o'clock the next morning. In the rush to get on the road, we inadvertently let Yoda escape from the house and spent the next four hours searching for him. When he eventually strolled out of a thick bush at the end of the yard, we scolded him, cuddled him, and gave him the sedative from the vet. After securing him in his cat box, we closed the door of the trailer.

I had intended to sit with him until he went to sleep, but we were now four hours behind schedule. We opened the car door, and the dogs jumped in happily, and we eased the car and heavily laden trailer into the street.

After twenty minutes we arrived at the neighboring small town of Randfontein. We drove slowly through the main street, and we noticed people turning to stare at the trailer hitched to the back of our car.

"What's wrong?" I said in alarm.

"I don't know, but I can't stop here." Rob braked at the only set of traffic lights, and then we heard it, the sound of a baby screaming.

"Oh no. That's Yoda," I said. "Why isn't he asleep?"

Sheba sat erect on the back seat, ears twitching. Her normally beautiful brown eyes glared at us. Candy lay in her favorite spot on the ledge underneath the back window. Her doleful eyes stared out at the trailer. Each time I turned to look back, she looked at me with tear-rimmed eyes.

As soon as it was safe to stop, Rob pulled over the rig, and I rushed to the trailer.

"Yoda, it's okay," I said. But it wasn't okay. Yoda lay on his side, clawing wildly at the wire netting, tearing at the wire with his teeth, blood leaking from his gums.

I lifted the frantic animal from the confines of his box and Rob snapped on his leash. I cradled the cat on my shoulder, trying to soothe him. He nestled into my neck, crying like a newborn infant.

"What can we do?" My tears soaked into his ginger fur. "We can't leave the door open. He'll tear up the van. Besides, we can't let him near Pedro." I glanced across to where our yellow canary sat in his cage, merrily chirping as he swung to and fro on his swing. At least the bird was enjoying the trip.

"Let's try him in the car," Rob said. "Once he calms down, maybe the sedative will take effect. Then we can move him back here." As we put him onto the back seat, both dogs gave him a rousing welcome. Sheba washed his face while Candy sniffed him all over, checking for injury. Yoda meowed and grumbled, obviously complaining of the way we had treated him.

As soon as the car moved, Candy jumped back onto the window ledge and went straight to sleep. Sheba sprawled on the seat, sighed, and closed her eyes. Yoda found a cool spot under the driver's seat, yawned, and allowed the medication to do its job. Within moments, all three were asleep.

Each time we stopped for a break, the two dogs leaped to their feet and Yoda scrambled from his hidey-hole. We received many strange looks as we walked all three on their leashes across the grass, the excited German Shepherd, the sedate Maltese, and the triumphant Yoda. He had fought a fierce fight and won. As a member of the family, he belonged in the car with the rest of us.

Three days later, we pulled up outside the new house. The couple who came to meet us stared in amazement at the back window. Three heads crammed out of the small space, taking their first look at their new home. Inside the trailer, Pedro trilled his song of joy. Yoda and family had arrived, ready to start their new life—together.

~Shirley M. Corder

The Huntress

Never interrupt someone doing something you said couldn't be done.
~Amelia Earhart

The local shelter called and asked if I would try to bottle-raise two kittens whose mother had been killed by a car. The babies were about two or three days old and required round-the-clock warmth and feedings. I took them on, toting box and blankets, hot-water bottles, and special formula to the office with me. I seemed to be a successful mom-cat surrogate except for the cleaning chores, for which I substituted a dunk in a bowl of warm water and a fluff-up with my hair dryer.

I found a safe, indoor home for the male kitten when he was old enough to be on his own. Miss Manners stayed with me. Actually, she was glued to me. I didn't know kittens could imprint on substitute mothers.

I wanted her to be a housecat, but she fussed so much when I went outside, meowing on a windowsill, trying to sneak out with me, that I relented. We live on a little-traveled road and behind the house we have a pond and acres of fields, woods, and brush. She didn't go far, and I had no trouble calling her back when I went inside.

One day a friend and I were taking a dip in the pond. Miss Manners, about six months old then, followed us to the edge of the water and watched us swim. She mewed and mewed and pretty soon had her front paws in the water. We watched, shoulder deep in the clear water, as she waded farther and farther, crying the whole time, until she struck out paddling for me. I caught her and carried the sopping cat to shore, shaking my head at what I'd just witnessed.

A month or so later, she ventured to the wooded wetland a hundred yards away. She came back carrying a weasel—a brown stoat—dead with two neat punctures at the nape of the neck. A naturalist friend looked at it and asked to keep it to mount for his native species collection. He said he had seen very few tracks of small weasels in the area. He added that this must have been an old or injured one for a cat to catch it, because Miss Manners was too young and inexperienced a hunter to outwit and out-reflex a weasel.

Summer wore on and one day I found a dead but intact bullhead fish, about six inches long, on my porch. Frowning, I could only think that a silly or energetic fish had accidentally jumped out of the pond and Miss Manners found it flipping on the lawn and brought it to me.

The next day another bullhead appeared on the steps. What was going on with the fish in the pond? While sitting in a lawn chair reading, I watched Miss Manners wade into the pond until she was more than belly deep in the water. She stood very still until, splash! She speared a small fish with her claws, brought it to shore, picked it up and carried it to the porch.

Her next triumph took place in the deep of winter. Again I was outside with her, brushing snow from the car, when she headed down to the wooded wetland, not at all concerned about the three inches of white, wet stuff she needed to march through. I was delighted to call my naturalist friend and tell him to come over if he wanted to add to his collection of native animals. Miss Manners had caught another weasel, this time in a white, spotted ermine coat.

As though she had proven a point and needed no further demonstration of her prowess, she retired contentedly to the house. With swimming, hunting, and fishing out of her system, she spent the next eighteen years as a cat should be—warm and dry.

~Ann E. Vitale

Battles of Normandy

My strength is as the strength of ten because my heart is pure.
~Lord Alfred Tennyson

I acquired my three-fourths Seal Point Siamese cat when she was six weeks old and I was a twenty-one-year-old college student. I saw an ad in our local paper advertising the kittens. When I called the number listed, I was told there were two kittens remaining, a male and a female. I asked them to hold the male kitten for me. I already had a name picked out — Norman.

After I arrived, the mom cat walked into the room followed by a healthy, rambunctiously romping kitten, the male. Following slowly behind came a much smaller kitten with shaky, bowed legs and a sparse dull coat, the female.

"That's the runt," the owner said. Although, the kitten was small and malnourished, she held her tail happily upright. I was shocked that the owners had never come to the aid of the little runt. Although I'd planned on purchasing the male, the little female needed me. Our eyes met and I felt an immediate connection. It was fate. I named her Normandy.

Normandy was so tiny a regular litter box was too big. I used the lid from a shoebox for her first litter box. I fed her a special mix of baby food, baby rice cereal and canned milk until she was big enough for kitten food. As she gained weight, her fur became soft and thick and her legs became sturdy and straight. She slept beside me on my pillow, curled up in the space between my neck and shoulder. She would wake me by attacking my eyelashes with her little kitten paws. Normandy grew into a healthy playful kitten that, if I tapped my thigh while wearing jeans, would climb up my leg and into my arms.

Normandy and I grew up together. She was with me through all of the major changes of my life. She was my comfort when my father passed away, and she helped me choose my husband. When I met my future husband, I told him he had to pass the Normandy test. My cat had to like him. She was a great judge of character and fell in love with him, too.

About a year after we married, my husband and I bought a house in a rural area. Normandy would finally have a yard to play in. She liked to keep me company while I worked in our new yard. She would roll in the dirt, chatter at the birds, and nap in the sun.

There were dogs that ran free and roamed the neighborhood. They were friendly dogs. Normandy didn't run from them so they didn't chase her.

One afternoon I was pulling weeds from the front flowerbed with Normandy sitting by my side. A medium-sized dog wandered up the street toward us. Normandy did something she'd never done before. She started walking toward the dog and situated herself between the dog and me. When I walked forward and called her, the dog started to back away and Normandy stealthily followed him.

The dog didn't quite know what to do with an aggressive cat and slowly kept backing away. When I moved toward the house, Normandy turned to follow me. If I stepped in her direction her, she went back toward the dog. I quickly picked up the gardening supplies and walked to the front of the house. Normandy followed with occasional glances over her shoulder to glare at the dog.

The next time I worked in the yard, a dog came over to visit and Normandy went at him like an enraged lion. The dog was shocked, but stood his ground until she flew into his face hissing and spitting. She chased that incredulous dog away. Once again, I had to retreat to the house before she would leave the poor dog alone.

Soon the neighbors were talking about that crazy, dog-chasing Siamese cat. I didn't know what had gotten into Normandy. She only went after dogs when we were outside together. After a couple of weeks of this unusual feline behavior, I found out I was pregnant. I don't know how she knew, but Normandy had known for weeks that I was pregnant and was protecting me.

Normandy was just as protective with my two daughters. When they were babies, she would meow to notify me when they woke from naps. She would hold vigil if they were sick. Wherever they were playing, she would be near keeping a watchful eye on them. She watched over our family for more than fifteen years. We loved her and she loved us.

When fate brought that needy kitten into my life, I never knew how much I would end up needing her.

~Deborah Wilson

Muffin the Warrior

Life is either a great adventure or nothing.
~Helen Keller

He was little more than a fluffy gray fur ball, crawling through the chain link fence to play with our children. We had promised the kids a pet as a way to soften the blow of our frequent moves as an Air Force family—a forever friend they didn't always have to leave behind.

I was unpacking boxes and organizing my new kitchen when the children came running in squealing, our oldest daughter clutching a tiny, wiggly, adorable kitten. Wasn't it interesting that we just happened to move in next door to someone with a new litter of kittens?

Though they were too young to be separated from their mother, the kittens squeezed through the fence to join our kids every time they went out to play. After about four weeks we had our new pet and the spell was cast.

Muffin was a longhaired, gray tiger cat with an enormous raccoon-like tail. In fact, people often mistook him for a Maine Coon cat. He loved to be with the children. They would tuck him down their shirts until only his little gray face and green eyes showed above the collar. They carried him around in a butterfly net, dressed him in baby clothes and took turns sleeping with him at night.

As he grew, his personality became apparent. He loved people and would sit on the front porch waiting for passersby. When someone approached, he would saunter down the walk, meow sweetly, and luxuriate in the attention. He soaked up the sun with his face uplifted and scrunched into an expression that looked like an imitation of Yoda.

Muffin refused to be an indoor cat. Like his father, the neighborhood tom, he was struck with wanderlust and full of courage. Muffin was a skilled hunter and very territorial. One day, our neighbor's dog, a Golden Retriever named Dusty, climbed onto his doghouse and jumped over the fence into our yard.

Muffin went on the offensive as the intruder entered his space. With the hair on his back raised, he crouched and stalked, preparing for his attack like a lion on the Serengeti. Then he went at Dusty full force, teeth bared, paws and claws like windmills twirling wildly in the air. Dusty outweighed Muffin by fifty pounds, but he was no match for this cat's ferocity. Muffin swiped and hissed until Dusty was dizzy from trying to avoid him. After running in circles and jumping constantly to avoid Muffin's razor-like claws, Dusty finally gave up and leapt straight from the ground over the fence and back to his yard. Muffin simply sat down calmly and began licking his fur as if to remove any speck of that dog from his universe.

As Muffin reached cat puberty he tested the boundaries. One evening, I heard a terrible cat fight outside. When Muffin didn't show up for breakfast the next morning I went to investigate. Tufts of cat hair and damaged bushes gave testament to the tussle, but there was no other sign of Muffin.

Days turned into weeks and still he didn't return. Searches and posters produced nothing, so we tried to comfort the children and move on. About a month later, the phone rang. Apparently, after losing the fight Muffin left to find his own territory. He traipsed through woods, fields, brambles and bushes until he was about ten miles from our house. Then, in the middle of a thunderstorm, he jumped up on the caller's kitchen windowsill, exactly as he did at our house when he wanted to be let in. He looked pitiful so she went outside to get him. At our reunion he was wet, bedraggled and full of burrs, but otherwise fine.

On our next move we chose to live on the Air Force base where all pets had to be leashed when they were outside. We honestly tried to keep Muffin in, but he would sit for hours at the window meowing mournfully. I finally relented and let him out. Imagine our chagrin as we arrived at the Officer's Club for an official function only to find Muffin sound asleep, ensconced on the wing of the airplane displayed at the entrance. We pretended not to see him.

The neighbors were actually grateful for Muffin's outdoor presence as he controlled the local mole population. He even entertained us at a ladies' brunch by catching a mole, tossing it in the air and batting it playfully as we tried to eat our quiche.

Muffin's greatest mole adventure by far occurred one afternoon just before the children returned home from school. I spotted Muffin sitting quietly in the yard and recognized his watchful stance; a mole was about to meet its fate. Then he tipped his head ever so slightly and pounced forward to seize the hapless mole in his claws. Before he could savor the moment, a hawk swooped down from the top of a tree, gliding soundlessly across the yard, just skimming the grass. Muffin never saw him coming. The hawk snatched the mole in its talons and took off. Ever the fighter, Muffin was not about to let this interloper have his catch. The hawk had one end of the mole and Muffin the other. As the hawk flew upward Muffin hung on. The hawk flew higher and higher, mole in tow and Muffin dangling below. I couldn't believe my eyes. Finally at about nine feet in the air, Muffin decided this was one fight he couldn't win. He let go and fell to the ground with nothing but his ego damaged. The hawk soared off into the woods with his prize.

As the children grew up and moved on, their forever friend was left in our care. So, at the age of twenty-one, Muffin, now blind, retired to Florida with us. Always the outdoor cat, we fixed a basket with a heating pad for him on the screened porch where he spent his final days prowling the perimeter of the lanai, enjoying the coastal breeze and sniffing the salty air.

As he sat in the sun with his long tail curled around him, eyes closed and face scrunched into his Yoda grin, I wondered if he was reminiscing about the adventures of his amazing life. Did he see himself as a young cat, climbing trees, chasing dogs, and challenging hawks? He lived to be twenty-three, a testament to those tomcat genes. A few days after Muffin died, a bobcat appeared at the edge of the pond across the street from our house. I e-mailed a picture of it to our oldest daughter, Muffin's original champion. She replied simply, "Mom, that isn't just a bobcat. It's Muffin's spirit returning to tell you he's okay."

~Liz Graf

The Veterinarian's Assistant

When a cat chooses to be friendly, it's a big deal, because a cat is picky.
~Mike Deupree

Our daughter, Melissa, first spotted the kitten suckling on its dead mother as we drove by the barn. "Stop," she said. "Maybe I can catch it."

She jumped out of the pickup and snuck over to the orphan. The kitten struggled as she pulled it from its mother's stilled body but calmed as soon as she cradled it between her palms. Glenn, my husband and a veterinarian, told her, "It can't be more than that three and a half or four weeks old. Let's take her back to the house. She needs a bellyful of milk."

Later that afternoon, after a couple of feedings, the young kitten gained enough strength to go outside with us. She crawled at our feet as we sat on the grass in the sun until Glenn accidentally stepped on her tail with the tip of his cowboy boot. Screeching, she ran off beneath dense shrubbery, hiding there beyond the reach of our arms.

Melissa knelt down, calling, "Come back, little kitten. Come back, Little Grey," but to no avail. Glenn felt worse than terrible. Melissa was bereft. "If she doesn't come out, the coyotes will get her."

Her dad comforted her. "If we're quiet, she may come out on her own."

Within a short time, the kitten crawled out and, to our amazement, clambered up Glenn's pant leg, up his chest, and all the way to his chin. Tapping her paw against his jaw, she looked him directly in the eyes, and squeaked a mew as if saying, "I know you didn't mean to step on me."

Stroking her, he told her, "You, little one, have a warm heart. I can tell you forgive me."

That's the day that Little Grey endeared herself to our family. It wasn't long before she grew into a shiny-eyed kitten that frolicked through our home. When friends visited, she'd rub against their ankles, purring affectionate hellos until they marveled, "This is the most people-loving kitten we've ever seen." Amongst the other pets in our household, however, our newcomer strode with her head high, her whiskers twitching with attitude as if she alone had regal status.

On Saturdays, our daughter helped at my husband's clinic. She wouldn't go without Little Grey, so the kitten always rode in the car with us cuddled up on Melissa's lap. At the clinic, "our princess" lay atop a tall counter greeting clients as they entered the waiting room with their pets to see Dr. Glenn. As she matured into an adult, most acknowledged our official greeter by name, saying, "Hey, Little Grey, how's it going this morning?" She'd either mew softly or reach out with a gentle paw and tap them on the arm. Our people-loving cat added a warm touch to the clinic.

In contrast to Little Grey's love for people, she was a choosy greeter when it came to the steady stream of animal patients. If a rambunctious Lab or a fussing lap dog spotted her and barked or yapped, our princess looked down on them from the safety of the counter, her gold eyes glowering in an unblinking stare. If the dog stepped closer, she growled, flattening her ears and flicking her pencil-thin tail, her way to remind all dogs to keep their distance.

One evening after Melissa left home for college, Glenn walked through the door of our home with a basket containing a red-and-white Jack Russell terrier named Mitchell. The owner had seen Mitchell in the fields with a rat hanging from his mouth, probably one dying from the effects of rodent control. Apparently Mitchell had ingested it and the poison ravaged his body: his stiffened limbs jerked, eyes twitched and body quivered. To control convulsions, Glenn hooked him up to IV fluids and administered sedation.

Little Grey must have heard the dog's whimpers because she stalked into the room, one hesitant step at a time, her angular face peeking from behind chair legs, her nose sniffing, as she approached the blanket-lined basket. Then her ears flattened. A dog! She hissed, snubbing our ill patient, and left the room grumbling, her dark grey nose in the air as she headed for the living room to curl up on the couch.

After monitoring Mitchell well into the night, Glenn finally climbed into bed, setting the alarm to awaken him every hour to assess the little dog's progress. After the three o'clock check, he lamented, "I'm not sure the little guy's going make it. I can't keep him warm enough."

At four, he called me downstairs. I feared the worst as I walked into the room, yet Glenn smiled, and said, "The vet's helper is here." I thought he was referring to me. But when I looked in the box, I found Little Grey, who had once been on the cusp of death herself, snuggled up close to the terrier, her front and back legs encircling him. Purring compassionately, she glanced up at us.

I looked at my husband, "Can you believe this?"

He smiled. "Wait until we tell Melissa about our new assistant."

As we dimmed the light, Little Grey laid her head on Mitchell's wire-haired back and we returned to bed knowing that we had another healer on our veterinary team.

~Karen Baker

My Maine Man

Most of us rather like our cats to have a streak of wickedness.
I should not feel quite easy in the company of any cat
that walked about the house with a saintly expression.
~Beverly Nichols

"**O**uch," I said, not from pain, but surprise. Tucker, a massive Maine Coon cat who deemed me worthy to serve him, nipped my ankles as I walked by. Tucker's motto reflects what a crazed woman in the movie *Fatal Attraction* said: "I will not be ignored."

Tucker is my "main man" in a household of one female person and one female cat. He prowls, struts, chases the other cat, and bites me.

He also adores me.

Strikingly handsome in his long coat of mixed brown, tan, and beige, he knows he is good-looking, and races to the cat brushes whenever I say the word "brush" so I can fluff his magnificent fur.

He weighs about twenty pounds, and has a huge head with mesmerizing green eyes in a face that is strikingly symmetrical, topped by two hairy, pointed ears. His fur is luxuriously soft. When he curls up in my lap, I'm instantly warmed by this giant plush pillow.

"Leave Gracie alone," I yelled at him for the umpteenth time as he relentlessly pursued the other cat, who only wanted peace.

But when Tucker is on a mission, he will not be denied. He goes into robotic mode, intent on completing his mission. If I discipline him to stop his behavior, he follows me and nips at my ankles. He doesn't hurt—in fact, it's kind of funny—but he makes his point.

Gracie, the tiny stray with stunted legs, is content to be subservient to Tucker's dominance. It's likely that Gracie was born under my back deck, where she survived harsh outdoor conditions before she gratefully made her home with me.

Tucker came into my life in a padded carrying case from his foster home, where he had been fondly groomed and nourished. His constant demand for attention in a household of many cats led to the family's decision to find another home for him. He entered my house with a sense of entitlement and wasted no time informing us that he was in charge.

One day this summer Tucker went too far in his bad conduct, so I carried him out to the screened-in patio. My cats enjoy being there, but that day I left Tucker in the patio for some relief from his escapades.

Freed from the mischievous monster, I completed my morning chores and prepared to go to the market. I debated about leaving Tucker in the patio. Usually I brought him inside when I was not at home, because even in the protected environment of the patio he found ways to disobey.

He climbed on the screens in an attempt to reach the squirrels or birds that fascinated him or the stray cats that agitated him. If Gracie was on the back patio and I wasn't there to supervise, he picked on her. If the door wasn't closed securely, he pushed against it in an attempt to escape.

However, the weather was pleasant, and Gracie was enjoying a snooze indoors, safe from Tucker's reach. Besides, I would only be gone a half an hour. So, I left Tucker on the back patio and drove away.

I didn't know it was a special triple-coupon value day at the market. Instead of buying the few items on my list, I went through all my coupons to take advantage of the extra savings. My few intended purchases ballooned to a basketful of groceries, and the half-hour venture took closer to one and a half hours.

During the time I was in the store, a thunderstorm had come and gone, apparently quite a doozy given the number of puddles and downed branches. Tucker, brute that he is, is afraid of storms. I worried about him as I hurried home.

When he is indoors and a storm strikes, he runs to a corner of the basement to burrow into coverings; on the patio, there are no dark corners or niches in which he can hide.

I dropped my groceries onto the kitchen counter, not taking time to put the frozen foods away, and hurried to the patio. I opened the door and called out "Tucker" as I searched under the furnishings. I couldn't find him. There were no holes in the screens, no signs of escape.

Had I forgotten that I brought him indoors before leaving for the store? I didn't think so, but I went indoors and scoured the house, calling "Tucker" throughout three stories of rooms. No Tucker, so I repeated the room-to-room search, this time getting down on hands and knees to look under furniture — still no cat. Did a neighbor hear him crying and take him in? Did a stranger find him and take him away?

I returned to the patio for another futile search. Perplexed and upset, I considered my options. I was about to search the yard when I heard a half-cry, half-meow from above. From above?

There was Tucker. How a mammoth cat could cram onto the shelf over the door behind a display of pottery, without knocking any of them down, defied logic. I couldn't coax him down until I offered his favorite treat. Clumsily, he emerged, dislodging ceramics, until I could reach him. He was soaking wet. His normally large pupils were enormous, and he trembled. I held him, trying to comfort and dry him at the same time.

He seemed so pathetic and — could it be true — humbled. For the rest of that day and all of the next, he was a changed cat, respectful and docile. I enjoyed his genteel demeanor, but only for a while. I missed the Maine Coon with the mean streak who never ceased to entertain me. Fortunately, Tucker returned to his former mischievous ways soon enough. I don't know if Tucker has a deepened respect for storms, but I am more tolerant of his naughty quirks.

~Linda Panczner

Reprinted by permission of
Bruce Robinson ©2010

For the Love of Fish

W hen I first moved to the little town of Portage La Prairie, Manitoba, I was lonely. I had my family and a few friends, but it was the first time I had lived alone. Although my place was lovely and had almost everything I needed, it did not have companionship.

After a month or so, I decided to get a pet. I went to the local pet store, but it only had fish. Although lovely, a fish was not what I was looking for. However while looking through the tanks, I saw an injured-looking Betta fish. It was a magnificent shade of royal blue with crimson spots on its fins. The poor thing was quarantined in a little net on one side of the tank.

The shop attendant explained that the other fish picked on it, but there was no room for it elsewhere. My heart went out to it. As a teenager, I was often the object of ridicule. I decided to take the Betta home. On my way home I chose the name Anshin, which is Japanese for peace of mind.

The following few weeks went more smoothly. I would come home and spend time watching Anshin swim around. I chuckled every time he puffed up his fins upon seeing his own reflection in his mirrored exercise floater. This was fine for a while, but there is only so much companionship to be gained from a fish.

I quickly fell back into feeling lonely and wondered what to do. By no small miracle, I overheard someone in the market speaking about abandoned kittens. When I asked her about them, she explained that she had found a box of kittens on the side of the highway. There had been seven to start, but five of them had died from starvation. I felt sick to my stomach just hearing about it.

She continued to tell me that she wanted to care for them, but she already had three dogs and four cats. My first instinct was to tell her that I would take them, but I was not sure I was ready for the responsibility. The only cats I had lived with belonged to my previous roommates. And I didn't know the first thing about caring for kittens.

My thoughts must have been transparent because the woman asked me if I might consider giving a home to them. The look in her eyes was desperate, and I thought she might start crying if I said no. When I told her I would, she burst into tears and hugged me tightly, right in the middle of the produce aisle.

Two days later, I was the proud and utterly terrified caregiver of two precious kittens. They were practically twins—all black fur except for one little spot of white on their tails. The only difference between them was one had one white toe. I named them Mika and Kyo.

I spent hours over the next couple of weeks researching proper care for kittens. I fed them special foods, took them to the vet, and litter trained them.

While similar in looks, they had very different personalities. Kyo was content to snuggle with me while I did my writing, but Mika always had to be doing something. She would seek out anything that moved, and unfortunately that also meant Anshin.

Fortunately, though, she did not appear to want to eat him. She was happy to watch Anshin swim around his bowl. Sometimes Mika would bat at the bowl if Anshin wasn't active. I worried that Mika would scare poor Anshin to death, but they soon grew fond of each other. Mika wouldn't even have to bat at the bowl to make Anshin frill his fins.

We had settled into a routine. When I came home, I would play with Mika and Kyo and brush them. Then I would sit down to write. Kyo would curl up on my shoulder and purr heavily into my ear. Mika would jump onto the desk beside Anshin's bowl and watch with wide eyes as he swam around.

Come summertime, my apartment became too hot to handle. I did not have air conditioning, and even with a fan in every room, it was way too hot. I opened all the windows, but noticed that one of them didn't have a screen. I didn't think much of this.

After opening the windows as much as possible, I went to take a cool shower. Upon returning to my living room, I was shocked to find a big purple pigeon waddling along my floor. I thought for sure Mika or Kyo would attack it, but they weren't fazed by its presence. Kyo sat perched on the couch giving herself a bath while Mika sat and looked out the window. I was so shocked that I didn't even move. I was trying to think of a way to get the pigeon out of my apartment.

After what felt like hours, Mika jumped off the windowsill and pranced over to the bird. She playfully nudged it with her face. It was as though she were trying to make friends with it. The bird was not put off, and instead wandered around my apartment. I assumed it was looking for something to eat, and that's when it spotted Anshin.

The bird flew onto my desk and waddled over to Anshin. Mika joined and watched closely. The bird started flapping its wings, and that was when I realized it was going to try to get Anshin. I was about to step in and try to scare the pigeon away, but I heard Mika hissing.

I stopped, as did the bird. The bird looked sideways at Mika and Mika stopped hissing. As soon as Mika stopped, the bird started attacking the bowl again. Mika began to growl this time. The bird backed off, but only for a minute.

This went on until, clearly, Mika had had enough. The pigeon had stuck its beak into the bowl and Mika took a fast swipe at it with her claws. The pigeon was none too happy and lunged at Mika.

Again, I was going to attempt to scare off the bird, but Kyo beat me to it. She had soundlessly left the couch and found her way to Mika's side.

The two of them ganged up on the bird and were winning. The bird retreated and started to fly madly around the living room. I hit the floor and covered my head until the noise had settled down.

When I looked up, I caught sight of the pigeon making a hasty escape through the window. I sat there, dumbfounded. When I looked over to see if my cats were okay, I found them purring and brushing up against Anshin's bowl lovingly.

The next few words came out of my mouth without even thinking: "Oh, for the love of fish!"

~Jazmyne Rose

I Can't Believe My Cat Did That!

Chapter

6

I'm Just Staff

Slow Learner

Most cats, when they are out want to be in, and visa versa,
and often simultaneously.
~Louis J. Camuti

When Bandit and Smokey came to live with me, they seemed happy with their new surroundings except for one pesky fact: whenever they were inside they wanted out, and whenever they were outside they wanted in.

This was problematic when I spent long hours at work and they were stuck where they didn't want to be, but evenings were even worse. I would sit in the kitchen grading papers near the sliding glass door. As soon as I got situated, one of the cats would come around, either pushing his nose to the glass from the outside, wanting in, or circling my legs and meowing, wanting out.

My new charges were driving me crazy! When friends suggested getting a cat door, I went deluxe and ordered a door that would be installed into the wall. I chose a model that consisted of double flaps, so that the cats had to go through the first flap, pass through a small tunnel about five inches long, and then through a second flap. This would prevent cold air from entering the house on winter days when the cats were particularly adamant about going in and out.

The next week a man named Jack came to install my door. As he sweated profusely in the August heat, the cats showed great interest in his enterprise, watching every movement. I was pleased with my sleek purchase. Having a cat door would simplify my life!

Jack warned me that it might take my cats a while to get used to the door, but he assured me that most pets adapted within a couple of weeks. As soon as he left, I nudged Bandit towards his new escape route.

Nothing happened. Bandit merely looked at me.

I placed him right against the flap.

"Come on, Bandit! Once you've mastered this, you can come in and out any time you like! You're going to love it!"

But Bandit squirmed when I tried to push him through the door, and Smokey got so scared watching me torture his brother that he hid behind the couch.

Despite Jack's reassurance, I was afraid I'd just wasted three hundred dollars.

When I came home from school the next day, I worked with the cats, pushing them through the cat door while holding the flaps open. None of these efforts appeared to make an impression on Smokey or Bandit.

About this time I met Fred. When he came over for coffee, he complimented my fancy door.

"It's a waste of money," I declared. "My cats won't use it."

"Sure, they will! But you have to train them. Come on! I'll stand outside and help push them in and out."

For the next half hour, Fred stood outside the house and I stood inside as we awkwardly passed the cats back and forth. They made piteous meows, as if the cold plastic flaps were painful to the touch, and sometimes we had to chase them down so that we could try again.

After Fred went home and I went back to doing homework at the kitchen table, they appeared, one by one, wanting out, wanting in, and I struggled to keep my concentration even though I was interrupted every few minutes.

For the whole next week Fred and I worked with the cats, but they didn't learn a thing. I resigned myself to the fact that I'd bought a useless door and stopped worrying about it.

One Thursday a month later, my afternoon meetings got cut short and I came home from school a couple of hours early. Although I knew darned well I'd locked Bandit in the house that morning, when I got home he was outside in the yard! He'd used his cat door! I hugged him and praised him. He had finally caught on!

"You're a good boy," I told him as I scratched his ears. "Now, be sure to explain all this to your brother. I'm afraid he's a slow learner."

Indeed, despite my best efforts to force Smokey through the door at least once a day, he resisted bitterly, meowing the whole time. I kept reminding him that these actions were for his benefit, but he didn't seem to care.

Several weeks later, I came home one day to find Smokey lying peacefully on the front porch basking in the sun even though I knew I'd left him inside on the couch. I was thrilled!

"You good boy!" I told him. "You finally did it! You're no dummy after all!" I picked him up and hugged him, twirling as I did so.

At that point my neighbor Matt stuck his nose over the wall. "Dancing with your cat?" he asked.

I was so happy that I ignored his taunts. "Celebrating! Smokey finally learned how to go through the cat door! I've been working on this for four months! Finally he won't be stuck inside when I go to class."

"You leave him inside when you go to school?"

"Oh, yes. In case he needs water or something."

Matt looked down at his feet, and I wondered if his tennis shoes were too tight. "I'm not sure how to tell you this."

"What? Is something the matter?"

"Nothing's wrong. But when you're gone, your cats get lonely. They over come here all the time."

"But… I don't understand."

"Your cat door," he said softly. "They've been using it for months. They figured it out right away."

"You're kidding!"

"As soon as you leave, they come over to visit me."

"You're telling me that these cats have known how to use this cat door since…"

"Since the week you got it."

That night when I sat at my table doing my schoolwork and the cats pressed their little noses against the sliding glass door, I gave them a stern look and continued what I was doing. No matter how hard they meowed, I refused to get up from my chair.

I may be a slow learner, but eventually, I do manage to learn.

~D.R. Ransdell

Ember's Bell

Since each of us is blessed with only one life, why not live it with a cat?
~Robert Stearns

As a single career gal and the owner of a new home, I wanted a pet and I was considering adopting a cat. However, I had heard all the usual stories from my dog-owning friends about how aloof cats are, how they cannot be trained, and how they just are not as intelligent or as "human" as dogs.

Being realistic, I knew that my erratic work schedule would not permit me to be home to walk a dog or to take it out as needed. So, despite all my friends' advice to the contrary, I visited my local animal shelter and adopted a fluffy eight-week-old tortoiseshell kitten with an orange star on her forehead. Since she reminded me of the flaming colors in my fireplace, I named her Ember.

Ember was a bright kitten from day one. She quickly learned not to jump on the counters. She also learned my getting-up, leaving-for-work, and going-to-bed routines. When I came home from work, she always met me at the door and brushed against me as if to say, "Hi, Mom... I've missed you." Also, she was an expressive kitty. I quickly learned to interpret her meows and to read the meaning of the positions of her ears and tail. She, in turn, seemed fascinated with my attempts to meow back at her.

Ember's very favorite toy was a single jingle bell, which I had threaded a string through and attached underneath the seat of a dining room chair. Ember would lie on her back under the chair for hours just swatting that jingle bell in all directions. If I awoke during the night, I could listen and hear the gentle tinkling of her bell as she played in the dining room.

One evening after working the second shift at the clinic, I walked into the house about ten o'clock, stressed, exhausted, and hungry. To make matters worse, I had to work the early morning shift at the clinic the next day. Ember greeted me at the door as usual, but I could tell by the tone of her meows that she was upset.

As I walked through the dining room, I noticed that the string that held her jingle bell to the chair had broken in two. She sat by the non-functional jingle bell staring up at me with soft, melting eyes. Too exhausted to even eat anything but a protein bar for supper that night, I just tied the two ends of Ember's string together with the promise to replace the string on the chair the next day after work.

After feeding Ember, taking a quick shower, and flopping into bed, I lay awake unwinding for a couple of minutes before closing my eyes. No sooner had I closed my eyes than I heard a faint tinkling close by. I switched on my lamp, and there sat Ember on the floor next to my bed, her eyes wide and soulful.

"Hi, Ember. Do you want to come up?" I said. That's when she took her front paw and patted the floor next to her three times. I looked down at where she was patting, and there laid the jingle bell and half the string. Apparently, the string had broken again. She picked up the bell in her mouth with the string attached and carried it into my bedroom so I could see that it was again in need of repair. My little Ember behaved just like a child with a broken toy... she brought it to her mom to be fixed. I was thrilled!

Exhausted as I was, I repaired Ember's jingle bell with a brand new string that night and tied it securely back onto the dining room chair. Ember deserved it.

~Diane P. Morey

Playing Dead

When my cats aren't happy, I'm not happy.
Not because I care about their mood but because I know
they're just sitting there thinking up ways to get even.
~Percy Bysshe Shelley

The cat collapses on the kitchen floor at my feet. Her eyes roll back in her head and her breath comes in short, shallow gasps. Her chest flutters with the effort of breathing as she raises one small paw in a final salute to life and all that is true and good in this world. Having mustered her last bit of strength for this poignant gesture, her head falls back against the floor and her body goes limp, every bit of energy spent in her final, fatalistic farewell. A faint "meow" lingers on the air.

"Move it," I say, stepping over her for the twentieth time that day. "You're not fooling anyone, you know."

The cat glares at me but pulls herself up and, dripping dignity, saunters down the hall.

"Dead Cat" is the new game of choice around our home. I don't know who started it, but I'm ready for it to end. It's becoming dangerous to even walk around the house. At any given moment a cat or kitten may fling herself at our feet and collapse.

We've analyzed the cats' behavior and have noticed "dead cat syndrome" is most likely to occur when we're ignoring them, the definition of "ignore" being that we have gone more than fifteen seconds without acknowledging their existence.

For example, we returned the other day from a forty-minute trip to the grocery store. I greeted the cats as soon as we entered the house and even stopped to offer a kibble treat before proceeding to put groceries away.

The cat sat in the kitchen doorway. "Mrow."

"Hi baby," I said. "I'm almost done here, then we'll play."

"Mrow."

"Five minutes, okay?"

The next time I looked over, the cat was lying belly up, like a fish on land. Her paws hung limply to each side. Her body was stretched thin and long, as if she'd been steamrollered.

"Oh, look at that," I said to my husband. "There's a dead cat in the hall."

"Bummer," he intoned. "But hey, maybe we can use her for a rug." He stepped over to the cat and raised a foot above her body. Miraculously, life flooded her limbs and she bolted down the hall.

The cat isn't alone in her road-kill impersonations. Cat and kitten appear to be rotating dead-cat shifts. The cat works on us in the daytime and the kitten takes the graveyard shift in our bed at night.

Cats are nature's original bed hogs. My husband and I huddle each night on opposite edges of our mattress, clinging to the sheet like rock climbers clutching a harness. We have been shoved to the edge of the bed by a twelve-pound feline who apparently uses a protractor to find the exact center of the bed then plops herself down, body splayed.

There is no budging her. I've tried to nudge her just an inch or two to the left, just enough so I can get one full shoulder on the bed. The kitten digs her claws into our bedspread and goes completely limp. The I'm-a-dead-cat feint adds a good ten pounds, making her almost impossible to move. I tap the kitten with my foot.

"Hey, scoot over," I whisper. She pretends not to hear me.

I sit up and scratch her ears, trying to charm her into moving. That doesn't work so I attempt to lift her. She counters by acting as if the life force has drained out of her and, if possible, goes even more limp. I retaliate the only way I know how. I kick and thrash my legs under the covers in the hopes of scaring her away.

"Ow, ow, ow!" says my husband. "Why are you kicking me?"

"Sorry. I was trying to frighten the kitten," I say.

"Talk to her about global warming," he suggests. "Or offer to cook something for her. Hey — ow!"

I'm at a loss. I simply can't pay attention to the cats 24/7. But seeing dead cats lying around the house distresses me. Don't my girls realize how much I love them? How truly distraught I would be were something to ever actually happen to them?

I decide it's a matter of miscommunication. Surely if I show the cats how upsetting it is to see someone they love "dead," they will stop this awful charade.

I talk to my husband and we plan our demise. That night at dinner, both of us fall out of our chairs and onto the floor in front of the cats.

The cats walk by with nary a glance in our direction. The only thing they seem distressed about is having to maneuver around us to get to their food dishes. Once they finish eating, they retreat to their favorite napping spots in the library. They plod across our lifeless bodies to take the most direct route possible.

Apparently "dead human" isn't anywhere near as upsetting as "dead cat." I should have known.

~Dena Harris

Left in the Dark

I had been told that the training procedure with cats was difficult. It's not.
Mine had me trained in two days.
~Bill Dana

Driving home from the movie theater one rainy evening, we saw something glowing in the dark. As our headlights illuminated the object, we realized it was a white cat. My husband pulled to the shoulder of the road, where I got out and approached the cat. She was hunched over, soaking wet and shivering. I expected her to run, but she sat stoically, staring straight ahead. I grabbed a small blanket from the trunk of the car, scooped her up and said, "Alexandra, you're headed for your forever-home."

It didn't take long for Alexandra to find a favorite chair on the screened-in porch where she could safely enjoy the sounds of the birds, the feel of the breeze, and watch the antics of the local squirrels. Some evenings she would sit by the screen room door and look out into the darkness as we watched and wondered what she envisioned to be out there.

One evening my husband and I were reading in the living room, comfortably settled in our chairs. Although Alexandra sat patiently by the door to the screen room, neither of us wanted to get up to let her out. Finally, she meandered off and gave up, or so we thought. Suddenly, the room went dark. I quickly turned, and saw Alexandra on the back of the couch, standing on her hind legs, reaching up the wall with her paw. She accidentally hit the light switch, leaving the room in darkness.

Now, if we wanted to continue reading, one of us had to get up to turn on the light. And, once up, open the door to let Alexandra out.

Although I am sure this first "light trick" was an accident, merely a consequence of a big cat stretch, Alexandra learned how to manipulate the family. From that night on, when she wanted out, she would jump onto the back of the couch, reach up to the light switch and leave us in the dark.

As the English artist Louis Wain said, "Intelligence in the cat is understated!"

~Mary Grant Dempsey

Boo Got Pulled Over

A black cat crossing your path signifies that the animal is going somewhere.
~Groucho Marx

At one time I had several cats and a job that could support them. They all had special personalities and interesting quirks, but one stood out. Boo was black with a white spot on her chest and the prettiest orange eyes I have ever seen on a cat. She was also scared of her own shadow, sudden noises, and new people that came to the door, hence the name Boo.

Boo loved to go for car rides. She loved to put her hind feet on the back seat, her front feet on the back of the driver's seat, and hang her head out the open window like a dog. I had lots of double takes and laughs whenever we went anywhere. And the faster we went, the better Boo liked it.

One day I was running late to the vet for her checkup and yearly shots, so we took the highway. As we drove, we passed a police car with an officer pointing his radar gun at the traffic. I didn't pay any attention since I was traveling the speed limit. I had forgotten about Boo and her hanging her head out the window—until I heard the police siren. He wanted me to pull over, so I did.

I handed him my license and paperwork. As he checked out the back seat I asked him what was wrong. He replied, "Nothing serious ma'am… Oh my God, it is a cat!"

He asked where I was going, and I explained. I added that I didn't know how I was going to get away with explaining that I was late for the appointment because my cat got me pulled over.

The officer rubbed his chin and replied, "If I give you a police escort and explain it myself, will you promise to stop by the station on your way home to verify why I pulled you over?"

I agreed. We arrived at the vet, Boo had her exam, and then we headed to the police station. When we entered, the officer at the front desk immediately started laughing.

She asked if Boo was the one that got pulled over on the highway. I said yes, and she asked if she could take the cat around the station to show her off. I sat on one of the benches to wait until she brought Boo back. When she did I saw that Boo was licking her lips. The office explained that it was lunchtime and many of the officers insisted on sharing their lunch with Boo. Not only did Boo get me pulled over, but she got a free lunch at the police station!

~Mary Brennan

Just Purr

To err is human, to purr is feline.
~Robert Byrne

My dad found Appleton's tail before we found Appleton. I was inside wrapping Christmas gifts when Dad rushed in with a beautiful, black fluffy tail. I was so awestruck that a moment passed before I realized what I was admiring.

"It was in the middle of the road," Dad said. He kept trying to hand the tail to me.

"Where's Appleton?" I asked, tearing up.

Dad shrugged and tried to hand the tail to me again.

I quickly slipped on my tennis shoes. I had to find my cat. Though I was wearing only a T-shirt and shorts, I was oblivious to the cold December air.

Dad and I walked the perimeter of the yard that abutted the woods where we knew my cats liked to play. Not too far into the woods I saw Appleton sitting on a log. His yellow eyes were huge and especially round, like two harvest moons. He watched us with fear and relief, if that's possible. I stepped toward him slowly and talked to him softly.

"Hey there, Apple. What happened, buddy?"

Dead grass and twigs crunched with each of my steps, threatening to send Appleton further into the woods. But he sat motionless.

When I reached him, he allowed me to stroke his head and neck.

Carefully, I slipped my hands beneath his front legs and carried him to Dad. While Dad cradled him, I ran to the house and called our veterinarian, who told us to bring in Appleton as soon as possible. After securing Appleton in the pet carrier, Dad and I sped to the vet's.

On the way there, Appleton sat in his carrier. He purred constantly. He purred the way he did when I brushed his soft, black hair or when he made figure eights around my ankles when he was happy to see me.

Dad noticed too. He said, "Apple purred the whole time I was holding him."

Dr. Holmes was amazed at how well Appleton was doing when we arrived. Appleton wasn't in shock; he had bled very little, and he appeared to be in no pain. Dad and I were a different story. Dad was still holding Appleton's tail, and I couldn't stop crying.

Dr. Holmes took the tail from Dad and said, "We won't be able to reattach it."

She also told us that Appleton might not survive. We would have to wait and see.

All this time, Appleton sat in the midst of us on the shiny silver examining table, wide-eyed, but very calm. And purring.

Months later, my little tailless cat, who I had begun to call Applebob, could run faster than ever before. Furthermore, he had developed a new strange habit, he backed up to everything: people, his food, his chair, the litter box. Quirkier and tailless, Appleton was more beautiful than ever.

Not long after all this happened I was reading a book about cats and learned that a cat purrs for many reasons, one being to calm itself in a stressful situation. This may have contributed to Appleton's survival. Then I thought about my varied and often hysterical reactions to stressful situations. I never practiced the human equivalent of purring—praying, chanting, humming, meditating, walking, or simply being still. When subjected to stress, I tended to cry, panic, become cranky, cuss, rush around, or hyperventilate. Although I still react this way occasionally, I have tried to slow down and think, "Just purr."

~Dana J. Barnett

What Zuzu Wants,
Zuzu Gets

The mathematical probability of a common cat doing exactly as it pleases
is the one scientific absolute in the world.
~Lynn M. Osband

On a warm Sunday afternoon almost two years ago, a panicked fifteen-ounce kitten darted onto a busy city street in front of our car. My husband slammed on the brakes, I snatched the little calico from certain death, and our life with cats, as we had come to know it, would never be the same.

We named her Zuzu. Bright-eyed and active, she stole our hearts immediately. The four aging cats that shared our home were appalled by Zuzu's arrival, but she ignored their hisses and rebuffs and went about settling into her new surroundings. She delighted in life and made everything a game. She pounced on the others while they slept, stole treats from under their noses, and interrupted their activities with toys.

"She'll outgrow the antics," I assured them. Tillie, growling and twitching, exited the room with Zuzu clinging to her back in a tiny chokehold.

Eventually, our other cats quit trying to teach Zuzu respect for physical and emotional space. I envisioned them having a group discussion that ended something like, "It's a waste of energy to try to teach her anything. And, besides, she is mildly entertaining, especially when her focus is on one of you." Whatever their reason, they decided to let Zuzu be Zuzu—not that she gave them much choice.

Because the older cats had voracious appetites, our only concern with them was limiting their food intake. However, for Zuzu, cat food wasn't interesting. In fact, my husband had moved her feeding dish to the bathroom so she would have the opportunity to graze without the others polishing off her portion.

One day I heard the sound of "tap, tap, tap" coming from the bathroom. After each tap, I heard the patter of little feet. When I opened the door, there squatted my husband, tossing small pellets of food against the wall. The pellets bounced and skidded across the floor, and Zuzu pursued the "prey" and gobbled it down. Tap, patter, gobble. Tap, patter, gobble.

"What are you doing?" I asked.

"She won't eat if you don't make it a game," he explained matter-of-factly.

"Breakfast is a meal, not a game," I said.

"That's not what Zuzu thinks," he said. "And look, you have to throw it just right. If you lightly toss it, she ignores it, but if you make it bounce against the wall so that it skids across the floor like an escaping bug, she traps and eats it."

My husband demonstrated the "how to" and "how not to" of cat food tossing. I left the room wondering how exactly Zuzu had taught my husband this new trick.

Although Zuzu had to be enticed to eat real food, she had no difficulty exploring the rest of the world through her sense of taste. My beautiful houseplants, some of which were over twenty years old, suffered under her onslaught. The ones that were toxic for cats were given to friends who did not live with plant-eating cats. The plants that were cat-friendly were pitiful sights indeed. My home, once beautifully adorned with lush foliage, now seemed stark and bare in comparison. Visitors were too polite to ask "Why is that scrawny houseplant wrapped in a little wire fence and encased in wax paper?"

And then there was fabric. Fabric was the love of Zuzu's small life. At first we didn't notice. Then one day I began to discover holes in items that had previously been intact. This included her most vora-cious project, a poncho-sized hole in a blanket that was protecting the sofa from cat hair. And she wasn't picky, for she consumed synthetic, blends, and cotton. If she could get her little mouth around it, she could make a meal of it. How she was able to pass such a massive amount of fabric is still a mystery to me—and to her veterinarian.

Besides the obvious physical concern for her health was the added concern of expense, because my husband never picked up after him-self. His clothes were fair game in Zuzu's mind. I had always picked up his dirty socks and underwear after they had been thrown on the bed or the floor. I carried his dirty clothes to the laundry, and I hung up the clean clothes he planned to wear again. His messy lifestyle had never been a source of contention because I long ago had accepted that he was un-teachable in this area. But, unfortunately, a time delay existed between the dropping and retrieving of clothes.

One day, while getting dressed, my husband noticed several large holes in his socks. He wiggled his foot at me and asked, "Do we have really big moths?"

As the weeks progressed, Zuzu consumed more and more of his clothes, including his socks, undershorts, and undershirts. Sometime later, he laid a pricey golf shirt on the bed while he showered. When he returned, one sleeve was missing a large chunk of fabric in the perfect shape of a cat palate. It was a favorite shirt now destined for the garbage with the other things Zuzu had managed to destroy.

I tried to offer comfort. "She's little and needs to explore and discover her world," I said.

"At the rate she's going, there won't be much world left," he grumbled.

Eventually, we managed to Zuzu-proof the house. Any new pur-chases I consider making, I stop first to ponder, "Would Zuzu eat this?" Nothing gets into our home if it doesn't pass that test.

And now, for the first time in over thirty years, my husband picks up after himself. He hauls his dirty clothes directly to the laundry room and leaves his clean clothes hanging until ready to put them on. Has he forgiven Zuzu for sampling his clothes and forcing him to change his messy habits? From the sounds of the two of them playing breakfast in the bathroom, I know the answer.

~Joan McClure Beck

The Missing Ring

By associating with the cat, one only risks becoming richer.
~Colette

O ur cat, Red, was sitting on the bathroom counter watching me spray lotion onto my hand. Red knew I was going away—he had watched me pack my suitcase the night before and even hopped into it. I had to lift him off the red sweater that he had snuggled into.

My husband and I needed a long weekend out of town. We work together, and from the moment we wake up in the morning until we go to bed late at night, work is the main topic of conversation. We were exhausted and looked forward to getting away to rekindle the romance in our lives.

Our original plans were to leave together, but an unexpected business meeting came up and Roger had to catch a flight the next day.

"Do you have everything? Your airline ticket, your wallet, your purse?" Roger asked when I was finally seated in the car.

"Yes, I do," I said as I checked once more in my carry-on bag. Then I looked down at my left hand. My wedding ring was missing. "Wait a second, I have to run into the house. I'll be right back."

I couldn't find it. The ring wasn't in my pajamas, and it wasn't on the bathroom counter near the bottle of lotion either.

With a heavy heart, I ran down the stairs and out to the car. "I can't find my wedding ring."

As my husband ran back inside with me, I noticed Red had a funny look on his face. With no time to spare, I didn't give it a second thought. We searched all over and turned up nothing. And the minutes ticked by on the clock.

"We have to go. You'll miss your flight," Roger said.

"I can't go without my ring!"

"I'll look for it later before I go to work. I'm sure it's here somewhere, don't worry."

But I did worry. As Roger concentrated on driving, I went over it in my mind. Where could it be? Cars were double-parked along the curb by the airport departure gates, so he didn't notice my eyes filling with tears as we kissed goodbye.

As soon as the plane touched down I ran to a phone and called him at the office. "Did you find it?"

"Not yet, but I'll search again when I get home."

Later that evening, he still hadn't found the ring and my heart was breaking. Could it have fallen down the drain of the sink? Did I throw it out with the trash?

"I'll do everything I can to try to find it, but my flight leaves early tomorrow morning," Roger said. "I'll see you there."

I didn't sleep well. I was up early and at the airport an hour before Roger's flight was scheduled to arrive.

I rushed up to greet him as he walked off the plane, and he wrapped his arms around me. After leading me away from the emerging crowd, Roger reached into his pocket and brought out a Kleenex folded not once or twice, but over and over until it looked like a tight ball of tissue. From the center he lifted out my dazzling diamond ring.

Looking into my eyes, he asked, "Would you marry me all over again?"

"Yes, I'd marry you all over again!"

Ceremoniously, he placed the ring on the third finger of my left hand. I threw my arms around him and gave him a long hug. "Where did you find it?"

"I reached over to pet Red last night and realized the basket he sleeps in was the one place I hadn't looked. There it was, under his blanket."

I must admit a treasure was found in all that confusion, and it wasn't just the missing ring. Did I give Red some extra love when I returned home from my trip? You bet I did. He taught me that sometimes you travel great distances to find what you've been missing, only to learn it's been there all along.

Maybe Red knew exactly what he was doing.

~B.J. Taylor

The Cat's Meow

Everybody started saying, well, this cat's not as dumb as people think he is.
~David Allan Coe

I never thought our cat Garfield was particularly smart, until the day I found him typing. It was the early 1990s, and although we owned a computer, we still had a typewriter. My husband loved to type. His morning routine typically involved waking up early, making a pot of coffee, and sitting down at our built-in desk in the kitchen where he would feverishly type.

Since our children were young and I was frequently up during the night, I usually stayed in bed most mornings while my husband typed away. One morning, I woke up early and couldn't get back to sleep, so I climbed out of bed and headed downstairs toward the strong scent of freshly brewed coffee and the clickety-clack of the typewriter.

I rounded the corner of the kitchen. Sure enough, there was my husband, typing away. I glanced down and smiled. Our bright orange cat sat at my husband's feet, resting his rather large behind on the kitchen floor, with only his front paws holding him upright. His head was tilted upward as he stared intently at my husband, who was oblivious to Garfield's gaze.

"Good morning," I said as I made my way to the coffee pot. Garfield didn't move, but my husband got up to give me a kiss, and went into the adjoining bathroom.

As soon as the bathroom door closed, Garfield sprang onto the chair in front of the typewriter. I watched in amazement. First, his right paw hit a key, or a couple of keys, his eyes completely fixed on the paper in front of him. Then, his left paw jerkily hit more keys. The rhythm was perfect. Clearly, this cat, who had led us to believe that sleeping was the only thing he excelled at, was smarter than I thought. I called to my husband, but the moment the bathroom door opened, Garfield jumped off the chair and resumed his pose on the floor.

"Garfield was typing!" I managed to say between giggles.

My husband gestured, offering more coffee, and said, "Sure you're awake?"

"Look at the typewriter," I said.

There were the letters, "po-ijk-sd-az."

Garfield played it cool for about a week after that, until one early morning when the phone rang. My husband had already left for work but the children were asleep and I was in bed. By the fourth ring, I picked up the phone. "Hello," I said very quietly.

"Did I wake you?" my mom asked.

"Hi Mom." I murmured. "It's okay, the kids will be up soon."

As my mother began talking, I heard what sounded like a baby crying in the earpiece.

"Mom, is Lauren at your place? I hear a baby crying." My mom sometimes cared for my infant niece while my sister worked.

But she insisted, "No, honey. It's on your end."

"I don't think so," I answered. "My kids are sleeping."

Mom continued to talk even though I still heard the muffled cries. By the time we hung up my children were awake so I reasoned it had been my younger who was only two at the time.

Busy with the children, I hardly noticed that Garfield was not around. Then, an hour later when I tried to make a phone call, the line was dead. I tried troubleshooting by checking all the phone lines in the house, but couldn't seem to locate the problem.

Then I remembered we had a corded wall phone in the back room of our basement, so I opened the basement door and went downstairs to check it out. I thought it was odd when I found the door to the back room closed. And I could still hear that baby crying.

I opened the door and there was Garfield—crying into the

receiver! He had obviously become trapped in the back room and knocked the phone to the floor when it rang that morning. I was shocked. Was my cat smart enough to know to "answer" the phone and try to communicate the fact that he was trapped? Unfortunately, since it took his owner so long to figure out the problem, I wasn't feeling as smart as my cat.

~Cari Weber

Bailey's Decision

*When a Cat adopts you there is nothing to be done about it
except to put up with it until the wind changes.*

~T. S. Eliot

After my beloved calico cat Chili died, it was six months before my husband and I were ready to share our lives with a cat again. However, this time I wanted two. I thought that Chili might have been lonely and I didn't want to have an "only cat" again. My husband Darrell reluctantly agreed we could have two.

We went to the local animal shelter to pick them out. I had decided beforehand that, in an effort to get Darrell more emotionally invested in our soon-to-be charges, we would each pick out one cat. We entered the room lined with rows of cages from floor to ceiling. To my eyes all the cats were beautiful. It was going to be a tough choice.

Not for Darrell. He walked around the room once, peering into each cage. Then, with a distinct lack of enthusiasm, he announced, "This one looks okay."

I walked over to see which one he liked. Sitting regally behind the bars of the kennel was a small, completely gray kitty with striking golden eyes. She was gorgeous. I agreed with Darrell, and one of the shelter workers helped him retrieve her from the kennel. They left the room to fill out the adoption paperwork and I remained to find our second cat.

Now that we had a female, I decided to select a male. The cats in this room were all allowed out of their kennels at least once daily and, for the most part, tolerated each other. A few were already out, sleeping in soft beds or playing on the floor. I got a laugh when one of the cats marched over and swatted the head of a sleeping, adolescent gray-and-white cat, who simply woke up and looked surprised—but did not strike back or even appear angry. That was quite a mellow kitty.

I quickly became overwhelmed with the number of male cats and kittens who were all possible choices, but I knew I could select only one. So after playing with or petting several of them, I narrowed it down to three: a shy, adult black-and-white guy; a pretty longhair; and the easygoing, adolescent gray-and-white cat.

The pretty longhair was affectionate and seemed to like me. I sat in a chair while he crawled all over me. He advanced up to one of my shoulders, and then to the top of my head.

The mellow gray-and-white teenager was playful, had a fetching pink nose, and was one of many siblings of the little female we had just adopted. By now he had returned to his open kennel in the highest row of cages and was napping.

I was also tempted to take the adult black-and-white cat since he was handsome, and so timid that I felt sorry for him.

My decision-making had come to an impasse. I couldn't even decide when forced to select from only three! Then Darrell entered the room. He'd completed the adoption process on our new girl.

"What's taking so long?" he asked, adding once again that we did not really need two cats.

I assured him I would be only a few minutes longer. He returned to the lobby and I remained in the room with the cats. I had to make a decision fast.

I had brought along two portable kennels. Our new girl was now in one of them waiting in the lobby with Darrell. The other one was with me.

Frustrated with myself for not being able to make a decision, I placed the kennel on the floor and opened its door.

"Okay," I said, looking around the room. "Who wants to go?"

Suddenly the adolescent gray-and-white cat woke up from his nap in his top-tier cage five feet off the floor, jumped down and stepped into my kennel.

Stunned, I laughed out loud and realized that my decision had been made for me.

I named him Bailey, and we soon learned this was the first of his many antics. He loves to play; one of his favorite activities is leaping three or four feet off the floor to catch a twist tie in mid air. He jumps on the bathroom counter every morning to watch me brush my teeth. When entering a room he announces his presence with a loud meow. He sits tightly against me on the couch every evening as if he can't get close enough to me.

And he often acts like a dog. I call him, and no matter if he's inside or out, he comes. He easily walks on a leash. He warms up quickly to almost any human. I have had years of experience with cats and can easily say that Bailey is one of the most outgoing and expressive cats I've ever known.

I'm so glad he jumped into my kennel.

~Tracie Hornung

I Can't Believe My Cat Did That!

Chapter 7

A Good Mousekeeper

A Kitten with Attitude

Let bravery be thy choice, but not bravado.

~Menander

The all-white kitten appeared one rainy afternoon. Seven weeks old at most, it had found its way up our mile-long dirt lane. Now it sat in the rain with plastered-down fur. No doubt some heartless person had dumped an unwanted litter on the country road below. When he mewed, I called "Hey, little fella!" from the porch, but he didn't turn his head.

I spooned soft food onto a plate for him, and as I tiptoed nearer to bring it to him, he continued staring into the woods. He didn't notice me until I set the dish down in front of him. Then he jumped and crouched in fear.

"Easy, boy, easy." I knew then. All-white male cats with blue eyes are often deaf, and his eyes were sea blue.

Poor little guy. Not hearing his littermates creeping off, he'd trudged alone in the rain, past hawks, foxes and coyotes that could have pounced on him unawares. After he gulped down the food, I bundled him into an old towel, brought him inside, and rubbed him dry. "Ozzie" trailed us in gratitude for weeks.

Once, while my wife was bathing the kids, Ozzie paced the edge of the tub and then deliberately stepped down into the three inches of water and walked around like he belonged there too. The children howled with delight, but their screams and splashes didn't faze the deaf kitten.

Deaf cats miss many cultural clues for proper behavior. We couldn't teach Ozzie not to climb the screen because he didn't hear our disapproval, and if we swatted him lightly with a paper, it scared him like a surprise attack. He didn't get that it was a deterrent. Our other cats were frustrated too. Ozzie didn't hear their growling signals, but kept pouncing on their tails or following them from room to room. When one whacked him, he looked shocked and hurt, with no clue why it happened.

Ozzie's deafness made him fearless about some things. The roar of the vacuum cleaner terrorizes most cats, but Ozzie liked its vibrations and hung onto the rubber bumper with front paws while I dragged him around the living room. If a dog visited, Ozzie, not hearing its barking and panting, bounced up to it spitting and clawing, and more often than not, the dog backed off.

One spring two black bears moved into our area. A mother with a second-year cub found our wild raspberry and blackberry bushes irresistible. Females with cubs are testy, and we hunkered in our house whenever they passed through.

One evening they must have smelled the food in our house because we saw the mother bear in our yard stand up to her full six-foot height and sniff. Then she trotted toward our porch with junior trailing. Her fur was glossy and rippled and her eyes were hard, black and cold. When you're ten feet from a lion or bear in a zoo, it's nothing like the moment a big, un-caged carnivore approaches you.

The female climbed our porch stairs confidently. I realized that she could burst through our screen door easily so I moved to shut the second wooden door—though even that might not stop her. Recently a bear in a nearby town had torn the siding off a house to get at a honeybee nest in the wall.

But before I reached the door, something white flashed past me. Ozzie flung himself against the screen, four paws spread-eagled, two feet up off the floor, as though the screen was only thing that had stopped him from latching onto the bear's muzzle and biting her nose. Then Ozzie howled. This was no meow, not even a deep growl. It was the howl a swamp beast might make before terrorizing a village. It was the sound of a werewolf getting a root canal. He yodeled and gurgled in his throat and translated to something like: "I will eat your face and spit out your beady black eyes!"

I stopped. What was I going to do? Slam the door and trap Ozzie between it and the screen? The huge bear could scoop him out for a snack. But Ozzie's fury made the bear pause. She swayed at the top step, looking at the howling white beast. Ozzie wailed, almost begging her to come into claw range. Finally the bear turned, padded gracefully down the steps and lumbered away, junior close behind.

Ozzie hung on the screen like a caterpillar and watched them disappear into the woods. His chest was heaving. I wanted to pick him up and praise him, but not quite yet. At the slightest touch now, he'd explode like a firecracker. And I didn't want to face the fury of our brave and deaf white kitten.

~Garrett Bauman

The Mimic

Cunning... is but the low mimic of wisdom.
~Plato

Scrapper, my outdoor mouser cat, had been missing for three days and I was beginning to get worried. She had just had a litter of kittens, and had been coming around for extra attention and food when she could snatch a moment away from her babies—which I still couldn't find.

Day four into my worry I was walking down our street when I heard these pitiful little mews coming from under the neighbor's front bushes. I began to piece things together. A coyote had been lurking around, and Scrapper must have been trying to keep her litter safe. Now three of the most adorable babies needed their mama.

Thus began a crash course in raising orphaned kittens. The boys were tuxedo-marked, gray-and-white kittens; the girl had the same tuxedo markings under a coat of gray, black and peach tiger stripes.

I loved bottle-feeding the babies that had now taken up residence in a large box in my kitchen. They would hear my voice and toddle up waiting to be fed. To all three of them I became "mama." They wanted to sleep on me, play with me, and follow me around. One of the little guys became known as Star, and he held a special place in my heart.

From a tiny, orphaned baby, Star grew up to be the biggest, meanest tomcat on the block. He felt it was his duty to protect not only our yard from the occasional visiting cat, but the neighboring hundred acres! Yet after he chased away the bad guys he came inside to be loved and petted.

Star's abilities never ceased to amaze me. He was an awesome babysitter when we added a new female kitten to the family. He made sure she didn't wander out of the house or yard until she was old enough to handle herself. He even taught her to mouse and hunt birds.

And Star was an amazing hunter. I would catch him crouching in the yard, waiting patiently, and then—quick as a flash—he'd pounce. He was always sharing his leftover "treasures" with us. Often he'd proudly display his latest kill on my back steps.

One day I learned the secret to his hunting success. It was a lazy day for Star, and for some reason he decided to stay inside on a bright summer day. He was perched in the window of the dining room catching some rays when all of a sudden his ears perked up. Some birds had come to rest on the driveway in front of his window. Without making a sound he turned and faced them. Then I heard it.

"Chirp chirp... chiiiiirrrrp!" I was surprised that the bird would come that close to the open window. I drew nearer to see it chirping.

"Chirp... chirrrrp!" But the noise wasn't coming from a bird. It was the cat!

Thankfully a screen separated them or I'm sure I would have witnessed a kill firsthand. I realized then that if his bird impressions worked as lure, it explained his amazing hunting abilities.

It wasn't too long after that the birds must have wised up. The number of birds Star brought to us decreased, and whenever Star was in the yard loud squawking from flocks of birds could be heard throughout the neighborhood. I'm sure they were saying, "Wait! Stop! Don't trust him! It's not a bird... it's a CAT!"

~Betsy Burnett

Reprinted by permission of Off the Mark
and Mark Parisi ©2005

Ghost Kitties

It is impossible to find a place in which a cat can't hide.
~Bill Carraro

My house is rumored to have ghosts. Ask anyone who has ever pet-sat for me and they'll tell tales about mysterious shadows that drift into the room as they're scooping the litter box, the eerie sense that they're being watched when clearly no one is there, and fleeing the house in fear due to the random flushing of the toilet when they are the only human in the house.

These tales of terror are one of my favorite parts of returning home from vacation. But I have a better answer than ghosts—cats. Five of them. Those felines are stealthy, sneaky and only make their presence known when they want to be seen. They fit in impossibly small spaces and like to hide in the basement ceiling, peering down at their caretaker, who is unaware of their presence. They'll spring out at any moment frightening the very person trying to care for them while I am away.

I call them CIA—Counter Intelligence Animals. These fur balls have taught me that nothing is impossible for a cat when it puts its mind to a task.

Many times I've fallen victim to the ghost theory.

The first incident occurred during the middle of the night. Loud voices pulled me from a deep sleep. Groggily I tried to make sense of what I was hearing. As my senses became more alert I realized the sound was coming from the television in the living room. My husband was snoring softly beside me and I figured he must have forgotten to turn off the television before he came to bed. But why was the volume so loud? Surely he wouldn't have been listening to a program at full volume, especially when he knew I was sleeping.

I made my way down the dark hallway and into the living room where the only light came from the glow of the television. The volume was deafening. I stepped toward the couch to grab the remote and was startled to see my calico, Buscemi, lying with her paw on the remote intently watching the television. She didn't seem to notice me until I slipped the remote from her paw. Somehow she had managed to not only turn on the television, but crank the volume as loud as it could go.

That was just the beginning.

Another night I heard thumping coming from the front of the house. I wasn't about to investigate the creepy sounds. In the morning I walked into the kitchen and stopped short when I saw two cupboard doors and one drawer hanging wide open. One cupboard held plates and bowls and was above the counter. The other cupboard was at ground level and contained pots and pans. The drawer held paper plates and aluminum foil.

I was baffled. What in the world were the cats looking for and how did they get those open?

My answer came a few days later when I heard the thumping sound again. I went to investigate and found my tortoiseshell standing on her hind legs on the counter trying to open the cupboard that held plates. She'd pull the door slightly open and it would thump shut. It only took her several more tries before the door remained open.

The creepiest incident was yet to come, though.

One weekend I pulled a box of books down from the attic to lend to a friend who had a sixth grader looking for books to read over the summer. After sorting through the box to make sure the books were age-appropriate, I replaced the lid and closed the attic door.

The next morning I was startled to see the lid off the box, the books rearranged inside it, and the attic door ajar. My mind jumped to the wildest of conclusions—I upset a ghost in the attic by taking the books.

Freaked out, I slammed the attic door shut and told my husband, who assured me it was a cat. I didn't believe him. I gave the books to my friend, and day after day I kept waking up to an open attic door. My friends were likewise convinced it was a ghost and one even offered to have a member of a local paranormal club come to my house. I declined as my husband insisted it was a cat, but every sound caused me to jump and I frequently looked over my shoulder.

I just couldn't fathom how a cat could turn a doorknob.

About a week later I was reading e-mail in the same room as the attic door when one of my tabbies, Petunia, started tugging on the bottom of it. I ignored her and suddenly I heard a click. I spun my chair around just in time to see her tail disappear through the partially open door.

There was my ghost! I learned that if the attic door isn't clicked shut, then all it takes is the vibrations from the cat shaking the door to release the catch.

The antics continue, but now when something goes bump in the night I can relax knowing fully well that it really is just a cat.

~Valerie D. Benko

The Guard Cat

The opportunity for doing mischief is found a hundred times a day,
and of doing good once in a year.
~Voltaire

When I was fourteen, my family moved from the city to a small farm. At last my mother could indulge her ambition to grow vegetables and fruit, especially strawberries, on a large scale. She had mastered flowers; her roses and dahlias were stupendous. The only drawback she saw to country living was the threat of snakes on the prowl in the berry patch or lurking under the squash vines. She was terrified of snakes.

The second summer we lived on the farm, a young black cat adopted us. We had no idea where he came from. There were few homes nearby. We inquired if someone had lost a cat. Most folks just laughed at us. It seems that people like to dump unwanted pets in the country to fend for themselves. We named him Blackie, fed him until he was plump and his ribs had disappeared under a shiny coat, and patted him when he would let us.

Blackie had one peculiarity: he wouldn't come in the house. Trusting humans, even ones who fed and cared for him, was beyond him. On the most frigid days he would come inside as far as the screened porch in back, but resisted all our efforts to introduce him to the delights of a warm kitchen. He seemed content to curl up on the daybed and wait until the weather moderated.

On hot summer nights—this was before air-conditioning—my

whole family would sit outside in the dark night air, hoping for a little breeze to cool us before we had to go to bed. Mom had invested in folding aluminum lawn chairs that had strips of woven plastic mesh to sit on. Blackie would come back from his nocturnal prowl, wander around checking to see who had invaded his domain, letting us pet him as he came by. He never lingered by one person for long.

Then the yelps would begin. Anywhere a bottom bulged through the mesh of the chairs was a worthy target for a swiped paw. We'd holler and reach under our chair to shoo him away. Of course, he had streaked across the yard by the time we reacted. This game of his would continue until someone nabbed him and made him sit in their lap to endure stroking until he began to purr or drop off to sleep.

Blackie would catch mice and rats in the barn and proudly bring them to the doorstep for us to admire. We'd praise him and reward him with a tidbit of cheese.

One morning I heard wild yelling from the back yard. Mom had been shelling early peas in the shade of the big pecan tree. Blackie had brought her his latest kill: a small black snake. He had presented it to Mom, who didn't appreciate the gift. Although the snake obviously was dead, Mom told me to kill it more and bury it in the pasture. I did as she told me. That wasn't the only time I had to rescue Mom. Women wore housedresses then. Often I would find my mother, screeching on tiptoe, with her dress held above her knees, facing another of Blackie's gifts.

By late spring, several hundred strawberry plants in their raised beds had covered the patch, almost obscuring the paths. Their white blooms above the shiny green leaves soon became luscious red berries in abundance. Picking berries is backbreaking work. Mom would kneel to pick the berries, first carefully parting the leaves with a long pole to check for the dreaded snakes she was sure were there. This would reveal the berries and she would harvest all within reach, then move down the row and repeat the process. I'm not sure of her plan if she had discovered a snake. It was too horrible to contemplate.

I was in charge of taking the containers of picked berries to the shade and keeping Mom supplied with empty boxes. I noticed that her constant companion was our half-wild cat. Blackie stayed just out of reach as he followed her up and down the rows. He would stare at her intently as she labored. I mentioned this to my dad. Without telling Mom, we began to observe this strange escort. Had Mom encouraged Blackie to come in the garden with her? Had he decided that snakes abounded in the strawberry patch, and if he were vigilant then Mom might unearth one for him to pounce on?

Strawberry season fortunately ended without a snake incident. Dad and I laughed privately at our Guard Cat. Soon, garden produce was filling our hours with picking, preparing and canning or freezing. Again we noticed that when Mom went to the garden, Blackie followed, moving along the rows with her. He never came into the garden with me or Dad, and never showed the least interest in our wellbeing. How did he know Mom needed his protection?

We laughed at Mom's aversion to snakes, but she didn't think it was a bit funny. Fortunately, she had our faithful Blackie by her side.

~Nancy Peacock

65

Life Saver

Kittens are angels with whiskers.
~Author Unknown

I was in my senior year of high school and we had a new kitten. I had named the kitten Ginger Baker after a drummer in a rock band with similar fluffy, ginger-colored hair. The kitten was frisky, cute, and the pet that I had wanted for so long.

I considered him exclusively mine, although I had five younger brothers, because I named him and he slept in my furry pink bedroom slippers by my bed every night.

I was sleeping peacefully one night when my mother jerked me awake.

"Quick!" she said. "Get up! The house is on fire! The living room is in flames!"

"What?" I stammered, half-asleep, trying to wake up.

"The kitten was crying and crying, and jumping all over me," Mom said. "I thought I smelled smoke. At first I thought you were in the kitchen baking and had burned something, but the kitty was frantic. Then I heard crackling. Thank God the cat woke me!"

I jumped up and ran behind Mom to the top of the staircase. The stairs led directly into the living room, where the picture window curtains were completely engulfed in flames. We looked down in horror.

We grabbed my two younger brothers from their beds, flew down the stairs, and then woke up my father who was a very sound sleeper.

Running barefoot in our pajamas, we woke up the rest of the family and ran outside.

Right after we took a head count and all of us were accounted for, we heard an explosion in the living room. We watched in disbelief and fear as our home and all our worldly possessions burned.

"Thank God we are all alive!" we said to each other.

The neighbors had called the fire department. We waited for the volunteer firemen to arrive, and then watched helplessly as they chopped holes in the roof and poured water into the house for three hours. They tirelessly fought the fire but were only able to save the shell of the house.

We knew we could always rebuild the house. The fact that we were all safe helped our aching hearts, but when the firemen searched for the kitten that had saved our lives, it broke my heart in two. My kitty had gone to the place he felt safe. They had found him seeking refuge in my bedroom slippers, where he died after he saved our whole family.

~Sharon Ann Harmon

66

Franklin and Berniece

Cats are mysterious kind of folk—
there is more passing in their minds than we are aware of.
~Sir Walter Scott

Berniece was a nondescript, faded gray-and-tan tortoiseshell cat with a squished face, puffy cheeks, and extra toes on her front paws. My husband had dragged her home, along with her brother, Franklin, at an estimated eight weeks old. They had been dumped on a road near our home.

Berniece was half the size of her brother and couldn't jump very well. While Franklin swaggered through the house and yowled for attention, Berniece would meekly follow. She was a seeker of peace and quiet, demanding no special attention.

Berniece and Franklin were a fascinating study in cat communication. They were devoted to each other first and me second. Although selfish and demanding, Franklin was the perfect gentleman with Berniece. He always let her walk through the outside door first, and she was always first into the cat dish. He protected her from dogs, cars and strangers, and would warn her not to go out in the rain. Together, they cut a swath through the arguments that cats are sneaky, fickle, self-centered, narcissistic, mean and nasty.

I watched them make many minor decisions. Who would get my lap, and who would get the couch? Who got what Christmas package under the tree they'd already re-trimmed together? Who was going to mess up the card game today?

I particularly loved Berniece, and she was devoted to me in return. Berniece would leave the warmth of her bed each morning to watch me brush my teeth and dress, adoration on her face, then walk me to the door to see me off to work. As soon as the door shut behind me, she'd scamper back to bed, joining my husband and Franklin.

One morning, during the toothbrush ritual, Berniece went crazy, scrabbling under a two-inch space under the shower, flipping and diving. Then she disappeared from the room. I thought no more about it until I heard the thunder of cat paws on the wooden walkway above.

In a minute, Franklin raced into the bathroom, straight to the shower crack and dove in with his paws. Berniece soon followed and they embarked on a frantic, ultimately futile, attempt to get whatever had captured their attention.

I pondered that event for many days. Berniece realized she needed help, so she raced upstairs and woke her brother. She must have communicated her concern and given direction, as Franklin beat her to the bathroom and went directly to the spot. Amazing!

Berniece and I also had an evening routine. She'd curl in my lap, never without an invitation, for an evening of television, and then we'd retire upstairs to bed. After I'd plumped my pillows and was comfortable, Berniece would crawl onto the bed. I would lay my hand on her, and Berniece would settle down, purr, and sleep.

One night, Berniece would not settle down. Instead, she mewed insistently and pushed against my face repeatedly. Finally, I gave up and got up. Berniece ran frantically down the walkway and stopped at the door at the top of the outside stairs. I followed and she turned to me with a loud mew. I was shocked; I'd never heard such a sound from my polite, shy Berniece. I looked out and there was Franklin, trapped in the rain, bedraggled, and unhappy. Berniece had recognized the problem, knew I could solve it, and was persistent in her plan to rescue Franklin.

Another time she came to his aid, Franklin had returned from an outside adventure beaten up. He had a deep gash on his face, walked with a limp, and obviously felt sorry for himself. During his convalescence he looked to, and leaned on, his nurse Berniece to help him with daily chores, such as grooming. She was patient and kind.

And Berniece went the extra mile. One day while washing dishes, I heard the unmistakable sound of cats in the cat food bag. I marched toward the open laundry room door to send those cats packing, but stopped and watched instead. Franklin was sprawled in front of the cupboard, sore leg outstretched. The cupboard door was half open, and I saw the big bag of cat food. Inside there was a steady crunch, as Berniece was helping herself. Soon a gray paw appeared over the top of the bag, and Berniece winged a piece of cat food to Franklin. He snagged it with a paw and, without getting up, munched it down. This was repeated several times before I retrieved Berniece from her self-service and re-filled the cat dish!

Berniece and Franklin were an amazing pair of cats that always had me wondering what they would get their paws into next.

~Ginny A. Lee

67

Bad Kitty

A cat sees no good reason why it should obey another animal,
even if it does stand on two legs.
~Sarah Thompson

I t was a beautiful sunny morning and I sat in my recliner, sipping my tea, watching the birds at the feeder on my deck. Sauza was perched on the chair next to me, intently observing the birds coming and going. I leaned forward to reach for my teacup when something moving on the floor caught my eye. It was a tiny mouse, slowly making its way across the carpet.

"Sauza! Mouse!" I cried. "Get the mouse!"

Sauza sat up and looked down to where my finger was pointing.

"It's a mouse!" I shouted. "Get the mouse!"

By this time I was on my feet and the mouse had made his way under a chair.

After stretching leisurely, Sauza jumped down, sat, and focused his attention on the area under the chair. Within a few seconds, the mouse continued its journey and headed for the massive bookcase next to the fireplace.

"There he is! Get him!" I said. Sauza yawned. The mouse had already disappeared under the bookcase.

In disbelief, I shook my finger at Sauza. "Bad Kitty! You're acting like a complete waste of fur!"

Sauza blinked at me with an innocent expression on his furry face. I narrowed my eyes at him.

"No kitty treats for you tonight!" He turned his back on me and proceeded to smooth an errant whisker.

That evening, when I told my husband Fred about the episode, he just shook his head. "Maybe mouse control wasn't on his résumé."

"I wonder how the thing found its way in here," I mused. "This is the second story and it's a big house."

All evening I couldn't stop thinking about the mouse lurking under the bookcase. How were we going to get him out of there? Then a thought occurred to me.

"Fred?"

My husband, concentrating on his laptop, muttered, "Uh-huh?"

"What's the poor thing going to eat? There's no food lying around here. We keep things put away. I don't want him to starve to death!"

Fred looked at me with a raised eyebrow. "Let me get this straight—you want the cat to kill him but you don't want him to starve to death?"

"No, I don't want Sauza to kill him. I want him to catch him and turn him loose outside."

"Right. Like that's gonna happen," Fred laughed. "At any rate, he's not going to starve. There are plenty of crumbs and things around here for him to eat."

As soon as Fred went up to bed, I put a peanut under the chair, back far enough so that Sauza couldn't reach it. When I checked the next morning, the peanut was gone. This nightly offering became my guilty routine.

A few mornings later, I was back in my recliner, sipping my tea, watching the birds. Since it was an especially warm day, I had opened the deck door and Sauza was outside basking in the sun. All was peaceful and quiet until I heard a sudden commotion and jumped from my chair in time to see Sauza come racing into the kitchen with a bird in his mouth.

I yelled, "Sauza! Drop that!" And to my surprise, he did. I snatched the tiny sparrow from the floor and looked closely at it. No blood, thank God. But it wasn't moving either. "I am so sorry," I told it, before locking eyes on the cat. "Bad Kitty!"

Sauza looked offended.

"I hope you're going to be okay," I told the little bird.

I set it down in a potted rosebush outside and watched from the window. It took a few minutes but finally the little sparrow took off.

I turned to the cat. "I hope you're satisfied. He's going to need therapy for years," I muttered. "You can't catch a mouse strolling by, but you can snatch a bird out of thin air? You're fired! No kitty treats for you until you get your act together."

Sauza turned his back on me and coughed up several feathers.

The days passed with no evidence of the mouse except for the disappearing peanuts. Until this point, my husband hadn't seemed all that concerned about the mouse but that changed one evening when I was out. Hearing Sauza playing with one of his cat toys in the kitchen, batting it around, throwing it in the air, then racing to catch it, Fred went in to watch the entertainment.

It wasn't a toy. It was the mouse. As Fred watched, the mouse went sliding across the floor, flipped over on his back, his feet stuck up in the air, assuming a very believable dead pose. Fred grabbed a paper cup, intending to scoop him up and take him outside, when the mouse suddenly flipped back over and raced out of the kitchen.

"Get the mouse!" Fred yelled. Sauza curled up on the rug and took a nap.

Finally one morning I woke to find the mouse dead on my bedroom floor.

"Oh geez," I murmured. "I'm sorry, little mouse."

Looking him over I didn't see any obvious wounds, so I calmed myself for a moment with the hope that it was a natural death. It was comforting to see that the little guy didn't look underweight at least. The cat observed me with interest from the bed.

"Seriously," I said. "You couldn't have just escorted him in here and handed him to me?" No comment forthcoming. Sighing, I gathered the little body into a wad of Kleenexes. Sauza watched and then meow-yawned an obvious question.

"I'm very conflicted about this," I told him. "We'll talk about the kitty treats later."

~Tina Wagner Mattern

68

O Captain!
My Ornery Captain!

The cat could very well be man's best friend
but would never stoop to admitting it.
~Doug Larson

Captain was not the most likable cat. In fact, that might be an understatement.

Rescued from the cruel intentions of a nutty neighbor back when I was just a teenager, I promised the little scruffy kitten I'd take care of her. I remembered how she looked me straight in the eye with her black bandit brow and silently accepted my vow.

"Don't worry, I'll take good care of you. I promise," I said. And when I make a promise I keep it... even if the recipient of that promise hisses and ignores me.

Captain, the little scruffy kitten, became part of our family and grew up alongside me in my mother's house through my school days, college years and then left the nest (with much elation from my family) when I got married.

She was an outdoor cat when I lived with my mom, but once I moved into my new home (with my "reluctant-to-have-a cat" husband) she stayed indoors. Being plain unlikable and having a cold detached personality was just what I learned to live with. (I'm referring to the cat, not my husband.) Although she didn't like to be held or cuddled, what impressed me about Captain was her loyalty.

She remained by my side, like a bodyguard, and walked beside me like a soldier lining up during his or her morning drills. Captain the ornery cat was loving, but just distant with her love. Some people are like that too. Not everyone wears their heart on their sleeve... or their paw.

Rarely did Captain meow. She had a little Bonnie Raitt type of rasp to her voice, but it was seldom heard. That's why on one particular night it stood out.

"Meow."

This was an unfamiliar sound in our house.

"Meow, Meow."

My husband and I were lying in bed perplexed.

"Is she hungry?" my husband asked.

I hadn't changed her meal plan in seventeen years, so it was doubtful.

So I asked, "What is it, Captain?" expecting an answer.

"Meow, meow, meow."

I sat up in bed and as I did this she took a few steps toward the bedroom door. She meowed again. I got up and she walked into the hallway. I could tell that she wanted me to follow her, so I did. Down the stairs we went.

Once we got to the kitchen, she repeated her raspy meows and stood next to the stove.

"What is it, Captain?" I asked again.

She meowed until I saw the flame on the stove.

And on the flame, was a pot. Once gray, now a dark charcoal color.

The pot! I had left a pot burning on the stove!

I remembered that I had planned to have a cup of tea before I went to bed but never got around to it.

Quickly, I rushed to turn off the back burner. The near miss of a house fire overwhelmed me. My husband and I would have been asleep in bed. The fear of what might have happened flashed through my mind.

Cuddle or no cuddle, I picked up this wonderful hissing hero and squeezed her with kisses and hugs. "O Captain! My wonderful ornery Captain! You saved the day!" She had earned her stripes and earned her name.

Although Captain was unable to show her affection in the ordinary feline tradition of snuggles and sandpaper-tongue licks, she had done something extraordinary. She showed her love that night in a heroic act of bravery.

~Mary C. M. Phillips

Seeing Eye Cat

A brother is a friend given by Nature.
~Jean Baptiste Legouve

Percival Putty Tat and Andie Pandi Dandi are my two Ragdoll cats that have truly shown me that taking my time doing things makes for a calm and happy existence. They are always calm and collected and move to a slow beat in life. But the real story is how I got the second Ragdoll, Percival, when I only could afford Andie.

Percival was a brother to Andie, and his breeder called me one day to say that Percival, cross-eyed and the runt of the litter, had been returned after being with a family for two months. I happily agreed to take Percival, and sure enough, he was very cross-eyed. Slowly he adjusted to his new family and was as loved as Andie, but I soon learned he had a few problems or "quirks" besides his eyes.

Ragdolls have the bluest of blue eyes and when Percival looked at me, I noticed that he often looked a little behind me. The vet said that Percival was trying to compensate for his sight, so it would often seem as if he were looking behind what he was trying to see.

Feeling sad for Percival, I asked if he could have surgery to correct his vision. The vet said no, that he had now learned to see this way, and it would only confuse him. However, during the examination, the vet found that Percival had a gum disease. All but his eyeteeth had to be pulled in a surgery to save his future health.

After the operation I noticed that Percival had an odd urge. He used his four front teeth to "staple" anything that happened to get in his way. This included soft shoe soles, magazines, letters, pillows, other cats, and students' papers.

Once I left out fifty student papers on the table that I had been grading, and the next day they had little staple marks all around the margins—he had had a busy night. He was still sitting in the middle of the papers when I found him. He should have had wings he looked so innocent. My students found his "stapling" very humorous.

But, as time has progressed, Percival had other adventures with his eye challenge. One happened a year ago, and continues to his day.

Percival often likes to lie in the sunroom and bask in the sun. The problem is that he does not seem to see very well after lying in the sun—much like a person who is in the sun too long without sunglasses and comes into a dark room.

On this Saturday, Percival had just completed his three-hour basking, and I was in the sunroom reading. As he got up, he stopped to scratch, and must have gotten turned around. He started to walk and ran right into his brother Andie.

I expected the "alpha dance" to begin between them, but Andie simply ignored him and tried to step around him. As soon as Andie moved, Percival moved in that direction and they collided again. This happened three times. Finally, Andie sat beside Percival and looked at him and let out an inquiring "Meow?"

They sat there for a while until, as on a silent signal, both of them got up, stood shoulder to shoulder, and started to walk forward together. Andie led Percival to the next room.

I soon found that this was no accident. I have seen Andie herding his cross-eyed sibling from spot to spot. I also noticed that Andie nudged Percival toward pieces of cat food that had dropped from the bowl he could not see or toward a toy, and arranged a pillow for them to share.

Today, when looking for Percival, look for Andie. They will be close together, one pair of blue eyes looking straight, the other looking a little behind.

~Pamela Tambornino

The Raccoon Hunters

The cat is domestic only as far as suits its own ends.
~Saki

Everyone knows someone with too many cats. For me it was my friend Kevin, and he elevated his cats to mythic status. Each cat had a title: Boots the Brave, Poogs the Stout, Yeen the Wise… I could go on, but you get the point. Kevin lived on a farm, and there was plenty of land for roaming. Somehow, over the years, they just kept acquiring cats. The issue was, I think, Boots, who was indeed brave, but alas not spayed.

Pulling into Kevin's driveway, my first impression was that a cat bomb had gone off. There would be cats splayed out in all kinds of positions, on their backs, on their sides, doing a split while washing up, lying on the driveway, on the car, in a tree, on the swing, the roof, the porch, everywhere. It was almost impossible to get an accurate count of his cats. Every time I thought I counted them all I'd see another.

As you can imagine, there was no rodent problem on that farm. The cats had the run of the place both inside and out. They even left the kitchen faucet on in the morning, at a slow dribble, so the cats could drink right from the tap. It wasn't uncommon to see a cat at your elbow on the dinner table, regarding you like you were the one who should not be there. They pretty much owned the place. But one summer night, there was bad news. One of the cats had been hurt.

Details were sketchy, but allegedly on the previous night, a commotion was heard out in the driveway, and Kevin's mother ran outside to find Poogs (the Stout) bleeding from his side, and limping. Something out there had dared affront the McFall cat clan.

Kevin and I made a pact that night: to protect his myriad cats in case this thing came back. What could it be, we wondered? Another cat? A skunk? Whatever it was, we were ready. We slept in the bedroom that opened onto the porch, so we could be out there quickly. We had baseball bats by our sides, and we slept with the windows open so we could be supremely vigilant.

It wasn't long past midnight when we heard the warning sound: a hiss. Kevin and I were soon running across the lawn in our underwear, baseball bats in hand. I saw the low, dark form of the thing dart out from a bush and run out into the street: a raccoon! It was big, and striped, and wore the characteristic bandit mask. The thing was in for a surprise, though. It had angered the wrong pack of kitties. From across the street came two of the McFall's cats, and the raccoon stopped, arched its back, and ran back the other way, even as more cats were pouring out from the farm. The raccoon ran down the street, was cornered beneath a streetlight post, and it began to climb.

The raccoon climbed all the way to the top, and there it clung for hours. From the base of the telephone pole sounded a chorus of meows. I finally had a chance to count Kevin's cats; there were nine that I could see. And all of them were circled round that pole, all nine tails flicking dangerously. We watched for over two hours, but there seemed to be a stalemate. We eventually got tired and had to go to bed.

In the morning all the cats were back to lolling about the yard peacefully, and there was no sign at all of any kind of excitement from the previous night. Now I'm no animal psychologist, but I'll bet that raccoon thought twice before tangling with Poogs the Stout again.

~Ron Kaiser, Jr.

I Can't Believe My Cat Did That!

Chapter 8

Love Me, Love My Cat

My Interior Decorators

Everyone carries his own inch rule of taste, and amuses himself by applying it, triumphantly, wherever he travels.
~Henry Brooks Adams

I walked into my kitchen and noticed a small corner of my brown grasscloth wallpaper below the chair rail was pulling away from the wall. No big deal. I rummaged through my junk drawer for a tube of wallpaper sealer. A small dab and the corner was flat again.

The next day, another bit of wallpaper was lifting off the wall. Another dab and the problem was solved. I ran my fingers across the wall, but the rest of the paper seemed firmly fastened in place.

The third day I found a small strip of paper fluttering, barely attached to the wall. I knelt down for a closer look. The paper was sheared away in a series of ragged slashes that looked suspiciously like cat scratches.

With three cats in the house, I was pretty sure I could narrow down the suspect pool to them. Unless, of course, they'd brought a mouse into the house again. No, the paper was ripped too high on the wall for rodents to take the fall for this. Definitely a feline felony. But which one was the culprit?

While I puzzled over the problem, Thomas came up behind me and head-butted me. Aha! I thought, my first suspect. Time for

Interrogation Techniques 101. All my years of reading mysteries and watching police shows was about to pay off.

I sat down on the floor and put him on my lap facing me. He immediately turned around and bunched his back legs in preparation to leap off me.

"Not so fast, Thomas. I need to see your eyes while I question you, not your behind." I gave him a quick spin and held onto him. "Listen carefully. No, don't lick me, just listen." I wiped my damp hand on my pants. "Thomas, did you or did you not tear a strip of my wallpaper?"

Thomas gazed into my eyes but didn't answer. I wasn't sure if that meant he was refusing to talk without his lawyer present or, as usual, wasn't listening to a word I said. I repeated my question. He repeated his silence. Realizing we weren't getting anywhere, I let him go, but not without a warning. "Remember Thomas, I'm watching you."

When I tried interrogating his siblings, I got the same results. However, I noticed that when I glued the strip down again, he was the only cat watching. Just to be on the safe side, I said, "Thomas, this is wallpaper. It's not a tree. Ripping wallpaper is bad. Very bad." I raised my voice loud enough for his siblings to hear. "That goes for the rest of you, too. No ripping of wallpaper." Thomas blinked and headed off to the sofa for a nap and possibly to cogitate on what I'd said. Or not. The others didn't respond at all.

By the end of the week, I had re-glued three more strips of wallpaper. Although I still didn't know who was guilty, I was ready to throw all three cats in jail. I restrained myself, partly because I'd miss them and partly because I worried about what bad habits they'd pick up while behind bars.

Instead, I decided to play detective. I choose the bottom step of the stairs just outside the kitchen for my stakeout. Not exactly a comfortable spot, but I was running out of wallpaper glue and patience, not necessarily in that order.

Just as my behind was getting a permanent indentation from the stair, I saw an orange-and-white paw stretch out toward the kitchen wall. I jumped up and raced into the kitchen.

"Aha!" I said, just as Thomas's claw sliced through the paper. "Caught you red-handed! Or is that orange-handed? Doesn't matter. You're busted!"

Thomas stared at me for a moment, then calmly licked his paw as if to say, "Who me? Certainly not."

"Don't play the innocent with me." I shook my finger at him. "Bad boy. Do not rip the wallpaper. Do it again and you'll find yourself wearing stripes."

Thomas looked at me, looked at the wall, and then sauntered off.

For two days after our talk, the wallpaper stayed where it belonged—on the wall. I began to wonder if I could get a job as a cat whisperer, since I was obviously pretty good at getting cats to listen. Must be my no-nonsense tone of voice. Or maybe the threat of wearing stripes got through to him. Either way, I chalked this up to a triumph of man, or in this case, woman over cat.

My pride, like my wallpaper, took a pounding on day three.

As I walked toward the kitchen, I saw not one, but two cats industriously pulling the paper off the wall. Thomas had co-opted his sister Sammy as his accomplice in crime. Tiger, cat number three, was ensconced in her usual position on top of the dining room table, ignoring her lesser siblings.

Mesmerized, I watched as Thomas stood on his hind legs and ripped from the chair rail down. Sammy, who's considerably smaller, worked from the baseboards up. If it weren't for the fact that they were wrecking my house, I might actually have been impressed by their teamwork. When Thomas ripped off a particularly large piece, my momentary paralysis vanished and I found my voice. "Stop!"

Before I could say another word, the feline felons raced past me heading for the basement. I was tempted to chase after them, but was too awestruck by the sight that greeted me. Between the two of them, they'd managed to pull most of the wallpaper off a three-foot section. There wasn't enough glue to put the tattered remnants back up.

As I wondered what the world would be like if Noah had barred cats from the ark, I gathered up the curls of paper on the floor. Then, almost without thinking, I sank to the floor and pulled off a few slivers still left hanging in that section. Then I pulled off a bit more to the left of the section, and then a bit more.

Half an hour later, there was no more wallpaper under the chair rail. Knees creaking, I stood up to see how bad it looked. It didn't. The entire kitchen looked lighter and airier without the dark brown weighing it down.

By then, both cats had slunk back upstairs and were crouched at the entrance of the kitchen, staring at me. I stared back.

"The only thing between you and the Big House is the fact that the kitchen looks better. But you only get one 'Get out of jail' card. Next time, you won't be so lucky. I'll be watching you."

Neither cat seemed impressed with my warning. Thomas gave Sammy a lick on the head, and they trotted off together for a long nap, no doubt dreaming of future felonies.

~Harriet Cooper

The Motown Cat

There are two means of refuge from the misery of life —
music and cats.
~Albert Schweitzer

When my little black cat Calpurnia died, I was bereft. She had been my companion for all but the first three months of her sixteen-year life, and the loneliness I felt when she wasn't there to curl up with me at night was palpable. After months of grieving, I finally summoned the courage to contact my local rescue group.

"Do you have any black cats?" I asked. I knew—and Dawn, the volunteer I spoke with, confirmed—that black cats were harder to place for adoption.

Calpurnia had been the runt of her litter, a homely little black fur ball that no one had wanted. She had grown into a beautiful, loving cat with a playful, comical personality. I couldn't hope to replace her, but I did want to give a cat a chance that might not otherwise be adopted.

The rescue group had one black cat named Sugar Plum. Someone had rescued her off the street when she was a very young cat with a litter of three kittens. In the year and a half that she'd been available, her kittens had grown up and been adopted, but no one had expressed interest in Sugar Plum, a chubby little thing with half a tail.

I brought her home a week before Christmas. I had learned the first time I'd interacted with her that she'd been mistreated. She was a friendly, curious cat, but if I tried to pet her anywhere but on her head, she would mew fearfully and reach back to gently nip my hand in warning. She had not been born with a shortened tail; someone had mutilated it. While she appeared ready to trust, her instincts told her to be wary of humans.

I understood. In the years before she came to me, I had suffered my own heartache and pain at the hands of ill-intentioned humans. I resolved to be patient with her, to help her feel safe.

Before she became comfortable in her new home, we moved to a cabin in the mountains. I had looked forward to this move as an opportunity to live amid nature, to get away from the clamor of a congested city, and to experience the quiet whisper of tall trees and birdsong. While the cabin didn't disappoint in regards to watching birds from the many wide windows on three different levels, the move itself was stressful for both of us, and Sugar Plum became clingy, following me from room to room, never far when I was at home.

One night after a particularly long day of unpacking boxes, I finally had a chance to relax in a hot bath. I left the bathroom door open, and Sug, predictably, followed me in and jumped on a tall cabinet, curling up on top of my clean pajamas. Her eyes were wide with anxiety, and I wanted to comfort her, but she was sitting across the room from me.

I thought of what had comforted me in the saddest times of my life, what had brought me solace when my heart was breaking, and I simply started to sing. I hadn't really given much thought to what I would sing; the words just spontaneously emerged.

"Sugar pie, honey bunch, you know that I love you…"

Then I sang The Four Tops hit, "I Can't Help Myself," which had been a favorite of mine since junior high.

Apparently it struck a chord with Sugar Plum, too. As I continued to sing, I saw her body relax. Then she curled her head around and rolled over on her back, belly up and paws extended.

It made me laugh to see her react in that way, but I convinced myself it was a fluke, that she really wasn't reacting to the song at all.

The next day when I came home from work, she met me at the

door as usual. I reached down to pet her, and out of curiosity I sang to her again, the same song. This time she flopped on her side from a standing position and again rolled over on her back, paws in the air.

In the weeks that followed, I tried every "sugar" song I could think of, but she showed little response—unless it was to walk away with her tail in the air. For some reason, that one song by The Four Tops was her favorite. As we both adjusted to living in this wild place, I would sing it to her whenever anything happened to frighten her, such as raccoons racing across the roof or the occasional bear peeking in the window. It always generated the same response.

Five years later, she still loves when I sing to her. So when she crawls under the covers with me at night, I often sing us both to sleep as she purrs happily beside me.

~S. Kay Murphy

The Cat Hat

I can't decide if I have a cat or a cat has me.
~Esther Marton

The frail black-and-white kitten nestled into the crook of my arm, closed his eyes, and fell asleep. He reminded me of a baby bird who had fallen from the nest. He barely weighed two pounds and his large head was balanced precariously above a thin body that was all ribs and claws. His nose was congested and crusted over, and his breathing was so loud that I could hear it even when I was on the other side of the room.

I'd only agreed to watch the kitten for the weekend until the rescue group could find a suitable long-term foster home for him, but I already knew I needed to adopt him myself. There was no way I could part with this bewitching, forlorn creature. I'd already given him a name: Rumi, after the Sufi poet.

Rumi was in terrible shape, but he was lucky to be alive at all. He'd already escaped death twice, and he wasn't even three months old. When he was only thirteen days old, his litter had been placed on the euthanasia list at the overcrowded city shelter. A rescue organization had saved him, his siblings and their mother in the nick of time. No sooner had they escaped from the shelter than they had come down with a serious respiratory infection. Several kittens had succumbed to the illness. Rumi had successfully fought for his life, but he had required nearly a month in the animal hospital to do it.

The weeks in the hospital had deprived Rumi of the essential education most kittens received automatically. Quite simply, sometimes he wasn't sure how to be a cat. The longer Rumi lived with me, the more painfully apparent this became. His sense of smell was almost nonexistent; later, his vet would surmise that the bones in his nose had been permanently damaged by his early illness. It took him a week to learn to use the litter box since he wasn't sure what he was supposed to do with it. Even minor changes sometimes threw him into such a panic that he puffed up like a Halloween cat and walked sideways like a crab.

However, Rumi had the sweet, calm disposition of his namesake. It was obvious that the staff at the clinic had fussed over him and handled him on a regular basis. When we returned to the vet's office for checkups, Rumi amiably allowed the doctors to prod him, poke him, and put drops in his eyes and nose. At home, he didn't blink when I clipped his nails or gave him pills. He was as cuddly as a stuffed animal, and he loved nothing more than to be picked up and carried around.

Above all, Rumi wanted to be near me. He met me at the door when I came home and followed me around the apartment. Rumi wasn't content just to sleep on the bed; he insisted on curling up on the pillow so he could be close to my face. And by the third week, he developed a very strange habit: when I picked him up, he scurried up my shoulder, perched on my head, and stayed there.

The first time it happened, I walked carefully to the bathroom, stared at myself in the mirror and laughed. It was a ridiculous sight: a two-pound kitten defiantly digging his tiny nails into my forehead. The second time Rumi settled on my head, I took photos so my friends would actually believe me when I told them about my Cat Hat. The third time, I began to worry that this was becoming a habit with Rumi, and that it might prove to be troublesome when he grew up and wasn't such a lightweight. A friend wrote a caption for one of the Cat Hat photos: "This is my smart human! She was smart enough to love me! I will hug her brain!"

By the time Rumi was four months old, he had perfected the Cat Hat stance. The posture was exacting: back feet on my shoulders.

Front paws on my forehead, claws retracted but toes splayed. Head alert. Weight evenly distributed. He figured out how to balance so precisely that I was able to walk around the apartment and do chores with him perched on my head. There was no way to remove him once he decided to stake out his place on my cranium; he'd firmly hold on with all four paws.

I soon realized that the Cat Hat pose was not a game for Rumi. He wasn't using me as a human cat tree. It was reassuring for him. Scampering around under my feet was a precarious operation. He couldn't always keep up with me. When he was perched on my head he could travel everywhere I went and see everything I saw. He could certainly ensure that he would not be forgotten: there isn't a good way to disregard a cat that is perched just above your forehead, after all. From his point of view, it made perfect sense: he was a little kitten, and he had to take drastic measures to make his presence known.

When I returned home after a long day at work, I could always count on Rumi to jump up and hug my head for a few minutes. The same held true when I had guests at the apartment. When he wasn't sure about strangers, Rumi invariably retreated to my head. When I adopted one of Rumi's littermates, a kitten named Bogie, the Cat Hat became an even more frequent occurrence. The siblings didn't remembered each other, conflicts arose, and Rumi reacted to the stress by hugging my head for all it was worth.

As Rumi grew, I realized something else: the Cat Hat game was reassuring for me, too. There were many things in my life that were completely out of my control, but for one little kitten, I was everything. He trusted me to look after him, and that was something I could do. Rumi seemed to sense when I needed extra support. If I was upset or sick, he spent a considerable amount of time perched on my head. If I went to sleep, he would curl himself around my cranium to guard me. In his own way, he was letting me know that he was there, and that he had my back.

Rumi is now two years old, and yes, he still transforms into a Cat Hat from time to time. He's grown into a fierce, active twelve-pound cat, but if something unsettles him, he'll run to his favorite perch. I don't mind. He doesn't just hug anyone's head, after all.

~Denise Reich

Snickers

I have studied many philosophers and many cats.
The wisdom of cats is infinitely superior.
~Hippolyte Taine

After I moved out of my parents' house and into my first tiny apartment, I went to the pound to pick out a feline friend. There were many kittens to choose from, but the little gal in the back of the cage caught my attention immediately. She was smaller than the rest of the kittens, and she stayed to herself. Believing she was the runt of the litter, I grabbed her right away. She snuggled under my chin, and I was instantly in love.

I named this precious little gift Snickers, because her fur was a variety of nutty colors with just enough chocolate shades to remind me of a Snickers bar. Snickers and I became fast friends. She remained timid, even in my home. I thought she would outgrow that once she got used to her new environment, but she never really did. She got better with me, but was shy around other people.

The older she got, the more comfortable our relationship became. She was there to welcome me home every time I walked in the front door. She comforted me when I was sad. She played with me when we both had an abundance of energy. When friends came over, however, Snickers usually stayed in my bedroom until they were gone. I got used to that. I understood her and would never make her come out of my room when she didn't feel comfortable. And it was Snickers' disposition that made what happened one day so totally unnatural.

The days of door-to-door salesmen were slowly coming to an end, but occasionally one would still come to my first-floor door. Hearing the knock, I ran to the door knowing I would try to get rid of this salesman as soon as possible.

A young man with a wide grin greeted me, telling me he had something I just "had" to see. I told him I wasn't interested, but he pushed the screen door a little open and held it there with his left leg.

I was angry because I had left the screen door unlocked and I felt threatened by the man's boldness. "Please," I said, in a frightened and heightened voice—and that's the only thing I was able to say. Before I knew it, my timid little Snickers came running out of my bedroom, jumped up on the man's calf and dug her claws deep in his flesh.

The salesman screamed and jumped back trying to throw Snickers off his leg in what looked like a feline dancing jig. After Snickers let go of the man's leg, she hissed loudly and chased him clear out of our apartment building complex.

Holding the screen door open for her, Snickers sauntered back into the house. She jumped up on the sofa like nothing unusual had happened and began giving herself a full body bath. I stood there for several seconds, scratching my head, searching my heart, and wondering if my timid little Snickers had suddenly been possessed by the spirit of Stephen King's Cujo.

Locking the screen door, I went over and picked up Snickers, cuddling her close and telling her I couldn't believe she had actually done that. I also thanked her for getting rid of the unwelcomed guest and gave her a special treat. From that day on I had a new respect for my feline friend, and I felt safer, much safer, living alone.

~LaVerne Otis

Toonsie to the Rescue

It always gives me a shiver when I see a cat seeing what I can't see.
~Eleanor Farjeon

To paraphrase Mick Jagger, you probably don't know what you want, and it doesn't matter anyway because you'll always get what you need. And sometimes what you need has fluffy black fur, lime-green eyes, and meows.

Whoever said that cats are aloof and independent must have been a dog owner, because Toonsie was high-maintenance. Little did I know that when a cat came running up to me in my yard, she would come to rule the roost. Once Toonsie maneuvered herself into our home, she became the proverbial only child. She demanded, and received, our undivided attention. Prospero and I rearranged our schedules to meet her needs. All meals were planned to include foods that Toonsie enjoyed, with a special emphasis on sushi from her favorite Japanese restaurant. And most importantly, we never, ever attempted to take another vacation once she became a member of our family.

Occasionally, however, we humans do have to have to treat ourselves to a good time, even if it means incurring her wrath.

Toonsie always knew when something was up that might upset her daily routine. So when she constantly meowed that sunny summer morning, we thought she was protesting our decision to spend the day at the Jersey shore. Being left alone for six hours is animal cruelty in her eyes. But she usually reacted by sitting in the middle of the living room floor and turning her back on us—the ultimate snub.

This day was different. Toonsie was making a racket in the hall-way that led to the bedrooms. The crying and meowing was nonstop. Finally, she decided to stick her nose in the electrical outlet. At first I thought it merely was a shameless bid for attention. Toonsie always tended to be a bit dramatic. But then my husband, Prospero, joined her on the floor and stuck his nose near the outlet too. What can I say? He always indulged her.

"I need a screwdriver," he said. At this point I felt like I needed a screwdriver, but not the tool.

Prospero removed the cover plate only to find a spark arcing from the outlet. He raced downstairs to shut off the circuit breaker, thus preventing an electrical fire.

Had it not been for Toonsie's keen sense of smell, we would have returned from our day at the beach to find our house burned to the ground. More importantly, our precious little cat would have been trapped in the inferno, and our hearts would have been broken forever.

Toonsie wasn't throwing a tantrum on that warm summer morn-ing, she was warning us of danger. I still cannot believe that a little stray cat—that we weren't sure about taking in—prevented a life-changing catastrophe. And as we came to know over and over again, we needed her just as much as she needed us.

Thank goodness for our fuzzy lifesaver. Toonsie saved the day.

~Lynn Maddalena Menna

Feline Caregiver

A meow massages the heart.
~Stuart McMillan

Born with the umbilical cord wrapped around a gangrenous paw, Sally underwent an amputation within hours of entering the world. Six weeks later, it was necessary to remove the entire limb. So in addition to being spayed, my young fighter returned home without one of her back legs.

After holding her through the night as she slept off the anesthesia, she woke up the next morning full of energy. Despite having only three paws, Sally could outrun, out catch, and out eat her brother.

At thirteen, Sally's adventures have included several relocations, a 1,500-mile trek on the dashboard of a U-Haul, a plane ride, an earthquake, and a second-story fall. Her biggest achievement, however, was the role of caregiver. When my mother came to live with me in her last days, Sally took it upon herself to share in the responsibilities. She took her role seriously and conscientiously.

Mom's nighttime routine usually began around seven o'clock. Within a couple of days after getting Mom settled, Sally had the routine down. First, there were things to be taken care of in the bathroom, then there was a time for reading or doing a crossword puzzle, some intimate conversations between mother and daughter, and finally sleep.

How she knew I have no idea, but every evening at seven, Sally approached Mom's chair with a gentle meow and soft nudge against her leg. Sally headed toward the bedroom, and if Mom didn't get up right away, Sally returned and repeated the summons—sometimes five or six times. Sally sat on the sink as Mom brushed her teeth, took her medicine, and washed her face. Jumping on the bed, Sally would lie next to Mom as she read. When it was time for our "bedtime chats," Sally came to remind me. Sitting between us, she listened and occasionally interjected her own reflections.

When the light was turned off, she remained by Mom's side until she was asleep. Was her shift over? Not by a long shot. I had a baby monitor in my bedroom downstairs so I could hear anything that might need attending to upstairs where Mom slept. Any time that Mom woke up to use the bathroom or get something to drink, Sally was up in a flash and following her every step until she returned to bed. Woe if Mom closed the bathroom door. Sally insisted on being within arms' reach of wherever she was, and closed doors were a no-no.

When hospice became involved, Sally's responsibilities increased. Whenever the hospice nurse arrived to check on Mom, Sally watched carefully as blood pressure was taken and heartbeats noted. She sat quietly and alertly on the arm of the sofa until the nurse closed her bag. Then Sally would turn to her and initiate conversation.

"Meow, meow, meow!" It was as if she was saying, "Look, Patty. You come in once a week. I'm here all the time. Let's compare notes!" Obligingly, the hospice nurse would turn her attention to Sally and listen mindfully to her input.

I'll never forget one afternoon when Mom was in bed and all her vitals were being taken. Immediately after Mom was done, Sally turned onto her back, right next to Mom, and stuck her three legs out. Sally wanted to have her vitals taken too.

When the end was near, Sally never left Mom's side. She barely ate and rarely moved from a spot just below my mother's hip. Two weeks passed and still she remained on watch. Occasionally, she would rise and look at Mom. Once in a while she would whine softly, and then lie back down, keeping vigil.

When Mom died, Sally didn't budge. She remained on her bed until the funeral home came, throughout the night and all the next day. Over the next several days, she continued her own process of grieving. In and out of the bedroom, in and out of the bathroom, curling up on Mom's rocking chair.

At seven o'clock in the evening, for over two weeks, Sally approached Mom's chair, meowed and sat there waiting. I began to clear out Mom's closet and Sally would have none of it. Sally was right. She wasn't ready and neither was I. There were slippers Mom wore in the closet, and I would sometimes see Sally sleeping on top of them. I put Mom's robe down by the slippers on the floor, and Sally would knead it as she softly moaned.

I cried often and hard. Whenever I did, Sally was there immediately. It was our custom to curl up on the couch or bed together. Sally had acquired an uncanny knack for soothing massage. My arm, neck, chest and legs were recipients of her sweet and loving sweep as I wept. After, she would lie next to me as close as she could while cooing and purring as I pet her.

It's been four years since Mom died. There are still moments of deep sorrow and Sally picks up on it in a heartbeat. I left one of Mom's slippers in the closet. Sally seems to sense the meaning of certain tears. When I am sad and missing my mother, Sally drags out the slipper.

~Dale Mary Grenfell

Lonely Leo

There is something about the presence of a cat...
that seems to take the bite out of being alone.
~Louis J. Camuti

Waving goodbye to the movers, I slid the patio door shut. The frozen smile I'd been wearing all day melted off my face.

"If war is hell, moving must be purgatory," I muttered.

My cat circled my ankles, willing me to pick him up. I knelt and rubbed his neck. "It's just you and me now, Leo, but let's cuddle later. You'll feel better once we get organized."

I scanned the stacks of boxes. Which one held his feeding bowls? A good guess found them and a bonus teacup for me. Another foray located the cat food and teabags.

"Let's start making this home, shall we?"

I chose a spot in my small apartment for his feeding area and poured his food and water. No interest on his part. More circling.

I brewed a cup of tea and headed for the couch. The boxes could wait. I plopped down and tapped the cushion. Leo jumped on my lap, hiding his head under my arm in his "gimme shelter" pose. I stroked his downy soft Maine Coon coat.

"I know, I don't like it either," I sighed, "but you learned to like our other new homes." A mental count brought me to six. Six new homes in his short ten years.

But this time, we were alone.

Husband gone; stepchildren gone; Rottweiler gone. I wondered who Leo would miss the most. One thing was for sure, it would be quieter, but this kind of quiet hurt. Leaning in, I pulled his cheek to mine. We needed this moment, he and I, the last remnants of family. The rays of a sinking sun cast shadows among the boxes. I blinked back tears. "You'll see," I whispered. "We'll make it."

The sprawling apartment complex turned out to be jammed with singles. Single. A word I had to get used to, but these welcoming people changed my world. Barbecues and poolside meets filled my nights. The quiet apartment sounded with music and happy chatter, and through it all, weaved Leo.

So many laps to choose from! So many willing hands for a stroke of the fur. More people at the door? Leo greeted each group with a wiggly flop on his back. "Here," he seemed to say, "scratch my tummy. That's the spot. I'll keep acting like a dog if you'll pet me."

The summer months flew by and I marveled at the quick adjustment we made. I was happier than I had ever been, and Leo was content.

Or so I thought.

I gave a sleeping Leo a quick caress on my way across the open patio. No time for more. The new girl, Laura, was hosting a Labor Day party, but I had only a general idea where she lived. My hurried pace soon turned to a stroll. The winding trail along two lakes allowed me the enjoyment of tiki torches, aromatic food grilling, and neighbors who tossed invitations to join their holiday revelry.

Laura's guests overflowed her tiny place, spilling onto the lawn. Reggae songs blared through extra-large speakers. Hours passed, wine flowed, and the music got louder. It seemed people couldn't resist turning up the volume when their favorite songs played. I left the lawn chair and went inside, seeking shelter from the assault on my eardrums. I joined a group of women chatting in the kitchen.

"I think I hear someone calling you," my friend said.

How could she hear anything over the din? A head popped around the corner and a hand clutched my shoulder.

"There you are," Laura said. "I've been looking all over for you. Leo's here."

I blinked. My eardrums must have been in worse shape than I thought. "What did you say?"

She shook my shoulder. "Leo. He's in the living room. I think he wants you."

Pushing my way through the crowd, I scanned the ground. There he was, in a forest of legs, looking up at each face in a concerted search.

I lunged and scooped him up, holding him baby style. "What are you doing here, you crazy cat?"

He went limp in my arms. I sensed relief flow through him. In what can only be called kitty adoration, he locked his tired gaze on mine. And deep in those green eyes was an unmistakable question. "Have you forgotten me?"

A rapid-fire picture show of the week's activities shot through my mind. Each frame showed me somewhere other than home. Work during the day, out each night, and the worst frame, brushing by Leo on my way out the door.

"I have to leave," I said past the lump in my throat. I clutched Leo to me.

"That's some cat," I heard someone say.

Leo made no attempt to leave my arms during the long walk home.

Some cat is right.

"How on earth did you find me? Did you check each of these parties along the way?" A guilty mother feeling swept over me. How lonely does a cat have to be to come find you in a sixty-acre complex?

I set him on his favorite "watch the world go by" patio chair, but he streaked toward the bedroom the minute I slid the door open. He stopped once to look back in his "follow me" pose.

I lay next to him on the bed, rubbing his chest and little paws. "I'm so sorry, Leo. Did the quiet get to you? I shouldn't have left you alone so much. How could I forget you lost your whole family, too?"

Long after my soothing words should have sent him to sleep, the slightest stir caused his eyes to open. "I'm here," I assured him, until his soft, even breath told me he would not awaken.

I studied him while he slept. I'm no animal expert, but I knew one thing for certain. His feline world was rocky and only I could smooth it.

The call went out the next day to my closest friends. From now on, we'd throw the shrimp on the barbie at my place.

"Leo's lonely," was all I needed to say, and these kindhearted people understood.

Soon, I wondered just who they were coming to see. Leo got the first hello, the last goodbye, and a million treats and cuddles in between. Okay with me. What can be wrong in a world with a contented cat stretching nearby?

Now when I close the door after the last guest has left, Leo and I watch the shadows of a setting sun nestled in a warm, peaceful, quiet.

Just right for a family of two.

~Sammie Callahan-Hutchens

Unforgiven

We do not quite forgive a giver.
The hand that feeds us is in some danger of being bitten.
~Ralph Waldo Emerson

We didn't want to leave him so soon. Really we didn't. But my husband Bill and I had made plans for a Caribbean vacation long before we rescued the shaky little eight-pound, black-and-white tuxedo cat we called Chuck.

Three months earlier, our new addition had come home with us coughing and sneezing and on the verge of what our veterinarian called "the cat version of a nervous breakdown." Chuck had been abandoned twice in the past year, and when the adoption call went out from our local animal shelter it was noted that in addition to being lethargic, he was refusing to eat. Two sets of owners had given up on him and now he was giving up on himself. Nonetheless, Bill and I saw something special in this little fellow and we vowed to soothe his trauma and give him the best home possible.

So, Chuck became our joint project. Together we nursed him through a respiratory infection, conjunctivitis, a psoriasis flare-up, and the worst case of fleas either of us had ever seen in our many previous years of cat ownership. It took a month and unmentionable expense until we found a brand of cat food that Chuck would agree to occasionally nibble, and eventually his weight did increase to a healthy ten pounds. No wonder his previous owners had returned Chuck to the shelter; he was a lot of work.

Yet our little Chuck had so much to offer. Each evening when I returned home from the office, he greeted me at the door then stood by my side as I prepared dinner. Afterward, he would chase a ping-pong ball or swat at a piece of string until, exhausted from his efforts, he would curl up on my lap and purr, practically vibrating with gratitude for his new home. Chuck was like a big, cuddly ball of love, and Bill and I were both smitten with him. That's what made leaving him for even one week so difficult.

Still, we convinced ourselves that Chuck would be fine in the care of my parents and we trundled him over to their house along with a large supply of food, his wicker basket, favorite toys, treats, and the name and phone number of not one, but two highly accredited veterinarians, just in case. After familiarizing Chuck with his temporary surroundings, Bill and I both kissed him goodbye and then proceeded directly to the airport. Securely tucked in my carry-on bag was a photo of our furry little friend.

I was the first to take out his photo as we sat in the airplane, preparing for take-off.

"I miss Chuck," I sighed to Bill over the roar of the engines.

"Miss him? We haven't even gotten off the ground yet," he answered.

But by the time we landed, Bill had asked to look at Chuck's photo twice, and when we found ourselves back on terra firma, our little friend somehow snuck his way into most of our conversations.

While swimming: "Ah, this beach is so serene. What do you think Chuck is doing now?"

While sightseeing: "Have you ever seen such a beautiful park? Chuck would love the shady spots under the trees."

During dinner: "This flounder is delicious. So well seasoned. Chuck would really enjoy a little nip of it."

And so it went for one week.

All too soon, though, our final day in the Caribbean arrived, and Bill and I strolled into town to do a little souvenir shopping, commenting of course, on how much Chuck would appreciate the cooling breeze. Suddenly, Bill stopped dead. Pointing, he turned my attention into a wide, shop window. "Chuck would just love this," he exclaimed, gesturing toward a wriggling, battery-operated toy muskrat. I noted the price: far more than either of us had spent on any souvenirs for ourselves. It was, however, for Chuck, and price notwithstanding, the muskrat was swiftly purchased.

Back at the hotel, I wrapped the souvenir and secured it for travel all the while imagining Chuck's delighted response to the return of his owners. In my mind's eye, I envisioned my little fur-ball running to greet me at my parents' front door. His purr would be on high speed.

When we arrived, I walked up the front walk barely able to contain my anticipation.

"Chuck! We're home!" I cried out. But, no Chuck. "Where's my cat?" I asked my mother.

"I think he's sleeping on the guest bed. That's where he spent most of his time," she said. "Except when he sat on your father's lap and watched television."

Bill followed me into the guest room, souvenir bag in hand. There lay Chuck atop the velour bedspread in a deep sleep, looking quite content. I petted his soft back. Chuck opened one eye, took a look at us and rolled over.

"I think he's giving us the 'cold-paw' treatment," Bill said. "He'll change his tune once he sees this gift." Bill took the muskrat out of the bag, laid it on the floor then turned it on. It wriggled in all directions. Chuck, however, remained supine.

I picked him up and placed him on the floor next to his new toy. "Chuck, it's for you. It's your souvenir from our vacation," I explained as I moved the muskrat closer to him.

Then, finally a spark of interest. Bill and I watched with bated breath as Chuck took a few cursory swats at the toy. Then he laid one paw atop the muskrat until it stopped moving, eyed it squarely, squatted on top of it, and promptly did his business all over it. Chuck had spoken. And Bill and I heard his message loud and clear. It was a long time before we left Chuck for a vacation again.

~Monica A. Andermann

79

Peach

*Cats look beyond appearances — beyond species entirely, it seems —
to peer into the heart.*
~Barbara L. Diamond

My husband Mike and our five-year-old son Aaron were visiting my family in Alabama for Christmas. Five months pregnant for the first time at the age of thirty-two, I was both thrilled and anxious. When I heard a faint mew through the raindrops thumping the tin roof of the beauty salon where we had taken my grandmother, I flicked my eyes to Mike, who was already staring at me with a barely suppressed smile.

"Did you hear that?" I asked.

Though Mike often wants to appear to the world as a man who tolerates his wife's obsession, he's as big a pushover for cats as I am. Out we went into the rain where we called, coaxed and, after a trip to town for some meat bait, captured the scrawny, screaming Maine Coon kitten who immediately relaxed into my arms. The kitten's mouth was badly damaged and we took it to a local vet who performed surgery that day.

I assured Mike I would find it a home. But as the days passed and time came for us to go back to Arizona, I knew I couldn't part with the kitten I'd named Peach. Telling me he knew from the moment we paid the vet bill that Peach had found a home with us, Mike and I discussed how to get the kitten home. We returned to the vet for both shots and tranquilizers for the flight.

Our attempts at bringing Peach home on the airlines in a carrier were foiled. Determined to bring her home, and after conferring with Mike, I tranquilized the tiny kitten and stuffed her into a fanny pack. Aaron was in on the secret and took great joy in telling our fellow passengers that his mom had a kitty under her shirt. Noting my bulging belly, they chuckled. It was only as the plane was circling to land at Sky Harbor Airport that she awakened and gave a loud meow, that folks started wondering if the little boy was right after all.

At home, Peach blended beautifully with our other cats, becoming everyone's baby. As the months passed she perched comfortably on my growing belly at every opportunity. She became my constant companion and I talked, cried, and shared my joys with this young cat, who stared straight into my eyes and seemed to understand everything I was saying and feeling. As we prepared the nursery for our baby's arrival, Peach tested the comfort of the bouncer, the changing table, the bassinet, the crib, and the car seat. She expressed her approval through purrs.

After an emergency C-section kept me away from home three days, I returned with baby Sam, and Peach leapt into my arms as I walked into the door. She stared into my eyes and blinked her love, then moved to the baby and put a paw atop his belly while making eye contact with me. It was if she was saying "I'll protect him for you."

And she did.

When Sam was six weeks old, Peach uncharacteristically awakened me with urgent meows and bats at my face. Half asleep, I followed as she led me to Sam's crib where he was struggling to breathe. We rushed to the hospital where he was immediately admitted and a chaplain was sent to comfort us. I remained at the hospital with Sam for two weeks as they treated him for severe respiratory syncytial virus (RSV). The doctors agreed that if Sam had not been treated, he would have died. Peach saved our baby.

Several months later, Peach woke me again when an electrical socket had caused a fire and the kitchen had filled with smoke. Mike discovered a faulty socket and some insulation material that had caught fire. If it had continued burning, we could have had a house fire. Peach saved our family.

Eight years later, my sister was released from the hospital to my home months after open-heart surgery. Her lungs had filled with fluid and caused her labored breathing. Rosie told me Peach helped her breathe through the fear. "It's like she knows I need her," Rosie said.

When my sister died a year later, Peach curled in my arms as I cried, her green eyes meeting mine. When I suffered migraines she placed her large paws on my head and stayed with me until the pain subsided. As my children grew, Peach was there, watching them with me, comforting, protecting, telling me with insistent meows when something was wrong.

Two years ago I said goodbye to my dear friend of eighteen years. Peach was a precious gift at a time in my life when I needed her most. She saved our son, saved our family, and gave us more comfort, joy, and love than I could ever imagine. Not a day goes by that I don't miss her with all my heart.

~Patti Wade Zint

80

Lost in Memories

*Cats were put into the world to disprove the dogma that
all things were created to serve man.*
~Paul Gray

"**Y**ou get the cat," I said to my wife Dotty. "I'll load
the car and buckle the kids." She nodded.

Fifteen minutes later, when Dotty hadn't
appeared with our rambunctious cat, I felt the flush on my face. Where
was she? I wanted to go into the house and release some of my anger.
We had a long trip ahead of us to get to Longboat Key on the west
coast of Florida, the opposite coast from where we lived.

We were starting a one-week vacation and were supposed to meet
another couple and their children for dinner. I shifted my weight in
the driver's seat, but remained seated. I didn't want to leave our seven-
year-old son and five-year-old daughter alone, and I was too lazy to
unbuckle them and take them with me back into the house.

Instead, I hit the horn with a fervor that surely would get Dotty's
attention. When she came out empty-handed, I was about to go into
a diatribe about what was taking her so long until I noticed the tears
in her eyes.

"I can't find the cat," she said. "Maybe she ran out when we
opened the door."

"I doubt that. She's an indoor cat and has never gone out before.
You stay with the kids and let me go look."

"I really searched everywhere," Dotty said. "She's not there."

I shrugged and put my arm around my wife. "We'll find her. Maybe fresh eyes will be able to spot today's hiding place."

Our cat had hidden a number of times before, but on each occasion we found her in short order. It was like she was playing hide-and-seek with us. When she appeared, the black spot on her white muzzle elongated as her cheeks puffed into a smile. At least, that's the way it always seemed to me.

As I walked into the house, I remembered that Dotty was usually good at sniffing out the cat. There was a lot of tumult getting ready for this trip, and our furry friend might not want to be found. Maybe she sensed this sojourn would entail her going into her cat carrying case, an event she never embraced. I hoped this wasn't the case, for it would make finding her difficult. I knew my wife, the animal lover, wouldn't leave without her. Truth be told, neither would I.

I checked the cat's usual haunts—behind the refrigerator, behind the washer and dryer, and on the shelves in my son's closet. I had no success. By then Dotty had brought the kids back into the house and was sitting at the kitchen table playing *Candy Land*.

I assured them, with little conviction, that I would find the cat before long. I initiated a room-by-room search for our feline. I checked under the beds, in the closets, behind the living room couch, and even behind the toilets and in the showers. I squeezed my hands together and shook my arms to relieve tension. After checking all possible hiding places in the family room, I sat on the couch, bent over and buried my face in my hands. I thought back to when we acquired this rambunctious cat. Maybe I should have left her where I found her.

• • •

I had just finished my residency in pediatrics, and as the Vietnam War had heated up, I was required to spend two years in the armed services. I would be stationed at Keesler Air Force Base in Biloxi, Mississippi, but first I had to spend three weeks getting some very basic training in Wichita Falls, Texas. We were put up in a motel with maid service while I attended classes in proper military conduct.

I only had three days of actual field training in the blazing heat of the Red River Valley. I guess they knew that was all the physical exercise that out-of-shape physicians who had just finished their medical training could handle. Most days, I was finished by late afternoon, and then Dotty, my infant son and I went to the mess hall for dinner.

One day, before supper, Dotty asked me to go downstairs and fill up the ice bucket. When I reached the machine, I heard a weak meowing sound. I looked around, and seeing nothing, I filled the bucket with ice. As I walked away, the meowing grew louder and more urgent. I still didn't see anything, but followed the noise to a bush on the side of the parking lot. Separating the leaves, I noticed a black-and-white fur ball with a black spot on its white muzzle, hiding in the branches. The meowing intensified, and she lifted up her head and stared into my eyes, beseeching me to help her. As frightened as she must have been, she emerged from the bush and rubbed against my leg. I poured the ice into the bush, scooped up the kitten and petted her as I placed her in the bucket.

When Dotty saw the kitten, she smiled. "How cute."

I told her how I had found the cat. "Why don't I go down and get her some milk? Then we'll put her back."

Dotty stroked the kitten under the chin, "No way. You know we wanted a pet. This one's so cute and sweet. Why don't we keep her? What do you say?"

"Are you sure?"

Dotty nodded. "We'll name her Wichita after where we found her."

I smiled. "I guess we've acquired a pet."

• • •

As I sat on the couch, I continued wondering if we had made the right decision. Look at all the trouble Wichita was giving us now. Then I remembered all the joy she brought—how she lay on our bed and purred as we stroked her; how she frolicked with the children, jumping up and down and licking their smiling faces; how she had won our hearts and had become a full-fledged member of our family.

Out of the corner of my eye, I saw the curtain behind me rustle. Wichita pranced out and rubbed against my leg. She looked up and her black spot elongated as her cheeks puffed into a smile. It was as if she knew I was thinking good thoughts about her.

I reached down and scratched her under the neck as she purred. "I'm glad I put you in the ice bucket," I whispered into her ear.

~Paul Winick, M.D.

I Can't Believe My Cat Did That!

Out of the Box

81

Mars Hatched My Babies

If a dog jumps in your lap, it is because he is fond of you;
but if a cat does the same thing, it is because your lap is warmer.
~Alfred North Whitehead

I never thought that a black cat sitting on my belly would be my pregnancy test. However, this is exactly how I found out I was pregnant for the second time.

During my first pregnancy my cat Mars decided he was responsible for hatching my daughter. Within weeks of conception, my belly became Mars's resting place. He nestled his stomach to my stomach whenever I would sit or lie in bed or on the couch.

This behavior may not seem odd, but he had been with me for three years and had never done this before. Mars would also become agitated if I had something else in my lap such as a book or a pillow. He would paw at the obstacle until I removed it to allow him open access to my lap.

As my belly had expanded with my first child, Mars shifted positions but he remained. She was not an active baby in utero, but whenever Mars was on top of her, she kicked. The black cat was in for a bumpy ride as she kicked, and probably punched too, in an attempt to knock him off her home. Mars won the king-of-the-mountain battle, sometimes at the expense of my belly, by digging in his claws and maintaining his balance with cat-like expertise.

Mars remained perched on his nest until the day his baby was born. We brought Morgan home from the hospital, walked in the door and set her in the car carrier on the living room floor. Mars ran over to Morgan and sniffed to make sure it was his baby. He looked up at me as if to say, "Yes. That's her." Then, he went on with his business of lying in the sun.

My belly was cold after Morgan's birth. Morgan had a permanent guardian angel though. Mars didn't leave her side for long. In most of Morgan's baby pictures, you will find Mars, his tail, or his paw.

After a year and a half, Mars resumed his perch. I didn't need a pregnancy test or a doctor's appointment to tell me I was expecting my son. Nine months later, Mars and I welcomed Dylan to the world and Mars remained cat guardian for his two babies.

~Lisa M. Wolfe

82

Magic and the Seagull

The phrase "domestic cat" is an oxymoron.
~George F. Will

Twenty years ago, I lived on a sixty-eight-foot steel cruiser on the River Thames in Windsor, England, with my husband, Peter, and our three cats, Lucy, Tabitha and Magic. The engine room was at the back of the boat, and although the cats were free to wander around the cruiser, this was their special area. There was a door at the back of the engine room leading outside, and we had put a chain on it so that it would open just enough for the cats to get in and out. They seemed to prefer using this door rather than the cat flap at the other end of the boat. As the central heating boiler was in the engine room, it was cozy and warm in there during the winter. The cats would often curl up close to the boiler and sleep for hours.

One summer's afternoon, there was a terrible clatter coming from the engine room. Although it became quiet for a moment, I soon heard a couple of bangs. I knew I had to go and investigate. As the boat was moored in a marina, we felt safe there, and anyway, it was the middle of the day. There were lots of people around, so I didn't think we had a burglar. It had to be one of the cats. Going into the engine room, I saw Magic dragging something in through the back door. Magic was the youngest of the three cats, and was Lucy's son. He was completely black and I thought him to be very handsome. He enjoyed hunting and often presented us with mice and sparrows, but what he was pulling in now looked enormous.

"What have you got there, Magic?" I asked nervously, stalling for time.

I knew that he wouldn't be able to answer, but I was loath to go and see for myself. Where was Peter?

Finally, I walked towards Magic, worried that the creature he had caught was still alive and could be dangerous. However, approaching it, I realized that it wasn't moving and was most probably dead. When I got close, I couldn't believe what I was looking at. Magic had brought in a large seagull. It was almost as big as he was, and he seemed extremely proud of himself. Magic glanced at me and then back at the seagull, waiting to be congratulated for his kill. I was reluctant to pick it up, but luckily I heard movement in the next room.

"Peter, hurry up. Come and see what Magic's caught," I shouted.

Peter came into the engine room and looked in disbelief at the seagull. I was relieved to be able to hand over the disposal of the bird to Peter. He confirmed that it was dead and managed to get it away from Magic without too much of a fight. Magic enjoyed bringing in his prey, but unlike the female cats, he wasn't interested in doing much else with them. To this day, I don't know how Magic was able to catch the seagull.

~Irena Nieslony

83

A Fitting Finale

I have felt cats rubbing their faces against mine and touching my cheek with claws carefully sheathed. These things, to me, are expressions of love.
~James Herriot

L aser was a therapy cat for more than twelve years, and in that time I was fortunate enough to see him do many amazing things and spread a tremendous amount of happiness.

One November evening, though, his gift of empathy surpassed every expectation I ever had. We were visiting the local children's hospital shortly before Thanksgiving. As we were hurrying to the elevator to visit the children on the oncology unit, a woman tapped me on the shoulder and asked if Laser could visit with her daughter in the lobby before we went upstairs.

Of course I said yes. She led me to a teenager in a wheelchair. Both the girl and her mother told me how much they loved cats, and how sad they were because theirs had died only a few weeks before.

Laser was a world-class snuggler. From the tiniest child, whose lap was so small that he had to do some serious contortions in order to fit, to the largest adult, Laser had a reputation at the hospital for always finding a way to curl up and cuddle.

That's why I thought it was so strange when Laser did not curl up on this teenager's lap. Instead, as soon as I placed him on the girl's lap, he climbed up and positioned himself with his chin resting on her shoulder and the length of his body pressed against her chest.

A big smile lit up the girl's features as she blissfully closed her eyes and rubbed her face against the soft fur of Laser's head and back.

It wasn't until I had been watching this happy interaction for several minutes that it suddenly dawned on me that the girl was not using her hands to pet Laser, and that in fact her arms were paralyzed.

Did Laser somehow know that this girl was unable to use her hands to pet him? Is that why he so uncharacteristically cuddled on her shoulder rather than curling up in her lap? I don't know, but I don't have any other explanation.

That encounter was especially poignant because it turned out to be Laser's last therapy visit. At age fourteen, he died very suddenly and quite unexpectedly just a couple of weeks later.

While I was devastated by his loss, the thought of all the joy he brought over the years and the difference he made in so many lives makes me smile. There could be no more fitting final chapter in the life of this amazing therapy cat than that experience at the children's hospital. I know Laser's spirit will live on not only in that girl's heart, but in the hearts and memories of everyone else whose life he touched.

~Nancy Kucik

84

A Face Only a Mother Could Love

Everything has beauty, but not everyone sees it.
~Confucius

I f you looked up the word "ugly" in the dictionary, I'm quite sure you'd find BT's picture beside it. BT's mother was a feral gypsy cat who waltzed in one rainy night, pregnant belly and all, and stayed around long enough to make sure her babies would be taken care of. When they were barely able to eat softened kitten chow, she disappeared into the shadows and was never seen or heard from again.

BT, the least attractive kitten in the litter, sought my favor early by being the most boisterous of the four kittens. With a meow that thundered above all the others, he had no idea what he looked like. He had fuzzy legs and a fuzzy tail, but the rest of him was smooth except for a tuft of long fur right between his eyes. He had a strange overbite and one front tooth stuck out at an angle.

Needless to say, finding good homes for his siblings was easy, but no one wanted BT, and he preferred it that way. He wanted to stay with me so he could chase tadpoles and bullfrogs around the old farm pond. I gave in and let him have his way. He captured my heart with "a face only a mother could love," and even that was questionable given the fact that she didn't hang around very long!

BT wasn't much on being petted. He was a loner who preferred staying outside, spending his days whiling away the hours on a hilltop under the shade trees near the pond. About the only time we saw each other was at feeding time, when he politely climbed the steps to the back deck, ate his food in silence, and then disappeared into the night.

Sometimes he would allow me the luxury of patting his head, but most of the time he preferred being left alone. Occasionally I would catch a glimpse of him chasing the moths that flew around the outside perimeter lights surrounding the front of my house.

As he grew older and wiser, BT figured out that living on my farm wasn't such a bad thing. He had a hearty helping of cat chow daily, as well as all the water, sun, and shade he could hope for.

In the winter he holed up in the hayloft, snuggling deep into the hay bales to keep warm. On a couple of occasions, when the temperatures dipped below zero, I tried coaxing him inside so he could snuggle up in front of the fire, but he must have had a fear of being a lap cat because he wanted no part of it.

Twelve summers have come and gone since BT came into my life. For the entire span of his life, he never left the property. Never neutered, he preferred for the girls to find him instead of romancing them from afar. Perhaps he knew he was ugly and had a hang-up about it—I don't know. But I do know he was always around at feed time. Never once did he miss a meal.

BT died three years ago from unknown complications. He simply laid his weary bones down beside a tree and slipped quietly into eternity. I know that's not anything for the world to be bothered over, but it upset me to know I would never again have the privilege of seeing him and patting his scraggly head. Without a doubt, he was the most loyal and trusting companion I've ever had. I buried him on his favorite hilltop overlooking the pond. For a headstone, I used a big flat rock and carved his name into it.

Spring of the following year rolled around and the fields around the farm were green with new life. As I passed by BT's grave, I noticed something strange. Growing right beside his headstone was one lone, ugly thistle.

Nothing had ever grown on that hillside before because it caught the rain runoff from the pasture and the topsoil was long gone. BT was sending me a message, I was sure. I knew that when the thistle bloomed it would proudly carry a beautiful lavender flower atop its lanky four-foot tall frame, letting the world know that even a weed is beautiful.

~Carol Huff

85

Baby Socks

He has become a much better cat than I have a person. With his gentle
urgings, he made me realize that life doesn't end just because one has a few
obstacles to overcome.
~Mary F. Graf

The gray tuxedo kitten decided he would live with my husband James and me after his feral mother was hit by a car and died. His tiny feet looked like he was wearing white socks so we named him Baby Socks. We fed him and talked to him until he finally trusted us enough to pet him and pick him up. We took him to the vet for his shots and had him neutered. Even with that, he was not an inside cat. He wanted to be outside where he could patrol his domain. However, when I would sit outside, he would jump in my lap, his white feet kneading my legs.

We were also owned by a ten-pound Yorkie-Poo named Sugar. Baby Socks eventually got used to her using "his" back yard and they formed a truce where she didn't chase him and he didn't hiss at her. Baby Socks grew and grew. He eventually weighed twenty pounds — twice the size of the dog.

At the same time, Sugar was getting older. By the time she was sixteen years old, she had cataracts in both eyes. But due to her age and numerous health problems, they couldn't remove them. Despite her blindness she knew how to navigate all the rooms in the house, and we left the furniture in the same place so she wouldn't get confused or hurt.

However we did worry about her going out in the yard. A slope led down to a creek, and there was the possibility that snakes or raccoons could harm her. We went with her on her bathroom trips and watched while she hunted for the right spot. Then we called to her so she could follow the sound of our voices and find her way back to the door.

Eventually Sugar also lost her hearing. We had to watch her every move when she was outside, and pick her up to bring her back to the house.

It wasn't long before we noticed that Baby Socks was following Sugar whenever she was in the yard. If she got too close to the slope, he got in front of her and nudged her back toward the house. When she was ready to go back in the house, he nudged her in the right direction and saw her safely to the door. He became her self-appointed "seeing-eye cat"! Sugar died when she was seventeen and a half. Baby Socks seemed to know that she was gone and not coming back, but he watched whenever we opened the back door, just in case.

He still patrols the yard, and when I sit outside he jumps in my lap, even though he takes up all the space and hangs over both sides. I tell him what a good cat he is and that, just maybe, we might get another dog someday. He doesn't seem impressed, but if that day ever comes, I'm sure Baby Socks will once more work out a truce, and maybe a friendship, with whatever new canine enters his domain.

~Bonita Chambers

86

Destructo-Cat

You may own a cat, but cannot govern one.
~Kate Sanborn

ogie has a knack for cuteness. He likes to sprawl across the carpet, turn his head completely upside down and put his paws up in the air. The resulting pose is adorable, and it never fails to make me smile. To look at him, you'd never guess that he was once a juvenile delinquent who almost set my apartment on fire.

I adopted Bogie as a companion for his littermate, Rumi. The first photo I saw of the little terror should have clued me in to the chaos to come. Bogie's siblings were photographed sitting sweetly on the couch. Bogie, on the other hand, was tangled in a Christmas tree in his picture. He had originally been named "Rogue" because of his affinity for escaping from his room and leading the other kittens to freedom. Bogie was long, lean and elegant; he sported white boots and had large, bat-like ears. He was apprehensive around strangers and fiercely loyal and affectionate to those he loved.

True to his original name, he was a roguish explorer, and his astonishing intelligence, inquisitive nature and mischievousness were challenging to handle. Bogie chewed through wires and ruined them. He snacked on glue, which prompted panicked calls to both the vet and the ASPCA's poison control hotline. After Bogie figured out how to open zippers, he filched a pack of birth control pills from my bag and left the crumpled foil sheet on the carpet. Some of the tablets were missing. Fortunately, he hadn't ingested any, but I didn't know that until I wasted a frantic half hour crawling around on the floor to locate every single pill. Bogie stole jewelry and hid it. I had to supervise mealtimes because he was so aggressive about eating that he scared Rumi. In sum, Bogie was a brat, and he forced me to continually upgrade the kitten-proofing around the house. No matter how much I played with him, how many toys he had or how many snuggles he received, he still behaved abominably. The vet gave him a clean bill of health, so he wasn't acting out due to illness. Frankly, he just seemed to enjoy causing trouble. I started calling him Destructo-Cat.

When Bogie grew large enough to jump up to the kitchen counters, we entered an exasperating new era of destruction around the apartment. I frequently caught him tiptoeing gingerly around the drainboard, nosing into the fascinating items on the counter or walking around on the top of the stove. He liked to sit in a ceramic serving dish, where he rather resembled an overgrown Christmas ham. I started finding refrigerator magnets in odd places.

I tried to discourage this behavior, of course. The way Bogie got onto the counters made me very nervous: he used the knobs of the stove as steppingstones to boost himself up. Every time he leapt to the counter or the stove, I immediately picked him up and put him back down on the floor. After a while he knew he was not supposed to be on the counters, and a simple glance in his direction or a stern word from me were enough to make him scurry out of the kitchen. However, my kitchen did not have a door, so I had no way to physically bar Bogie from the area. I frequently came home to find paper towels, cups and other items strewn about, which made it crystal clear that Bogie was entertaining himself in my absence.

On the morning Bogie decided to turn on the stove, I woke up uncharacteristically early. I like to think that my guardian angels were looking out for me. All I know is that when I opened my eyes just after sunrise, it was with a sense of urgency. I knew had to get up immediately because something was seriously wrong. As I sat up in bed, I began to cough. The horrible stench of rotten eggs permeated the air. It smelled exactly like the gas from the stove, in fact. The stove!

I bolted toward the kitchen. The odor of gas was overwhelming, and a small blue flame was merrily flickering on the front burner.

I knew without a doubt that Bogie was responsible. The oven had been safely turned off the night before. Nobody had visited the apartment while I slept. And since Rumi was still too little to jump to the counter, Bogie was the only one who could have reached the knob for the burner. For the next few days, Bogie slunk quietly around the house, refrained from his usual mischief and pointedly avoided the kitchen, which confirmed his guilt.

I was beyond grateful that nobody had been asphyxiated and that the apartment hadn't burned down. I was also genuinely relieved that I was not going to have to describe the incident to my landlord or the fire department. It would have been embarrassing, to say the very least. How do you explain that it wasn't your fault that the kitchen caught on fire, because your cat turned on the stove while you were sleeping? Let's face it, nobody is ever going to believe that your sweet-looking kitten is a pyromaniac in training.

Once the apartment was aired out, I had to tackle the question of securing the stove from future cooking attempts by Destructo-Cat. I found knob guards intended for babies, but they would have been way too easy for Bogie to defeat. They were designed to stop little hands, not to withstand the ten-pound impact of a leaping kitten. I finally settled on a bizarre stove modification. I pulled the knobs off and taped pot lids over the bare handles. Whenever I used the oven, I fished the knobs out of the junk drawer and restored them. When I finished cooking, I replaced the "Bogie-proofing." Friends who visited my apartment just raised their eyebrows and shook their heads when they saw my handiwork. Bogie never did turn the stove on again, though, so it served its purpose.

Strangely, the incident with the stove was a turning point for Destructo-Cat. It seemed to scare him enough to curb some of his more exasperating conduct. Perhaps he felt that playing with fire was a suitable grand finale to his life of crime. In addition, Bogie was diagnosed with a puzzling allergic condition called eosinophilic granuloma complex. As the EGC was treated and Bogie started feeling better, he gradually settled down and became less destructive.

Bogie is still being treated for EGC, but he is happy and healthy. He's far more inclined to greet me at the door with a head-butt than he is to leave me a trail of debris. However, he is still a roguish, nervy Destructo-Cat at heart, and every now and then he needs to get it out of his system. It explains the shredded toilet paper, chewed up boxes and ransacked bookshelves I find every so often. At this point, I take it as a normal part of life. If I didn't find a mess every so often, I'd worry that Bogie was unwell. And I'd worry even more about what he might be plotting.

~Denise Reich

Two Journeys

What greater gift than the love of a cat?
~Charles Dickens

"Sammie! What are you doing here?" I couldn't believe it. My neighbor's cat was at my back door, gazing at me through the glass. This wouldn't have been unusual if it weren't for the fact that Sammie had moved across town with her family the week before.

I immediately called Sammie's owner, Laura. Laura told me that Sammie had been missing for two days. We came to the only possible conclusion—Sammie had walked the three miles from her new house back to her old neighborhood. Although it's possible that Sammie remembered me feeding her a few times, Laura and I agreed that there was more to it than that. The cat missed me.

Sammie and I had become friends over the previous few months. I would sit on my front steps every afternoon and call to her. She'd come running over from her house. Then I'd scratch her ears, chin, and lower back. She would purr, and look deep into my eyes, as if to tell me how grateful she was. The feeling was mutual.

Now I had a big decision to make. Should I offer to keep Sammie? It seemed clear that she wanted to stay with me, but I had my reservations.

After my boyfriend's death a few years earlier, I'd retreated deep within myself. I didn't see my friends very often, and I tried to limit my commitments. I worked from home and didn't go out much. Then, when my mother's cat passed away, a cat I was also very fond of, I'd subconsciously made the decision to not have a pet. I didn't want any more loss in my life. Although I loved Sammie, I just wasn't sure I wanted to take on the commitment of caring for her, both physically and emotionally.

However, when I discussed it with Laura the next day, we decided that the best thing for Sammie would be for her to stay with me. We certainly didn't want to risk her trying to return to me if she went back to her new home. We knew that whatever route she had taken, she would have had to deal with traffic, other animals, and who knows what other dangers. So there it was. I had a pet.

Today, Sammie is thriving. We have multiple "scratchie" times a day, and we both are happy to have each other. She spends a lot of time on the deck, but also comes inside to sit on the couch. Sometimes she walks across my keyboard, inadvertently typing for me.

I have taken on the commitment wholeheartedly, and I know I came to the best decision. I now understand that it is always the right thing to open up to the possibility of love, even with the knowledge that loss often follows.

Sammie made an incredible journey when she walked from her new house back to me. But I made a significant journey, too, when I went from a closed heart to a wide-open one. Sammie seemed to know what I needed more than I did.

~Carol E. Ayer

The Day I Let the Cat Out of the Bag

There is no love sincerer than the love of food.
~George Bernard Shaw

erhaps my favorite part of the day is coming home from work to the warm reception I always receive from my two cats, Misty and Stormy. One day, however, as I walked up the path, I was confused about what I saw through the tall, narrow windows that frame the front door. As I got nearer and peered in, I confirmed my growing dread: my tuxedo cat, Misty, was lying on the bottom step of the staircase leading to the second floor, her head tightly wrapped in white plastic!

My heart nearly stopped. For a few seconds I couldn't breathe. My mind raced, trying to make sense of what I was seeing. What had happened? Who had done this to her?

I shook off my shock and with a trembling hand jammed my key into the lock, my eyes never leaving her still form. The noise of the key usually brought both cats running, but this time there was no movement from the limp body on the stairs—nor did Stormy make an appearance.

Oh no—they were BOTH dead!

I opened the door and stepped inside, slowly approached Misty, and called her name. My relief was overwhelming when she raised her head feebly, dazedly, as if awakened by some distant sound that she couldn't quite place. She was alive!

I rushed forward and knelt beside her, noting in a split second that her head was completely encased in a small, opaque bag of sturdy white plastic, her ears flattened against her head. How long she had been like this, I could only guess. The bag was repeatedly sucked against her face and then released as she struggled to breathe. Something about it looked familiar, I thought, yanking it off her head.

From the neck up her black fur was slicked down with sweat, making her look like a seal that had just surfaced from a pool of water. I picked her up and cradled her, grateful she was alive. I barely noticed that she reeked of several unpleasant smells—fear, urine, and... turkey? I carried her into the kitchen where the overturned garbage pail told the whole story.

Misty is what my dad would call a "chowhound." Even as a tiny kitten, she would nudge her littermates away and hog their mother when she wanted to nurse. Once weaned, she'd quickly gobble up all her food and then start on the bowl set out for Stormy, who was less aggressive when it came to eating.

She would greet me with wails as soon as I awoke each morning. The message was clear: why was I so slow to prepare her meal when she was starving? She'd underscore her impatience by ripping out and devouring bits of the bathroom rug (apparently an appetizer) while waiting for me to shower and go downstairs to fix her breakfast.

Dinner was much the same. Even after she was fed, she'd jump on the kitchen table and try to eat my food, too—not only the meat or fish, but salad, pasta, cookies, juice—it didn't matter what. I had always feared that her tendency to eat almost anything might one day do her in... and it nearly did.

From the evidence left on the kitchen floor, I surmised that she had managed to circumvent my dumpster-diving precautions and dig through the trash for an empty plastic sleeve that once held ground turkey. She must have shoved her face inside to lick the remains, pushing her nose ever deeper into the bottom of the sleeve; but once in there she couldn't remove the tight-fitting sleeve from her head. Thank Heaven there were microscopic holes in it so she could breathe—albeit not well.

I was so relieved to find her unharmed that I didn't even mind discovering (well, not much, anyway) that she had peed all over the floor below the step where I found her, soaking the furry bedroom slippers I had left there. This olfactory deterrent is what had kept Stormy, who I found hiding under the bed, from rushing down the stairs to greet me.

I'll be forever grateful to Misty's guardian angel for watching over her while I was at work. That day my little chowhound used up at least one of her nine lives—and one of mine, too.

~Susan Yanguas

Taming My Ogre

Love makes your soul crawl out from its hiding place.
~Zora Neale Hurston

I sat in the folding chair across from Tom in his auto body shop. The subject of our discussion, my rusted Austin Healey, seemed the last thing on his mind. Did I imagine a flirtation?

My mechanic Steve had referred me to Tom for some restoration work on my classic car. I didn't realize at the time Steve acted as a clandestine cupid trying to bring his two single friends together.

"Do you have children?" Tom asked.

"No. I have cats."

"Cats?" He spat the word as though spewing curdled milk.

Uh-oh. Not a cat lover? I moved to the edge of my chair, ready to skedaddle at his next criticism of my beloved felines.

Tom softened a bit. "How many?"

"Two tuxedo cats. Brother and sister, named Sebastian and Squeakette."

"What's a tuxedo cat?"

"They're black with white markings, which resembles a tuxedo, hence the label."

He pursed his lips and nodded.

I scooted back in my chair again. Okay, he isn't a full-blown ogre, but can I change him into a cat-tolerating person?

I made daily visits to see the progress of my car's restoration and, in those three months, Tom and I became friends. The subtle flirtations led to an invitation to the Austin Healey's welcome home party.

Tom delivered the finished car and didn't show his anti-cat posture when he came inside. Sebastian, the shy cat, went to Tom instead of hiding under the bed—his usual protocol when I had visitors.

Every visit thereafter, the cat followed him around with a "let's do guy stuff" attitude. Good thing Tom didn't smoke cigars. Sebastian would've been puffing away on a Montecristo right along with him. Squeakette worked her magic on Tom, too. He enjoyed watching her hop—Pepé Le Pew style—through the ferns in my back yard. Her lizard-hunting prowess never ceased to impress him.

"Real men don't have cats," he said stroking Sebastian's back.

"Is that so?" I answered with a tongue-in-cheek smile. My "real man" had a cat in his lap.

As Tom's opposition to my pets waned, he rarely spat the word "cats." I actually heard him use the term "kitties" once or twice.

We married two years later and bought an old bungalow in South Tampa. It had twice the number of windows as my previous home, delighting Sebastian and Squeakette with a panoramic view of the neighborhood. And, I might add, twice the repair issues.

An electrical short in the ancient wiring damaged the motion detector. Tom set up his six-foot ladder the next day to climb to the eight-foot ceiling and into the attic to replace it.

When he finished, he came into the kitchen shaking his head in amazement. "I was lying on my stomach with barely enough room to work in the corner of the eaves," he said. "I heard this crunch, crunch, crunch—small footsteps behind me. I looked over my shoulder, expecting to find a rat ready to gnaw on my arm. Instead, I came face-to-face with Sebastian."

"Really?" I headed to the hallway to see the attic opening. "How'd he get up there?"

"Same way I did." Tom then pointed to the ladder. "And if we need to replace a motion detector again, Sebastian's our go-to cat. He watched every move I made."

That night, I awoke to paws walking across my belly. In the pale moonlight, I saw Squeakette creeping toward Tom.

My husband folded the sheet back, without waking, and exposed his underarm. Squeakette nestled into his armpit. She purred and pressed paw to flesh, kneading him like biscuit dough. Tom stirred once or twice, but continued to snore with his arm over his head. Had she trained him to do that in his sleep?

The next morning, Tom raised his arm in front of the mirror. Running a hand over his flesh, he commented, "I get this prickly rash every once in a while. What do you think it is?"

I choked back a chuckle. "I don't know. Try some aloe on it." Note to self: Clip Squeakette's claws.

We'd been married seven years when Sebastian passed away. Squeakette followed her brother fourteen months later. Tom mourned their loss with me.

I thought being cat-free and living in a home without cat hair or the all-too-frequent fur ball would please Tom. But a pair of ten-week old tabbies at a pet supply store stole my husband's heart the following Christmas. He insisted on bringing them home.

I argued with him, knowing his previous aversion to cats; but he would not budge. Those kittens were ours.

I named the shorthaired kitten Pixie. Tom named her longhaired sister Feathers. "She's so soft," he said. "It's like petting a feather duster." He didn't know naming a cat is a sign the cat now owns you.

I came home from work one day to find Tom with a measuring tape outside the back of the house.

"What are you doing?"

"I'm going to build a Kitty Kabana. Then the girls can go outside without the dangers of being outside."

The girls? Did he just refer to the cats as "the girls?"

The Kitty Kabana became a wrap-around screened porch with tiled flooring and its own tin roof attached to the back of the kitchen. Nothing's too good for Tom's "girls."

Five years later, Tom began kitchen renovations. He wouldn't allow Pixie and Feathers near that room. "It's too dangerous," he said. "Besides, I'll have to take out the Kabana for this project."

My bottom lip protruded. "But you worked so hard to build it."

"That's okay." He dusted off his sledgehammer. "I'll build the girls a better Kabana."

I scratched my head. "A better Kabana?"

Tom nodded. "With two levels." He locked the door to the kitchen.

Feathers paced behind the door, pawing at it. She meowed her protest — loudly.

Tom shot a concerned look at me. "Poor kitty. Do you think she needs counseling?"

Of course, he was joking, but I had to wonder what happened to the ogre I married?

I can't believe it took four cats: Sebastian, Squeakette, Pixie, and Feathers to tame my ogre for me. Well done, kitties, well done!

~Janet Ramsdell Rockey

Inside Out

If purring could be encapsulated, it'd be the most powerful
anti-depressant on the pharmaceutical market.
~Alexis F. Hope

I still remember the first time I saw her: a tiny kitten with white paws and an orange smudge above her eyes. She was hiding at the back of her enclosure, making herself as small as possible and trying to disappear from the world. One by one, all of her more outgoing brothers and sisters were taken, until she was left on her own. It seemed no one wanted the scared, reclusive kitten in the corner, but I knew straight away she was the one for me. Amber, the kitten, however, needed a lot of convincing.

She cried all the way home and every night. She hid under my bed, behind the fridge, somehow squeezing into every corner of our house where no one could reach her. Slowly and carefully, I gained her trust. When she finally ventured out from under my bed to eat, the sound of her crunching her kitty biscuits was music to my ears.

Over the years, we became inseparable. Amber was at the door whenever I got home from work or university, she stayed up late with me when I was studying, and she even scratched on the bathroom door and meowed if I'd been in there too long. I, in turn, respected her boundaries. I could scratch her head and under her chin, but I couldn't rub her tummy or pick her up for cuddles.

A few short years into our friendship, I was raped, and I started a rapid downward spiral into depression. I stopped going to work and school and stayed in bed. I became a traumatised soul hiding in darkness, making myself as small as possible to disappear from a dark and cruel world.

Amber never left my side. She was a warm, furry bundle of comfort when no one or nothing else could reach me. Once, at my lowest low, her cold, wet nose on my cheek made me lift my head from my tear-soaked pillow. There was Amber, with one of her ears turned inside out. She looked so completely absurd, this elegant feline, paws tucked daintily underneath her, tail curled perfectly around her, with one ear inside out... that laughter gurgled up through all the darkness and pain and overflowed.

That moment was the turning point for me. I got out of bed, opened the curtains and pulled myself together. I went back to university and to work, and started seeing a counsellor. It was a long road to recovery, but I am here today, walking that road because Amber dispersed the darkness long enough for me to get back on my feet.

Throughout our years together, Amber has brought a lot to my life. But I will never forget that when I lost faith in humanity it was a cat who was able to give it back to me.

~Shireen Wahid

I Can't Believe My Cat Did That!

Chapter 10

Eight Lives and Counting

Decorating Paws

Cleanliness is next to impossible.
~Author Unknown

After forty-five years of marriage, there aren't many projects my husband and I have done that did not turn out successfully. We've planted gardens, built a dark room, raised six children, and finished many decorating projects. Not all of the latter were easy, however. There was a time we wallpapered a room and I was certain it would end in divorce. Projects with spouses take work and they certainly educate you on the rules of give-and-take.

I'll never forget our very first decorating project. We were newlyweds, and we redecorated the dining room at our first home in Delaware. When finished, the room was painted a light golden hue that left it feeling warm, and the windows sported new off-white drapes with golden flecks that perfectly complemented the color we had chosen.

"I love it," I said, as I slipped an arm around Don's waist and hugged him.

"The next project is the kitchen floor," he declared, as we beamed over the outcome of the beautiful new dining room. "We can cover that ugly old linoleum with new vinyl tiles. It's not a difficult job, and I can do it myself."

A few weeks later we purchased the vinyl tiles for the kitchen, and Don began the preparations to install our new floor. We had added a sweet little black kitten to our family just days before, and had not yet given him a name. I was keeping the kitten in the basement with a litter box some of the time until he learned to use it.

The kitten was in the basement the morning my husband began spreading the black, goopy glue on the kitchen floor for the new tiles. The basement door was at one end of the kitchen, and the entrance into the newly decorated dining room was at the other. Just as Don took his trowel and smoothed the sticky glue on the last section near the dining room entrance, he saw something streaking towards him across the black glue and realized it was the kitten. He had forgotten to close the basement door!

"No!" I heard him scream. I turned to see him grab the kitten before it could reach the dining room carpet, and at the same time he dropped his gallon can of black, goopy glue. The can hit the floor and the contents shot across the dining room carpet, up the newly painted wall, and splattered all over the lovely new drapes.

"Oh no!" I yelled over and over as I saw Don dashing out the back door of our row home into the yard with the messy, struggling, glue-covered kitten. The kitten scratched at his hands and arms as he stretched out one arm to hold it away from him. He knew he needed to clean it before it ran away again and tracked the black glue all over the carpet in every room of our house. Still holding onto the frightened, frantic cat, he gingerly climbed through the basement window with it.

The only thing my husband could find in the basement to remove the tar-like substance from the cat's paws and the entire under portion of its tail was a can of paint thinner. He quickly put some on a clean rag and began wiping the cat with it. Upstairs, I was in tears over the disaster in the dining room.

Suddenly I heard a blood-curdling caterwaul followed by my husband's "Ouch!" (And a few other choice mutterings.) Then I heard the kitten running up the basement steps.

Once again, he burst through the basement door with a "Mee-yowl!" and sped across the black and sticky glue, through the dining room and into the living room. My husband yelled at the top of his lungs from the basement, "Catch the cat!"

The kitten was still howling as he dove under our television set in a corner of the room. I could tell he was in great distress, and I began to cry even harder.

My husband came bounding in the back door holding a towel on his wounded hand where the cat had bitten a chunk out of his skin. He was mumbling something to himself, and then yelled in my direction, "Grab him, before he runs everywhere!"

"I am trying," I cried as the cat meowed and weaved dizzily in the corner of the room. He looked drunk, and I felt he might keel over any minute. When I saw and heard the kitten in distress, I just cried more and yelled at my husband, "You've killed my kitten!"

"Hey... he bit me!" Don emphatically replied. I was afraid to reach for the kitten in case he might take his frustration and fright out on me, too. I quickly ran upstairs, grabbed a bath towel, a Band-Aid and first aid cream for my husband's hand, and ran back to the frantic pair. Luckily I was able to gather the kitten in the towel while Don grabbed the car keys so we could rush to the vet's office.

The cat was examined and we were told that the paint thinner had temporarily stung his sensitive paws and backside. After a bath, he was just fine. Thankfully, my husband's hand was not seriously injured either.

The dining room, however, did not fare so well. Our kitchen tile endeavor turned into an extended mission that involved redecorating the dining room.

It certainly was not comical at the time. But forty-five years later, we can tell the story and laugh about our first year as newlyweds and how our first home improvement project went awry when a little kitten moved in.

I wanted to name him Tarbutt, but the family decided that Midnight was a better name!

~Beverly F. Walker

The Ghost of Truffles

There are very few monsters who warrant the fear we have of them.
~Andre Gide

In the days of my youth, when I was still known as Billy, my namesake and beloved Uncle Bill made a long trip to visit us. Bill was a railroad man, my father's older brother, a kindly man who told exciting stories of his work with the giant steam locomotives of the day.

Back in those days, such visits were infrequent, at least in our family. This was Uncle Bill's first, and as it turned out, only visit to his brother, and it proved to be memorable, all because of Truffles the cat.

Truffles had arrived at our house one blustery winter day and decided to stay. She was a nondescript feline, of numerous indeterminate colors, and exhibited a similarly undefined, almost nonexistent personality. Truffles blended into the background, as nearly invisible on a richly colored Persian rug as on a drab linoleum floor. Truffles ate and snoozed. She gave and asked for affection in equally minimal measure. Truffles was a cat who was not there, even when she was. But Truffles could play the piano.

One day, exploring our small house, Truffles wandered into the basement. My father had built a recreation room in the basement, and the centerpiece was a well-traveled upright piano. Dad was a piano player. Obeying his masterful magic fingers, that old piano had sent out a million ragtime tunes, tangos, waltzes and polkas that would rouse the dead. Our recreation room had hosted countless neighborhood parties where the dancing began at eight o'clock and ended in the wee hours, the old house shaking with the pounding of the dancers' feet.

Truffles may have observed my father playing the piano, and connected the sounds to the moving fingers, or more likely she jumped on the keyboard and made a "Eureka" discovery. What we do know is that one day we heard a melodic tinkling of the keys—somewhat discordant—but the notes went up, then down, then back up the keyboard. My mother and I peeked through the door, and there was Truffles, vaguely visible, walking back and forth on the keyboard. She was clearly enjoying the sounds she was creating. As time passed, Truffles' piano concerts became a part of our lives.

Uncle Bill arrived, and after a long day of great stories and Mom's best recipes, Bill was tired and asked where he was going to sleep. The only guest bed was a pullout sofa in the recreation room, so Bill headed downstairs, and soon all of us were in our appointed rooms, dreaming pleasant dreams.

In the dead of night, on little cat's feet, a musician sat down to play. Because Truffles was an invisible cat most of the time, Uncle Bill had not seen her, and did not know she lived among us. Bill woke with a start, sometime after midnight. The piano on the far wall was playing. Faint light from the sunken window to the street showed the white keys moving up and down, with no apparatus to make them do so. He explained later, he came to believe the unseen piano player was making an attempt at Beethoven's "Moonlight Sonata," but doing it badly. Dark basements and invisible piano players? Bill quickly came to the logical conclusion: a ghost!

"Be off!" he cried, "Leave me be!" He slapped the bedclothes.

Truffles, possibly insulted by this negative review, ceased playing. Slowly Bill allowed himself to believe this had been a nightmare. Invisible sonatas indeed! Pulling the covers over his head, he returned to fitful slumber.

But Truffles' concert was not finished. She began again, high notes, sharps and flats, fast twinkle-toed notes. A Mozart concerto?

The unearthly music penetrated Bill's senses, leaving him too terrified to cry out. He shrank against a wall, silently pleading with the spectral pianist to leave. Through dark hours this torture continued. Then, after a pause, Truffles began her finale, and with a leap, all four paws sounded out the opening chords of Chopin's "Funeral March"—which Bill swears to!

Realizing now that he had been "sent for," Bill shouted out, "Help, help, no, don't take me, not now!"

Reacting in panic, he threw books, a lamp, and whatever was handy at the ghostly player. This commotion woke the household. Soon, my father and mother and I had rushed down to the recreation room. The lights came on showing a shaking, hollow-eyed Uncle Bill.

"GGGGGhost... piano playing... funeral..." he stammered, unable to speak coherently.

As quickly as we guessed the culprit, who was currently invisible, Truffles, alarmed at the uproar and confusion, made her escape from the top of the piano. With a bound she landed upon the deep base keys, sending out a thunderous, resounding roar.

We then explained to him about Truffles and her piano playing. Uncle Bill laughed and joked about how silly it was to let his imagination get the best of him, but he did sleep on a tiny couch in the upstairs living room for the rest of his visit.

~William Halderson

93

The Zen Cat

The cat has nine lives: three for playing, three for straying, three for staying.
~Proverb

My little grey tabby cat Misha loved to prowl the neighborhood by day but she always came home at night. So I was frantic when she didn't come home one evening. In Victoria, Canada, cats often get attacked by raccoons. Just a month before, my friend's cat had been mauled to death, and I was terrified that something horrible would happen to Misha. I wandered the neighborhood, calling her name and shaking her treats loudly. I shone a flashlight in the bushes around my home, but to no avail.

In the morning, I called the Humane Society. I almost dropped the phone when they told me a cat was brought in the day before matching her description. It was dead. Hit by a car in my neighborhood. They asked me to come to make a positive identification. Knowing I would be an emotional basket case and unable to drive, a friend offered to drive me there.

The friendly staff at the Humane Society told me the cat wasn't mangled, so I wouldn't be too shocked. The minute my friend and I walked into the room, I fell to my knees. It was her! I started to bawl. My friend started praying and put his arm around me. My precious Misha! Life would be so lonely without her!

The Humane Society agreed to keep her for a few days while I figured out where to bury her. My friend consoled me for hours while I told stories about Misha and her antics.

"She sits on my shoulder when I walk around the house! She sleeps curled up beside me every night! When my car pulls in the driveway, she runs to the door of the house to greet me! My life will be so empty without her!" I cried on and off for two days, calling all my friends and family and sharing the terrible news.

A family in the neighborhood said I could bury Misha in their backyard pet cemetery. They were very good friends and agreed to have a burial ceremony for her too. After five days of grieving, I bought a box that I decided to decorate as her coffin. I planned to do some colorful artwork and attach some Misha photos to make the burial box special. In all my years of having cats, this was the most elaborate funeral planning I had ever done. Misha was unique.

She and I had an instant connection from the moment I got her ten years before. I had been travelling the United States in a 1968 Volkswagen van, visiting the national parks. In Virginia, I stopped at a hippie farmers' market and noticed a box of free kittens. The minute I saw her little pink nose and brown eyes peaking out at me, I fell in love. I picked her up and she immediately pulled herself onto my shoulder. She wouldn't leave. I wanted to keep her, but I was travelling in a van and heading back to Canada.

I asked her owner, who looked like Bob Marley's twin brother, if I could walk around with her for a while and think about it. Everyone I talked to said we belonged together. She was so tiny; she fit right on my shoulder with her face nestled in the side of my neck.

After much deliberation, I decided to give her back to her hippie owner.

"I just can't travel with her in the van and there's the issue with taking pets across the border."

"You gotta keep her," he said. "You two belong together; your eyes are the same. It's so Zen!"

I didn't know exactly what "It's so Zen" meant, but he convinced me to keep her. Misha loved travelling in the van with me and a few weeks later we made it safely across the border into Canada.

Now after ten years of adventures and a move across the country together, I was bidding farewell to my Zen cat. I would never find another pet like her.

With a sigh and a heavy heart, I got the art supplies out of the closet to prepare Misha's coffin. Before beginning my painful art project, I noticed a light flashing on my answering machine.

"Uh, yeah, this is your roommate from your old house. Misha just showed up at our door. You wanna come over and get her? We've got her in the house."

I rushed out of the house, jumped in my car, and sped to my previous address. It was six months since I'd lived there. I couldn't believe that Misha would go back there after all this time!

No one was home. I looked through the window and saw Misha sitting in the middle of the living room, completely relaxed and looking at me as if to say, "What? So I was gone a few days... so what!"

Crawling through the open window, I grabbed her in my arms, weeping with joy, and scolding her for making me worry all this time! I wanted to wring her neck for giving me such a scare. Instead, I brought her home and pampered her with treats and a warm blanket.

The next day, I called the Humane Society to tell them that Misha had returned and that I couldn't believe an identical female cat had died in my neighborhood on the same day I lost her. They agreed—it was quite a coincidence!

~Kathy Linker

94

Ragtime Cat

If music be the food of love, play on.
~William Shakespeare

Eight-year-old Chris picked out the kitten, the runt of the litter, with soft black fur and a sweet face. We named her Emily, for Emily Dickinson, Belle of Amherst. Within a few weeks it became apparent that Emily was not a proper name for the sleek male of Siamese grace and lithe power that the kitten became. We decided to call him Amherst, since "Dick" didn't suit him at all.

Amherst was very much his own cat, with distinct and sometimes unusual likes. His favorite yogurt flavor was raspberry, although he would lick any container if given the chance. He was greedy about sipping the leftover juice from any honeydew melon rind, but not at all interested in cantaloupe or Crenshaw melon. He worked for days perfecting his leap from the top of the refrigerator onto the kitchen table, despite being reprimanded every time he tried it.

His most unusual quirk, however, was his passion for the music of Scott Joplin. Whenever I sat down at the piano to play some ragtime, Amherst jumped immediately onto the piano next to the music rack, curled up and listened. If anyone had the audacity to leave, say, homework on his piano space, he would disdainfully sweep it to the floor. His very favorite rag was "The Cascades." When I would play it, he couldn't keep still. He would walk around the piano, ending up on my lap, pressing the top of his head under my chin, purring raggedly. Bliss!

When Amherst was nearly grown, we moved to a different house half a mile away. When the time came to load the car, Amherst was nowhere to be found. We looked and looked, and came back daily to the old house, armed with raspberry yogurt or honeydew melon, but we never found the cat.

Jump three years ahead; we've moved again, easily a mile from either of our former homes, across a busy highway. Chris came in from school one day and announced, "Amherst's home. He's on the front porch." I accompanied him out to see and found a big bruiser of a tomcat, one ear slightly chewed, a disdainful expression on his big round face. "Oh, honey, I don't see how this could be Amherst. Amherst was a much more Egyptian-looking cat, slender and long-legged. This fellow looks like John Wayne!" In any case, Chris—a cross between Dr. Dolittle and St. Francis of Assisi—fed the big black cat every day.

Whoever the cat was, he was polite, never asking to come inside. He just sat on the porch. One fine afternoon, a week or so after he had appeared, I decided I'd determine once and for all that this big cat was not Amherst. I propped the front door open, sat down at the piano, and proceeded to play "The Cascades." The cat walked in, gathered his twenty-pound self up and sprang to the top of the piano. Alas, he didn't fit in his favorite spot any more, nor was there adequate room for him on my lap, but he gave it every effort, purring vociferously. Later when the music was finished and he'd eaten half a carton of raspberry yogurt, I was convinced. I couldn't wait for Chris to get home from school so I could tell him, "Chris—Amherst's home!"

~Sue Zendt

Surprise!

One small cat changes coming home to an empty house to coming home.
~Pam Brown

"**S**urprise!" That was the word that introduced me to the black kitten my daughter gave me for Mother's Day. I was expecting a box of candy. But my daughter Spring had decided a cat would be good company for me after she left for college.

We named the kitten Surprise. I welcomed him into my life and my home. After all, how much trouble could one kitten be?

Surprise thought the entire house had been designed as a giant playground for him. I'd never seen so much energy in such a small ball of fur. He could leap off the top of the recliner, hit the coffee table, slide across the table, and bounce across the sofa ten times in four seconds. He seemed to be everywhere; at times I felt as if we had ten kittens instead of one.

At night I would put him in his cat bed, but in the morning I would wake up to find him sleeping on top of my head, draped over it like a fuzzy black wig. During the day he'd crawl up the back of my chair and drape himself over the top of my head to take his nap. I didn't mind it so much when he was little, but when he was full-grown I couldn't walk around with a ten-pound cat on top of my head.

It was my daughter's last weekend at home before she left for college and we decided to spend it at the beach. We were going to leave early Saturday morning, spend Saturday night at a hotel, and come home Sunday night. I left plenty of food, treats, and water for Surprise and knew he'd be fine overnight. I made sure the windows and doors were locked and the house was safe and secure.

My daughter and I had a wonderful weekend and I hated to see it end. We were exhausted when we arrived home Sunday night and decided to wait and unpack the car the next morning.

As we approached the house the light went on in my bedroom. We both stopped.

"There's someone in the house!" I whispered.

The light in my bedroom went off and a minute later the light went on in my daughter's room.

There was no doubt about it. There was a burglar in the house and he was going from room to room robbing us!

We hurried across the street, hid behind a fence, and called the police. We told the police we'd been gone for the weekend, had just returned home and someone was inside our house. The police told us to stay where we were and if someone came out of the house, not to confront them.

A few minutes later two police cars arrived. I gave my house keys to one of the officers. Two policemen went to the back of the house; two other policemen banged on the front door and shouted, "Police! Open up!"

When the burglar didn't answer the door the police opened the front door and rushed inside. Suddenly lights came on all over the house.

"We've found the burglar, you can come inside now," an officer shouted.

My daughter and I crept into the house expecting to see some dangerous looking criminal in handcuffs.

A policeman was holding Surprise and petting him.

"Here's your culprit," the officer said, and sat Surprise on the nightstand next to my bed.

Surprise put his paw on the lamp, which was a touch light, and it lit up. He touched it again and it turned off. He continued using his paw to turn the light on and off while he watched the light bulb with fascination.

"Do you want to press charges?" an officer joked.

"He's young; let him off with a warning," I said.

~April Knight

96

Nine Lives

In nine lifetimes, you'll never know as much about your cat
as your cat knows about you.
~Michel de Montaigne

People often talk about a cat's independence, but what about the cat's friendliness, and capacity to forgive? My cat Morris made me a lifelong cat lover at a young age because I learned from him a lesson in humanity.

When both of my grandparents died unexpectedly my family and I flew to California for their funeral. We left in a hurry, and I closed up my crawlspace hideout beneath our house without thinking that it might be occupied. But it was. For two weeks, my cat Morris was stuck under there in the dark.

When we returned from California I opened up the crawlspace door and found an emaciated Morris lying among a pile of insulation. He'd survived by eating paper, insulation, and carpet. We brought him to the veterinarian. He stayed overnight, was already improving by the next day, and we were able to bring him home.

But there was one strange side effect of Morris' containment: forever after his head was tilted to one side.

The vet though he might be deaf in one ear or blind in one eye, but neither proved to be true. Although we felt bad, none of us could keep from chuckling when we saw Morris trotting down the hall, his head turned at a 90-degree angle. We called him Sidewinder after that. Somehow he still maintained perfect balance, never stumbling or missing a jump. He was his old self. Or so we thought.

Before he became trapped beneath the house, Morris was the cock of the walk. We'd hear him outside mixing it up with the neighborhood cats, dogs, or whoever. Many times I saw Morris just take off down the street upon seeing another cat. The other cats always ran away, and no dog ever challenged him that I saw.

And after the accident Morris still got in scraps. In fact one night I found him on the sidewalk, his face all bloody. My first thought was that his face had been scratched, but then my neighbor across the street yelled to me.

"Hey! Your cat just ran into a car!"

"You mean he got hit?" I yelled, afraid.

"No, he ran into the side of a tire of a moving car! He hit the hub cap, I think!"

I picked up Morris and brought him in the house. He looked pretty bad. I couldn't even see his eyes or nose; his face seemed they had been destroyed completely. I sat crying, waiting for my parents to get home from shopping. I gently touched his face. My finger found fur beneath the blood, and I wiped a little away. Then more. In fact his whole face was coated in a layer of thick blood from a cut on his forehead. I wiped the blood away, and there were his eyes and nose, perfectly fine.

Despite all the calamities Morris went through, his attitude never once changed. When he walked into a room we were in, his tail shot up in greeting, every time. He still rubbed against our legs, still licked our fingers, with the occasional love bite. Morris never let life make him bitter, even when he nearly starved, and nearly had his eyes gouged out. Morris has been gone for years now, and I can only hope that when I'm tested in life, I'll fare as well as him.

~Ron Kaiser, Jr.

97

Traveling Partners

No heaven will not ever Heaven be
Unless my cats are there to welcome me.
~Author Unknown

Had I known that my parents would spend eternity in the Knobs Baptist Church Cemetery with cats nestled at their feet, I would have taken comfort in knowing they would never be alone. Though Christianity teaches us that Christ offers forever companionship, the cats were visible partners that would accompany them to the great hereafter. Like ancient Egyptians, my parents were laid to rest with one thing they cherished—my father with Kee Too and my mother with Jake.

Unusual news travels fast. As I checked out of the local motel the day after Dad's funeral, the lady at the desk expressed her condolences and then asked, "Is it true that your father was buried with his cat?"

The day before, less than an hour before it was time to begin the funeral, Cousin Gary had happened by the camper business, the one my father had started with my brother. It was closed that day for the funeral, but Gary had stopped by to check on things and discovered Kee Too, the gray tortoiseshell cat, had died in the night outside the building. No visible marks, but dead just the same.

He phoned my brother, who phoned the undertaker, and yes, there was time to bury the cat with my dad. Gary brought Kee to the funeral home and he was placed inside the casket, next to my father's feet. In our grief we had to smile. Only the supernatural could conjure such coincidence.

My father had always liked cats, from his days as a boy in Canada, sneaking the family cat into his room in a cold tenant house on the Alberta prairie in the depth of winter. Stinky Davis was the cat he liked to talk about. And later, as a young married man, Honey, the barn cat he and my mother had befriended, a cat with less than pristine grooming, which he dubbed Honey-Under-His-Tail.

It would be twenty-odd years before we would adopt another cat, Hanny Honey, a pure white tom that would put up with childish antics, including having glasses and stripes drawn on his fur with watercolor markers.

More cats came and went, and by the time I left for college, my parents had become cat-obsessed, collecting every stray that came along. Dad befriended two tortoiseshell cats, Jim Olson and Mrs. Olson, another named Louie Hoo Hoo, and years later, Kee Kee, a cat that commanded a $500 reward when he went missing one winter. Dad's newspaper ad for the missing tabby drew attention from local reporters, and eventually the Associated Press, that put the story on the wire: "Illinois Man Willing to Pay $500 for Lost Cat."

After months of false sightings and charlatans wanting to claim the reward money for any old feline, the real Kee Kee was returned by a boy my father actually knew. The cat had somehow wandered a few miles from home. Dad paid the reward and all was well with the world.

A later tabby cat, Kee Too, was acquired to fill the void of Kee Kee who had died of feline leukemia. Kee Too hung out at the camper business well past the day my dad left in failing health. The cat remained in the building except for that one night he wandered and was found dead the next morning, the morning of my father's funeral, by my cousin.

During the funeral, the preacher mentioned how my dad prized cats, how he paid good money to find his lost one, like the Biblical shepherd seeking a lost sheep. Preaching from the pulpit, located next to my father's casket, the preacher had no idea that one of Dad's cat buddies was tucked away with him for eternity.

Three years later, when my mother followed my father to the cemetery, we would place her prized stuffed animal, Jake, with her. As a result of her dementia, she had thought Jake was a real cat. It seemed only fitting to allow her the pleasure of a cat too, in the afterlife.

One with a real cat, the other with a fake, buried with cats like Egyptian mummies. And so they went.

~Tamra Wilson

The Instigator

The belly rules the mind.
~Spanish Proverb

I t started innocently enough when I decided to rescue a cat from our local animal shelter. Even my husband had agreed to the plan. With the kids grown and out of the house, things were a little too quiet. A cat would be a great companion for all of us, including our elderly Schnauzer, Indy, who slept too much and played too little.

As I wandered past rows of cages in the shelter's cat room, I felt a tap on my shoulder. A gray tiger-striped tabby had stretched out a paw from between steel bars to get my attention. I looked at the card attached to his cage. Apparently he'd been in a foster home with dogs. The note went on to say that the animals played together and appeared to get along well. Intrigued, I opened his cage door and the cat leaped into my arms, purring like a motorboat as I stroked his soft fur. Who could say no to that? So I filled out adoption papers and took Bogey home.

The first hurdle we conquered easily. When Bogey met Indy, neither of them raised a hair. They sniffed and eyed each other for about five minutes. With introductions complete, they became as comfortable as two best friends reunited after a long separation. I breathed a sigh of relief.

I knew cats were agile, but soon discovered Bogey combined the energy of a lightning bolt with the dexterity of Houdini. He climbed the drapes to become King of the Curtains, conquered the curio cabinet, and maneuvered himself to the top of the foyer closet. It seemed the cat could do anything. Indy couldn't follow all the places Bogey led, but it soon became clear that years had rolled off my aging dog's life. He bounced around the house as though he were a puppy again, while Bogey sprinted circles around him. It seemed a perfect arrangement until a few strange things began to happen.

I found a chewed water bottle lid on the floor. I must have dropped it, and with Indy's newly rediscovered puppy energy, he'd done the rest. My fault, though it surely seemed that I last saw it sitting on the counter top.

The next day I found a plastic clamp chewed to pieces—then a pencil. How in the world did Indy get hold of all these things? He hadn't been so destructive in years. Then I caught Bogey pawing a rubber eraser from the table to the floor where Indy waited. Apparently the two had become colleagues in crime. As a result, I no longer left things on tables or countertops.

Bogey had other talents. Cabinet doors were a favorite. I watched him stand tall on his hind legs and grab the top of the door with his front paws to pull it open. This activity apparently provided endless amusement. Whenever I'd return home, there would be half a dozen cabinets standing in perfect imitation of open-mouthed amazement.

Not long after Bogey's first birthday, I started a backyard project that required running in and out of the house. After several trips back and forth, I found the sliding glass door open. Both Bogey and Indy were gone. Horrified, I scoured the area until I found the two of them hanging out under the neighbors' deck two doors up the street. I brought the runaways home and shut the door firmly. Bogey scampered straight for it and pawed with the talent of a true cat burglar. Indy watched him with ears pricked forward and tail at stiff attention. In no time at all, Bogey had worked the door open. I now keep it locked.

But soon another issue came along that overshadowed Bogey's behavior. I complained to my husband.

"Our refrigerator is getting too old. The magnet doesn't hold the door tight enough anymore. Please be sure to close it completely. I don't know how many times I've come home lately to find the thing standing wide open."

He looked bewildered.

"I could have sworn I closed it before I left for work today." But like any smart husband he quickly amended the comment. "Yes, dear. I'll be sure to shut it next time."

Only a few days later I found the door open again. This time my blood pressure achieved never-before-seen heights. I touched the top shelf. It felt practically room temperature with the motor chugging loud as a freight train. Worse yet, when I examined the contents for spoilage, I noticed my beautifully prepared salmon dip had been plundered.

I tapped my foot in aggravation. My husband had not only left the door open again, but he had also sneaked a sample of something he shouldn't have. He knew I'd made that dip for a party. When he got home, he'd certainly get an earful from me.

I fumed silently for a while, but soon noticed the house seemed eerily quiet. I crept toward the kitchen and saw Bogey stroll to the refrigerator. Then he nonchalantly flopped on his back and pushed his paws against the refrigerator door's rubber tubing. Only a minute later, it swung open. Indy joined his pal as two noses sniffed the shelf at muzzle height. Bogey went for the salmon dip while Indy lapped leftover ham salad. My eyebrows shot up and I hurried to stop them. Indy backed away, but Bogey didn't budge, emitting a few loud and proud meows. Better than a dead field mouse, this box of delights had evidently become the catch of the day, his crowning achievement. I could only shut the door and shake my head.

Perhaps every Baby Boomer needs excitement, even if it comes in the form of a four-footed juvenile delinquent. Things have certainly changed since Bogey came to live with us. Indy got a friend and regained his youth. I became much more nimble trying to outguess a cat who thankfully does not have opposable thumbs. My husband has someone else to blame for unfortunate household incidents. He describes Bogey quite accurately.

"That cat is like a two-year-old with four-wheel drive."

Meanwhile, until the refrigerator is finally replaced, we keep a chair propped in front of the door. Lucky for us, Bogey hasn't yet learned to move furniture.

~Pat Wahler

Reprinted by permission of Off the Mark
and Mark Parisi ©2002

My Protector

A beating heart and an angel's soul, covered in fur.
~Lexie Saige

My husband and I lived in the wilderness of the northern New Mexico mountains. He was a therapist who worked down in Santa Fe. And at home, I tended the woodstoves we relied on for heat, grew produce in our greenhouse and garden, and watched over a bevy of cats while chopping wood, chasing the line laundry down the hill on a windy day so that the neighbors' goats wouldn't eat it, and setting pots simmering on the stove for the evening meal.

Powder Puff was a longhaired calico, mainly black with some white, and an orange spot set over each of her golden eyes. I had raised her from a kitten along with a great longhaired gray cat with green eyes that I nursed to health from distemper when he was just a few weeks old.

Whenever I hiked in the canyon, along the ridge of the chasm, or up into the mountains, Powder Puff would shadow me, hiding in bushes all along the way. She often called to me plaintively, reminding me that I was straying beyond the territory where she felt comfortable, but she would not leave my side until I was once again within plain sight of our house.

In fact, she seemed to shadow me at all times, except when I had to drive to the city to go to the bank and run errands. Once when I returned from one of those trips, Powder Puff met me at the car as I pulled into the gravel driveway.

She mewed at me plaintively as I got out of the car and carried my grocery bags through the gardens on the way to our adobe house. As I strolled past a bed of chrysanthemums, she suddenly stiffened and pressed her body against my leg.

"What's wrong, Powder Puff?" I asked. A low warning growl came from her throat and, as I bent to see what she was staring at, a thick unmistakable rattle stuck right up through one of the chrysanthemums and shook with a menacing sound.

Startled, I jumped away, called to her to come into the house and made it inside the door. But Powder Puff stood her ground and led the rattler on a frightening series of maneuvers with her jumping over it again and again as it crawled onto a strip of grass and coiled and struck, missing her again and again.

Still when I called to her, she wouldn't come into the house. I tried throwing rocks at the snake, which only seemed to make it more aggressive. In desperation, I called Tomas, one of our friends at the Pueblo reservation. My husband was due home that night from an out-of-state convention, and I didn't have any way to get rid of the rattler—could he please help me? Tomas came with his rifle and killed the snake.

After he'd chopped off the head, he let me pet its sleek soft body, more like feathers than scales, not slimy but smooth. I felt bad that it had to be killed, but I also knew Tomas would make use of the pelt and the meat. Powder Puff seemed unaware of the great service she had done.

Several years later, her adopted sibling Sam developed a severe kidney disease. Doctors told me there was nothing we could do, but I couldn't bear to put him down. I kept him near me in a basket by the woodstove and fed him from a medicine dropper as long as he would take nourishment. When he began to bleed from his urinary tract and stagger across the room, I cried as I told my husband that perhaps the only kind thing left to do would be to put him to sleep. Before we could make arrangements, one night I heard him meowing faintly. I got up and went to see what I could do, but he struggled on spindly legs, staggered toward me and, as I bent to scoop him into my arms, died.

My husband and I waited until the next day to bury him next to the St. Francis shrine in our garden. That night, I lit a candle near the shrine on our adobe wall. To my amazement, Powder Puff jumped on the wall and there she stayed, settled on the wall by the candle until morning came.

For several more years, Powder Puff was my closest companion. Then one night, during a cold and blustery winter, I had gone to sleep. My husband was again out of town, but Powder Puff slept in her bed by the corner near the woodstove.

I dreamed that night that Powder Puff crawled on my pillow and spoke to me—though it wasn't with words. Rather, it was as if she had shared her thoughts, transmitting them to my mind.

"I am going away," she said softly. "But you mustn't be afraid, and you mustn't look for me any more." In my dream, she pressed against my face. "Thank you," she said. And then she disappeared.

When I awoke, she was nowhere to be found. Not in her bed, not in the house, and although I wandered about outside calling her and filling her dish, she did not come. When I went back into my house and began tidying the rooms, making my bed, I saw on the pillow beside my own a wisp of Powder Puff's hair.

In the days that followed, we searched everywhere and called for her in vain. I never saw her again and we never knew what had befallen her. But I take comfort in the fact that she seemed to know that she was leaving, and in her own way, served as my protector yet again when she said goodbye to me.

~Anne Wilson

Kittens in Transit

It is impossible to keep a straight face in the presence of one or more kittens.
~Cynthia E. Varnado

I was not even remotely pleased with the way the afternoon was going. My two kittens, Rumi and Bogie, just needed a simple veterinary follow-up, but it was probably going to take hours. Things always seemed to be complicated with them. I'd recently adopted the two black-and-white tuxedo brothers from a local cat rescue, and they were still receiving medical care from the organization. I was grateful for that, but the veterinary practice that the rescue used was on the other side of Manhattan, and it was going to require several bus and train changes to get there.

I was tired, run-down and sick of winter, and the very last thing I wanted to do was go on a long subway ride, particularly at rush hour. However, there was no way around it. I sighed as I loaded Rumi and Bogie into the carrier, tucked a warm blanket around them and gave them a toy to share. They were only four months old, and they were so tiny that they could easily share the space. I bundled up and trudged into the cold January afternoon, kittens in tow.

School had just gotten out, and the bus was packed with kids. The ones sitting closest to me were being loud and somewhat disrespectful. I rubbed my head and winced as their laughter and shrieks burrowed right into my brain; the beginnings of migraine were hovering just behind my eyes. Neither Rumi nor Bogie seemed to mind;

they simply peered out of their carrier with their large amber eyes and took it all in.

One of the girls looked in my direction and noticed the kittens. Her friends followed suit, and suddenly, their rudeness dissolved into a chorus of "Oh, cute!" "Look at the cats!" "There are two of them!" "Awwww!" "How old are they?"

They crouched down to get a better look at the kittens. Rumi and Bogie had somehow disarmed their teenage bravado and replaced it with the wonder of children. I was stunned as I fielded question after question from the eager girls.

On the first subway train, I stood close to the conductor's booth and held Rumi and Bogie's case protectively against the wall. The noise and motion frightened them, and they began to yowl. When we changed trains at Lexington Avenue, the kittens kept up their loud, indignant serenade all the way through the corridor, down the escalator, and along the platform. I wearily leaned against the station wall and held their carrier in front of me.

As we waited for the number 6 train, Rumi and Bogie settled down. They converged at the front of the case again and stared solemnly out at the platform. And for a reason I couldn't explain, once again, people noticed them. I started to become aware that several of the haggard commuters around me were turning their heads and smiling. A man in a business suit approached, leaned down and beamed at the kittens. A woman came up and talked directly to them. Another man eagerly told me about his own cats. Two teenagers stopped to look at Rumi and Bogie and comment on them.

What on earth was happening? I was in a subway station in New York City. There's one protocol there: you mind your own business. It was incredibly hard to faze or impress an NYC commuter. Street performers did back flips—literally—and danced down the aisles in the subway cars, and some people didn't even look up from their newspapers. You could board the train with a tree, a harp, a set of skis or a puppet that held a conversation with you, and nobody would blink. You could be dressed in a clown, chicken or zombie costume and you'd be met with indifference. The golden rule for mass transit never changed: you minded your business, you didn't make eye contact with anyone, and you certainly didn't chat anyone up. As cold as the custom sounded, it was necessary for survival in a crowded, busy metropolis. I followed it myself.

Rumi and Bogie didn't know subway etiquette, and apparently, they had uncanny ability to make others forget it, too. They were simply two small black-and-white kittens with amber eyes, and all they were doing was sitting in their carrier and looking out at the world. But they were somehow compelling my fellow passengers to temporarily venture outside their protective bubbles for a second or two. In the course of five minutes, I probably conversed with more strangers in transit than I had in the past five years.

The moment we stepped onto the 6 Train, Rumi and Bogie's hold on their audience seemed to break. We were swept back into the anonymous underground stream of commuters, where we were close to hundreds of others and interacted with none. As I rested the kittens' carrier on my lap, I couldn't help noticing that my migraine had dissipated. I wasn't feeling quite as tired anymore, either. The positive energy that had been directed toward the kittens seemed to have benefited me.

The trip to the vet's office took a solid hour, two trains and a bus. In the course of that journey, Rumi and Bogie managed to bring a moment of joy to a gloomy subterranean world. For that alone, the journey was worth it.

~Denise Reich

The King's Guard

True nobility is exempt from fear.
~Marcus Tullius Cicero

Finishing the last of the morning dishes, I glance out the window, dreaming about the upcoming change of season. Spring will be here soon. I watch for movement high above the trees or across the fallen limbs that line the 108 acres of woods behind our house. All is still.

As I turn to put the last pot away, something catches my eye. There in the sky is a beautiful red-tailed hawk. Soaring above the naked treetops I watch as it gracefully circles above.

After a few minutes it slows its circuit and descends into the woods. I see it fly in between trees, occasionally landing on a heavy limb. I know it has honed in on dinner and I am torn between letting nature be and running to the rescue of the poor bushy-tailed animal that it has its sights on.

"Survival of the fittest," my daughter would always tell me as I cried over some poor creature I had found that had been attacked.

I look around to see what it has zoned in on. What was holding its attention? I see a rustling in the hardened pachysandra. Something is marching through the woods towards the house. With intensified horror, I see that it is Gizmo, my neighbor's cat, flaunting itself in the wild. Walking without a care in the world.

I'm torn. Do I run outside and signal Gizmo? Should I warn him that he is about to become hawk meat? Oblivious to any danger, he has stopped to groom himself. The sun has peeked through the empty branches and is shining on him, almost like a spotlight leading the way for the hawk.

"Look, Jack," I say to my husband. "Gizmo is about to buy it."

The hawk has now descended deeper into the woods. With no leaves on the branches, it is easier for him to maneuver—periodically landing on a well-chosen branch where he can keep an eye on the unsuspecting bundle of gray fur still cleaning his paws.

Just as I am about to grab my jacket lying by the front door I hear Jack shout.

"Wait, check it out. Gizmo's not alone."

"What? Who's with him?"

"Not who, what. Look to the left of him. By that huge fallen oak."

A flash of white catches my attention. I see it. A deer.

"Look again," Jack says.

I look and see two additional tails waving. Then, to the right of Gizmo, closer to our house, I see two more white flickers. Five deer.

I think back to the winter before when we saw Gizmo outside entertaining three deer on the front lawn. Periodically, Gizmo and his entourage have been seen touring the neighborhood.

"Looks like his following has grown by two," Jack says.

We watch to see what happens next. With carefully calculated movements, the deer surround him. Once encircled, the King and his troops parade across the wood's edge and stop at the fieldstone wall that acts as a fortress on our property. When he stops, so does his guard. He takes a moment to reflect and then jumps on top of the wall. Taking a few steps, he positions himself in the middle of the wall, the gray of his long Maine Coon fur blending in with the aged fieldstone.

The deer take this as a sign to stand down. Two deer fall back and lie in the pachysandra adjacent to the wall. The other three stand guard nearby.

Jack and I are so shocked by what just transpired that we have totally forgotten about the hawk.

I look up and into the woods. No movement.

"Do you see him?" I ask.

"No, I guess this time the king has been spared."

~Jeanne Blandford

I Can't Believe My Cat Did That!

Meet Our Contributors
Meet Our Authors
Thank You
About Chicken Soup for the Soul

Meet Our Contributors

Debbie Acklin is a professional writer living in Alabama with her husband and her two children. Her current feline family member is three-year-old Duchess. Contact her at d_acklin@hotmail.com.

Valerie Fletcher Adolph is a writer and speaker. She teaches and blogs about writing and gives presentations to volunteer and employee groups. Her book, *The Story Solver*, helps speakers use stories effectively. Published internationally, she is a teacher and mentor specializing in speech editing and evaluation. Learn more at youreawriter.wordpress.com.

Teresa Ambord writes articles for business full-time from her rural Northern California home. For fun she writes stories about her family and pets. She is fully owned by the cats, small dogs, and foster dogs that inspire her writing and decorate her life. Her volunteer work with animals is through ACAWL.org. E-mail her at ambertrees@charter.net.

Monica A. Andermann lives on Long Island with her husband Bill and their cat Charley. She is a frequent contributor to the *Chicken Soup for the Soul* series. More of her work can be found in such publications as *Sasee*, *Skirt!*, *The Secret Place*, and *Woman's World*.

Elizabeth Atwater lives in a small town in North Carolina. She discovered the pleasure of writing at a very early age. She was encouraged to write by her teachers who thought she had a "gift for words" as one of them put it. Her "gift" brings her endless hours of pleasure.

Carol Ayer is a freelance writer and poet living in Northern California. Her credits include *Woman's World*, *The Christian Science Monitor*, and several *Chicken Soup for the Soul* books.

Karen Baker lives with her veterinarian husband and their dogs, cats, cattle, sheep, and horses in Napa Valley, California. She is a past recipient of the Jessamyn West Writing award and her stories about animals appear in the anthologies *My Dog Is My Hero* and *A Cup of Comfort for Dog Lovers II*.

Dana J. Barnett is a writer and English teacher. Her favorite things to do are writing, reading, hiking, watching movies, junking, and doting on her cats. Currently, among other projects, Dana is working on a children's book. Please send good thoughts her way. Contact her at dbarnett25@gmail.com.

Jane Barron received her Bachelor of Science degree, with honors, in Elementary and Early Childhood Education from the University of Alabama. She taught school until 2002 and is now a full-time mom and author. Her story "Stickers" appeared in *Chicken Soup for the Soul: Grieving and Recovery*. E-mail her at jbarron9@bellsouth.net.

Garrett Bauman lives a mile from the nearest road in the Finger Lakes region of New York, where bears are becoming regular visitors. A retired professor from Monroe Community College, he has published two college textbooks and stories for many books and magazines. Contact him at Mbauman@retiree.Monroecc.edu.

Joan McClure Beck has a master's degree in education. Retired as a reading specialist, she also has taught at the community college level and in a GED program. Joan has several publication credits, including two prior Chicken Soup for the Soul stories. Besides writing, she loves watercolor painting and volunteering.

Valerie D. Benko is a Communications and Community Relations Specialist from western Pennsylvania. She is a frequent contributor to the *Chicken Soup for the Soul* series and has been published in other anthologies and online. To see all of her publishing credits, please visit her at valeriebenko.weebly.com.

Jeanne Blandford has found her dream job as an editor at Chicken Soup for the Soul. When she is not reading inspirational submissions, she and her husband, Jack, are visiting their two children, working on documentaries, writing and producing children's books or volunteering for OPIN, a local animal rescue.

Verna Bowman is a writer, a speaker and has been involved in ministry to women for many years. She and her husband Jeff reside in Pennsylvania and have four children and five grandchildren. Her personal experience stories have appeared in several devotionals and publications.

Mary Brennan has taken writing classes on and off for several years, and lately the teacher and several students seem to like many of her stories and have encouraged her to submit some. This is the first story that Mary has published professionally.

Caroline M. Brown lives in Maine with her two cats, and would like to see if any more stories can be published. She enjoys reading, old movies, walks on the beach and watching the sun come up over the ocean.

Debra Ayers Brown, a marketing professional, has received numerous project, design and writing awards on a national and international basis. She graduated magna cum laude from UGA, earned her MBA degree from The Citadel, and was recently included in the Stanford Who's Who. Please follow her blogs at DebraAyersBrown.com.

Betsy Burnett lives in Illinois with her husband and four children. This homeschooling mom enjoys writing, reading, and bike riding. Active in her church, Betsy oversees the children's ministry. To nurture her creative side, she teaches craft classes as well as organizes scrapbooking events. E-mail her at burnett.betsy@gmail.com.

Sammie Callahan-Hutchens is a freelance writer living in Odessa, FL with her husband Greg. A member of the Christian Writers Guild and the Florida Writers Association she enjoys writing short stories and historical fiction.

Hana Haatainen Caye, aka Green Grandma (www.greengrandma.org), is the agency principal for Speechless (www.wordsinyourmouth.com), a company specializing in voice-overs, copywriting, creative writing and editing services. A multi-published journalist, award-winning poet and author of short stories, Hana presents writing workshops at conferences and leads a monthly writing group in Pittsburgh, PA.

Mary C. Chace lives with her family and menagerie in Northern California. She enjoys the company of her husband, their six children, a horse, dog, hamster, tortoise, and of course, Sophie, the cat. Besides freelancing, Mary helps students improve their college admission essays and timed writing skills. E-mail Mary at mary.chace@gmail.com.

Bonita Chambers is the office manager for St. John Lutheran Church in Angleton, TX. She has always enjoyed writing and photography and works part-time for *Image Magazine*, a reflection of Brazoria County living. E-mail her at bonitachambers@gmail.com.

Linda S. Clare is the coauthor of three nonfiction books and author of a novel, *The Fence My Father Built* (Abingdon Press, 2009). She teaches writing at Lane Community College in Eugene, OR, and for George Fox Evangelical Seminary. She lives in Eugene with her family and three wayward cats. E-mail her at Lindasclare@gmail.com.

Harriet Cooper is a freelance writer. Her topics often include cats, health, exercise, diet, family and the environment. A frequent contributor to the *Chicken Soup for the Soul* series, her work has also appeared in newspapers, magazines, newsletters, anthologies, websites and radio. E-mail her at shewrites@live.ca.

Shirley Corder is a registered nurse, cancer survivor and freelance author. She lives near the sea in Port Elizabeth, South Africa with her husband Rob. Her book, *Strength Renewed: Mediations for your Journey through Breast Cancer*, is due to be released September 2012. Contact her at www.shirleycorder.com.

Mary Dempsey, a former teacher and bookstore owner, now resides in Bluffton, SC. Her writing has appeared in newspapers, magazines and in a recently published *Chicken Soup for the Soul* anthology. She does freelance writing for a local newspaper and recently published a book of her short stories. E-mail her at marydemp27@yahoo.com.

Sally Desouza received her Bachelor of Arts degree from the University of Oregon and Educational Specialist degree from Lewis & Clark. Before a recent move to Virginia, Sally worked as a school psychologist near Seattle. She is currently traveling and writing about her experiences. Contact her through sallydesouza.wordpress.com.

This is **Cynthia M. Dutil's** first published story. Cynthia has always loved pets, and is living in a nursing home. She hopes to write more stories.

Susan Peterson Gateley sailed Lake Ontario with her cats for several years and published a book about her three cats' cruise to Canada,

Twinkle Toes and the Riddle of the Lake, available from www.chimneybluff. com or Amazon. E-mail her at susan@silverwaters.com.

Liz Graf is a retired high school biology teacher with three grown children. She and her high school sweetheart are now settled in Palm Coast, FL. Liz loves seeing and translating the world through the written word. She strives to make every day a Sunshine Day. E-mail her at linesbyliz@gmail.com.

Wendy Greenley graduated from the University of Delaware and the Villanova University School of Law. She is a member of the SCBWI and her love for animals works its way into many of the stories she writes. E-mail Wendy at wbgreenley@gmail.com.

Dale Mary Grenfell is a prolific freelance writer, educator, storyteller and workshop facilitator. She loves living in the foothills of the Rocky Mountains and actively volunteers in her community. She graduated with honors from Regis University in sociology and with a minor in religious studies. E-mail her at grenfell@q.com.

Bill Halderson received a B.A. degree from California State Polytechnic University, and an M.A. degree in government from Claremont Graduate University much of a lifetime ago. Bill retired from a career as a corporate manager and trainer. He lives and writes in Cookeville, TN. E-mail him at billandmonica1943@frontiernet.net.

Maryanne Hamilton has enjoyed the company of mischievous and loving cats since childhood. She is a published author and an artist/ art therapist with children and adults. In her leisure time you may find her traveling, creating art, writing children's books, or playing her clarinet in a very large marching band.

Sharon Harmon has published numerous short stories, articles and 120 poems. She has been published in *A Patchwork Christmas*, *Birds & Blooms* and *Swimming With Cats*. She lives in the woods with her husband and cat and is working on a memoir. E-mail her at sharonannharmon@peoplepc.com.

Dena Harris' book *Who Moved My Mouse? A Self-Help Book for Cats (Who Don't Need Any Help)* has been translated into six languages. A writer and in-demand speaker, Dena owns a freelance copywriting business, runs ultra marathons, and frightens her husband and cats with her experimental cooking. Learn more at www.denaharris.com.

Karen R. Hessen has been published in *Chicken Soup for the Soul: Divorce and Recovery*, *Chicken Soup for the Soul: Food and Love*, *Guideposts*, *Vista* and many others. She and her husband Douglas live in Forest Grove and Seaside, OR. Karen can be reached at karenwrites@frontier.com or visit her website at www.karenrhessen.com.

Rebecca Hill's cat, Saddie "Spot" Wilson, was respected by all and loved by an elite few. Her biggest fans were Tom Caufield, Chip Wilson, Kandy Hill, Laura Gorenstien-Miller, Cindi and Faye Toth, Jini Durr, Nicole Damato, Darnell (from Dr. G's office) and Gary and Sherry Guinn. Spot is missed greatly.

Tracie Hornung is a former award-winning reporter, a freelance writer, and a volunteer at cat shelters and wildlife rehabilitation organizations in the Pacific Northwest. In addition to writing about animals, she enjoys hiking, bicycling, boating, and nature photography. Visit her website at thcommunications.net.

Carol Huff is a frequent contributor to the *Chicken Soup for the Soul* series as well as other well-known publications. She owns Sudie Belle Animal Sanctuary in Northeast Georgia and spends most of her time taking care of rescued and special needs animals. E-mail her at herbiemakow@gmail.com.

BJ Jensen is an author, inspirational speaker, dramatist and music-signing artist. She directs Love In Motion Signing Choir (www.

signingchoir.com), which travels internationally. BJ is happily married to Dr. Doug Jensen and they live near their son, daughter-in-law, and three precious granddaughters in San Diego, CA. E-mail her at jensen2@san.rr.com.

Ruth Jones lives in Cookeville, TN with her husband Terry and a very fat calico named Annabel.

Ron Kaiser lives in the foothills of the New Hampshire White Mountains with his wife Meghan, whose beauty and intelligence exceed the writer's ability to describe. They have a wonderful son together, named William, who is silly as all get out. Ron is currently at work trying to publish a fantasy novel. E-mail him at kilgore.trout1922@gmail.com.

April Knight is an author and artist. She loves cats and believes every cat she has owned has enriched her life. She is currently living in soggy, dreary Seattle where the sun never shines. Learn more at www.cryingwind.com.

Kimber Krochmal lives in a small town in North Carolina. When not writing, she enjoys drawing, painting, and spending time with her large family. Her children, including her "fur children," are her biggest inspiration as an artist and a storyteller.

Nancy Kucik and her husband Dennis, both Wisconsin natives, live in Alabama with their two mixed-breed dogs, and two cats—eighteen-year-old Fluffy and a new kitten, Mocha. Nancy works as an editorial assistant at a medical journal and enjoys reading, running and writing in her spare time. E-mail Nancy at nancykucik@yahoo.com.

Joyce Laird is a freelance writer living in Southern California with her menagerie of animal companions. Her features have been published in many magazines including, *Cat Fancy, Grit, Mature Living, I Love*

Cats and *Vibrant Life*. She contributes regularly to *Woman's World* and the *Chicken Soup for the Soul* anthology.

Ginny A. Lee lives on about 230 wooded acres along Minnesota's Mississippi River. She shares her life with a variety of cats, dogs, horses, cows, chickens and the occasional donkey or sheep. She finds it a singularly satisfying life, supported by therapeutic and able-bodied riding lessons.

Kathy (Kat) Linker has a B.A. degree in psychology, a graduate degree in clinical art therapy and a master's degree in education. She has traveled the world extensively but found her true home in Hawaii. She is currently writing inspirational stories about her life and travel adventures. E-mail her at kathylinker@hotmail.com.

Virginia Maher, of Halifax, Nova Scotia, is a long-term wife, mother and grandmother. She enjoys these three roles tremendously most of the time and prefers to approach life's challenges with a sense of humour. Virginia enjoys writing, reading, traveling, sewing, knitting, photography, gardening and spending time with her family.

Irene Maran, a retired high school administrator from the Montclair Kimberley Academy in New Jersey, enjoys writing humorous essays. Irene writes a bi-weekly column for the *News-Record* of Maplewood/ South Orange and *The Coaster* in Asbury Park. She directs two writing groups at the Jersey Shore. E-mail her at maran.irene@gmail.com.

Alice Marks retired from a career in Early Childhood Education in Roseville, MN. In 2005, she and her husband moved to Port Aransas, TX. She joined a writers' group, Port A Pens. Inspired by this group, she writes regularly. Other passions include people, pets, and volunteer work at her church. E-mail her at amarks001@ centurytel.net.

Tina Wagner Mattern is a Portland, OR writer who is married to a great guy, has two awesome kids and is the adopted parent of a bad kitty named Sauza. She is grateful to have been published in four other *Chicken Soup for the Soul* books so far. E-mail her at tinamattern@ earthlink.net.

Linda Mehus-Barber lives with her husband, two dogs, and a cat in the seaside community of Crescent Beach in Surrey, British Columbia. She teaches English and Ancient History to energetic middle schoolers, and writes as a way to relax.

Lynn Maddalena Menna is a freelance writer and former educator. She is a columnist for *Main Street Magazine* and writes for *NJ Education Now*. Lynn lives in Hawthorne, NJ with her husband, Prospero. Sadly, Toonsie passed on to heaven, but lives on in their hearts. E-mail Lynn at prolynn@aol.com.

Diane Morey received her B.S. degree in Dental Hygiene with highest honors from the University of Louisville and an M.S. degree in Education from the University of Wisconsin Oshkosh. She has published professional articles, is retired, and lives in Rhinelander, WI with her mother and her two cats, Ember and Cinder.

Lisa Kirkpatrick Mueller is a psychology major at Liberty University. Lisa and her husband, Ian, currently reside in Kennesaw, GA with four felines: Leo, Budd, Snowie, and Smokie. Lisa enjoys writing, cross-stitching, reading, and watching movies. The stories in this book are Lisa's first published work. E-mail her at lisakmueller@hotmail.com.

S. Kay Murphy is a writer, high school teacher and lover of black cats. She can be contacted at kayzpen@verizon.net—and if you enjoyed her story, please find Sugar Plum on Facebook and let her know!

Irena Nieslony was born in England and received her B.A. degree in English and Drama from the University of London. She now lives in Greece with her husband and numerous cats and dogs. As well as writing short stories, Irena is working on her first novel. E-mail her at irena_nieslony@hotmail.com.

LaVerne Otis lives in Southern California where she loves writing, photography, bird watching, reading and spending time with family. LaVerne is recently retired; taking classes at a local community college. She has been published several times in *Chicken Soup for the Soul* books and various magazines. E-mail her at lotiswrites@msn.com.

Linda Panczner teaches composition at The University of Toledo and tries to practice what she preaches through freelance writing. Her cats provide ample inspiration for some of her prose because of their pleasing, sometimes perplexing, personalities. Whereas writing can be a challenge, reading is pure bliss.

Mark Parisi's award winning "off the mark" cartoon appears in newspapers worldwide. His work also appears on calendars, cards, books, T-shirts and more. Visit www.offthemark.com to view 7000+ cartoons. Mark resides in Massachusetts with his wife and business partner Lynn, along with their daughter Jen, three cats and a dog.

Nancy Peacock is a retired librarian who loves to read and write children's books and spy novels. Her short stories have been published in several anthologies. Her husband and daughters love to read anything she writes and are her best critics. Her critique group members call her the "Punctuation Police."

Award-winning columnist/novelist **Saralee Perel** is honored to be a multiple contributor to *Chicken Soup for the Soul* anthologies. Her book, *Raw Nerves*, is now available as an e-book on Amazon.com. E-mail Saralee at sperel@saraleeperel.com or visit her at www.saraleeperel. com.

Mary C. M. Phillips is a caffeinated wife and mother residing in New York. Her work has appeared in the *Cup of Comfort* book series and *Bad Austen: The Worst Stories Jane Never Wrote*. Mary is currently writing her first Austen-inspired novel. With enough coffee, she may finish it. Learn more at caffeineepiphanies.wordpress.com.

D.R. Ransdell got her starter cats a decade ago and has kept a house of felines ever since. To read Bandit's version of the story, please consult *The Secret Lives of the Pink House Cats: Prose Poems by Five Felines* or visit pinkhousecats.com.

Denise Reich practices flying trapeze, dances, and likes to paint. She can be seen dancing in the "mob" in five episodes of the TV show *Mobbed*. Denise's most recent writing credits include several *Chicken Soup for the Soul* titles, the anthology *She's Shameless*, *The Pet Press*, *Bunker Hill* magazine and *Goodkin*.

Bruce Robinson is an award-winning, internationally published cartoonist whose work has appeared in many consumer and trade magazines, including *National Enquirer*, *The Saturday Evening Post*, *Woman's World*, etc. He is the author of the cartoon books *Good Medicine* and *Bow Wows & Meows*. Visit www.BowWowsandMeows.net or e-mail him at CartoonsByBruceRobinson@hotmail.com.

Janet Rockey is president of CWG/Word Weavers-Tampa Chapter and is a member of Florida Writers Association. She lives in Tampa, FL with her husband and two cats. Her writing withstands a full-time job, constant home improvements, and her feline "children," all inspiration for her stories. Visit her blog at rockeywrites.blogspot.com.

Lynn Rogers lives on a small farm in Central Kentucky with her husband and various critters. She enjoys writing in her spare time.

Jazmyne Rose has been writing since she could hold pen to paper. It has always been her passion and she hopes to unite people all over the world through a love of literacy. For more works by Jazmyne check her out on Facebook or Myspace!

Linda Sabourin lives in the River Valley of NW Arkansas. She shares a home with her brother, her boyfriend, several cats and one dog. Formerly an accountant, she now spends her time going to auctions and selling vintage items on eBay. E-mail her at vintage6468@aol.com.

Kelly Boyer Sagert has published eleven nonfiction books, most recently *Icons of Women's Sport* (ABC-CLIO). She has also been commissioned to write three full-length historical plays. Kelly and her family now own four beautiful cats: Char, Coal, Milo and Dylan. E-mail her at kbsagert@aol.com.

Ayesha Schroeder lives in Texas, where she does web content writing by day and plays house by night with her two Bengal cats and husband. She enjoys writing, scuba diving, cooking, and blogging. E-mail her at ayeshaschroeder@gmail.com or visit her website at ayeshaschroeder.com.

Mary Z. Smith is a regular contributor to the *Chicken Soup for the Soul* anthology as well as *Guideposts* and *Angels on Earth* magazines. She resides in Newton Falls, OH, enjoying penning praises to God.

L. Stewart is a freelance writer from the Midwest. She loves teaching and working with college students, writing plays, and hang gliding with her dad. She loves her God, her family and her writing, in that order, and never plans to retire.

Susan Sundwall is a freelance writer and children's playwright. She is working on her first novel, a comic cozy mystery. E-mail her at scsundwall@gmail.com.

Pamela Tambornino teaches English full-time at a tribal university.

She has a B.A. degree in English, MLS and M.A./English. E-mail her at bookwormbugg2002@yahoo.com.

B.J. Taylor can't believe how Red helped her find romance again. She is an award-winning author whose work has appeared in *Guideposts*, more than two-dozen *Chicken Soup for the Soul* books, and numerous other publications. You can reach B.J. through her website at www.bjtayloronline.com and check out Charlie Bear's dog blog at www.bjtaylorblog.wordpress.com.

Karen Teigen is a retired library director who has worked in school and public libraries. She wrote this story as part of a leisure learning course on non-fiction writing. She enjoys reading, traveling, crocheting, and spending time with her children and grandchildren.

The cartoons of **Andrew Toos** have been anthologized in numerous cartoon collections, such as *Lawyers! Lawyers! Lawyers!*, *Cats, Cats, Cats* and *Modern Employment*. His cartoons appear in textbooks, trade paperbacks and books published by Cambridge University Press, Simon & Schuster, Warner Books, Contemporary Publishing, Gibbs Smith and many others.

Ann Vitale has been a microbiologist, a dog trainer, and a car dealer. Previously published by an educational press, Chicken Soup for the Soul, and local newspapers, she is working on a mystery novel. Her interests are wildlife, teaching in adult schools, and art. E-mail her at ann.e.vitale74@gmail.com.

When she was eight, **Shireen Wahid** fed a pregnant stray cat that wandered into her backyard. Since then, their antics and purring companionship have been a constant in her life, seeing her through some rough times. Shireen lives in Sydney, Australia. E-mail her at shireen.wahid@gmail.com or visit her blog www.shireenswriting.wordpress.com.

Pat Wahler is a freelance writer from Missouri who has published stories in multiple venues, including both local and national publications. Pat balances a full-time job, family, and writing with varying degrees of success. She blogs all things animals on Critter Alley at www.critteralley.blogspot.com.

Beverly F. Walker lives in Tennessee with her retired husband. She enjoys writing, photography and scrapbooking pictures of her grandchildren. She has stories in many *Chicken Soup for the Soul* anthologies, and dedicates this story to her cat Audrey, who once belonged to her late son Donnie.

Samantha Ducloux Waltz is an award-winning freelance writer in Portland, OR. Her personal stories have appeared in the *Chicken Soup for the Soul* series, numerous other anthologies, *The Christian Science Monitor* and *Redbook*. She has also written fiction and nonfiction under the name Samellyn Wood. Learn more at www.pathsofthought.com.

Whether through words or photographs, **Cari Weber** is passionate about telling stories. She is a freelance writer and award-winning photographer whose work has been published in several books and magazines. Cari finds beauty in the ordinary and especially enjoys nature and wildlife. Visit her website at www.cariweber.com.

Anne Wilson teaches at University of San Diego. She has published/ won prizes in poetry since 1996, and during the 1980's published articles in spiritual/religious magazines and academic journals. Powder Puff was her cat in Northern New Mexico, where she lived with her husband until the 1990's.

Deborah Wilson resides in Everett, WA with her husband and two cats. Deborah is a graduate of the University of Washington and a member of Toastmasters. She and her husband enjoy hiking and biking in the beautiful Northwest. Other passions include reading, writing, cooking and knitting.

Tamra Wilson lives in North Carolina and has been published in more than fifty literary journals and anthologies. She earned her Master's of Fine Arts degree from the University of Southern Maine and released her collection, *Dining with Robert Redford*, in 2011. E-mail her at tamra@tamrawilson.com.

Paul Winick, M.D. lives in Hollywood, FL with his wife Dorothy. He practiced there for thirty years and is currently Professor of Clinical Pediatrics at University of Miami medical school. This is his eighth *Chicken Soup for the Soul* contribution. His second memoir, *Cancer Dreams*, has just been released. E-mail him at paulwinick@pol.net.

Lisa Wojcik teaches literacy and art to low-income elementary grade children through a Florida public library system. Degreed from The University of New Mexico, Lisa is a science researcher, artist, and writer. Her short stories, poetry, children's literature, and research work can be seen at www.t4studios-bd.blogspot.com. E-mail her at lisawojcik@hotmail.com.

Lisa M. Wolfe is a freelance health and fitness writer. She is also the author of six fitness books and one Christian fiction novel. Lisa and her two children remain active and healthy. Mars passed away in 2010 and they miss him every day.

Susan Yanguas received a B.A. degree with honors and distinction in all subjects from Cornell University. She lives with her two cats in Maryland, where they help her write by manipulating her mouse and walking on the keyboard. Susan (with feline assistance) has also written two novels that are currently seeking publication.

Sue Zendt holds an MFA degree in Theatre; she is a playwright and a retired teacher of Theatre, Composition, and Literature. She can't imagine a home without cats in it.

Patti Zint is a freelance writer and private college program director.

Home is shared with numerous pampered cats and two wish-we-were-cats dogs. She is the proud mother of one amazing teenage daughter, one inspiring Marine son, and one awesome twenty-something son. E-mail her at is pwzint@cox.net.

Meet Our Authors

Jack Canfield is the co-creator of the *Chicken Soup for the Soul* series, which *Time* magazine has called "the publishing phenomenon of the decade." Jack is also the co-author of many other bestselling books.

Jack is the CEO of the Canfield Training Group in Santa Barbara, California, and founder of the Foundation for Self-Esteem in Culver City, California. He has conducted intensive personal and professional development seminars on the principles of success for more than a million people in twenty-three countries, has spoken to hundreds of thousands of people at more than 1,000 corporations, universities, professional conferences and conventions, and has been seen by millions more on national television shows.

Jack has received many awards and honors, including three honorary doctorates and a Guinness World Records Certificate for having seven books from the *Chicken Soup for the Soul* series appearing on the New York Times bestseller list on May 24, 1998.

You can reach Jack at www.jackcanfield.com.

Mark Victor Hansen is the co-founder of Chicken Soup for the Soul, along with Jack Canfield. He is a sought-after keynote speaker, bestselling author, and marketing maven. Mark's powerful messages of possibility, opportunity, and action have created powerful change in thousands of organizations and millions of individuals worldwide.

Mark is a prolific writer with many bestselling books in addition to the *Chicken Soup for the Soul* series. Mark has had a profound influence in the field of human potential through his library of audios, videos, and articles in the areas of big thinking, sales achievement, wealth building, publishing success, and personal and professional development. He is also the founder of the MEGA Seminar Series.

Mark has received numerous awards that honor his entrepreneurial spirit, philanthropic heart, and business acumen. He is a lifetime member of the Horatio Alger Association of Distinguished Americans.

You can reach Mark at www.markvictorhansen.com.

Jennifer Quasha is an award-winning writer and editor. She is a published author of more than forty books, including three dog books: *Don't Pet a Pooch... While He's Pooping: Etiquette for Dogs and their People*, *The Dog Lover's Book of Crafts: 50 Home Decorations that Celebrate Man's Best Friend*, and *Sew Dog: Easy-Sew Dogwear and Custom Gear for Home and Travel*.

She graduated from Boston University with a B.S. in Communication and has been writing ever since. Jennifer has been a contributing editor at *Dog Fancy* and *Dogs for Kids* magazines, and has written monthly columns on rescue dogs, etiquette, and travel. Jennifer has also been published in Chicken Soup for the Soul books and is thrilled to be a co-author of *Chicken Soup for the Soul: I Can't Believe My Cat Did That!* and *Chicken Soup for the Soul: I Can't Believe My Dog Did That!* She also was a co-author of *Chicken Soup for the Soul: My Dog's Life* and *Chicken Soup for the Soul: My Cat's Life*.

In her free time Jennifer loves to read, travel and eat anything anyone else prepares for her. She lives with her husband, kids, and two dogs, Sugar and Scout. You can reach her by visiting her website at www.jenniferquasha.com.

Thank You

Thank you cat lovers! I owe huge thanks to every one of you who shared your stories about beloved cats that have touched your lives. You have made me laugh, cry and nod my head. My heart brightened when you got a new kitten; I chuckled at your teenage cat's shenanigans; I was touched by the amazing variety of ways that your adult cats love and share your lives; and I promise that I cried with you when old age or sickness took your best friend from you. I know that you poured your hearts and souls into the thousands of stories and poems that you submitted. Thank you. All of us at Chicken Soup for the Soul appreciate your willingness to share your lives with us.

We could only publish a small percentage of the stories that were submitted, but we read every single submission—and there were thousands! Even the stories that do not appear in the book influenced us and affected the final manuscript.

A special thank you goes to Chicken Soup for the Soul editor Kristiana Glavin. This book could not have been made without her diligence, input, and well-oiled knowledge of what makes a great Chicken Soup for the Soul story. Amy Newmark, Chicken Soup for the Soul's whip-smart publisher, had my back during every stage of creating this book and guided me gracefully and with quick replies. I also want to thank Assistant Publisher D'ette Corona for managing the whole production process, and editors Barbara LoMonaco and Madeline Clapps for their proofreading assistance.

Thank you to cartoonists Mark Parisi, Bruce Robinson and Andrew Toos for giving us eleven reasons to giggle throughout the book. Lastly, I owe a very special thanks to our creative director and book producer, Brian Taylor at Pneuma Books, for his brilliant vision for our covers and interiors.

~Jennifer Quasha

Improving Your Life Every Day

Real people sharing real stories—for nineteen years. Now, Chicken Soup for the Soul has gone beyond the bookstore to become a world leader in life improvement. Through books, movies, DVDs, online resources and other partnerships, we bring hope, courage, inspiration and love to hundreds of millions of people around the world. Chicken Soup for the Soul's writers and readers belong to a one-of-a-kind global community, sharing advice, support, guidance, comfort, and knowledge.

Chicken Soup for the Soul stories have been translated into more than forty languages and can be found in more than one hundred countries. Every day, millions of people experience a Chicken Soup for the Soul story in a book, magazine, newspaper or online. As we share our life experiences through these stories, we offer hope, comfort and inspiration to one another. The stories travel from person to person, and from country to country, helping to improve lives everywhere.

Share with Us

We all have had Chicken Soup for the Soul moments in our lives. If you would like to share your story or poem with millions of people around the world, go to chickensoup.com and click on "Submit Your Story." You may be able to help another reader, and become a published author at the same time. Some of our past contributors have launched writing and speaking careers from the publication of their stories in our books!

Our submission volume has been increasing steadily—the quality and quantity of your submissions has been fabulous. We only accept story submissions via our website. They are no longer accepted via mail or fax.

To contact us regarding other matters, please send us an e-mail through webmaster@chickensoupforthesoul.com, or fax or write us at:

Chicken Soup for the Soul
P.O. Box 700
Cos Cob, CT 06807-0700
Fax: 203-861-7194

One more note from your friends at Chicken Soup for the Soul: Occasionally, we receive an unsolicited book manuscript from one of our readers, and we would like to respectfully inform you that we do not accept unsolicited manuscripts and we must discard the ones that appear.